ISBN 978-0-243-47313-7
PIBN 10800751

THE TUNNEL
THRU THE AIR

—

W. D. GANN

LOOKING BACK FROM 19

BY

W. D. GANN

Author of "Truth of the Stock Tape" and
"Speculation a Profitable Profession"

FINANCIAL GUARDIAN PUBLISHING C(

80 WALL STREET, NEW YORK

DEDICATED

TO THE MEMORY OF MY MOTHER

SUSAN R. GANN

AND

TO AN OLD SCHOOLMATE IN TEXAS

MY NATIVE STATE

FOREWORD

"Happy is the man that findeth wisdom, and the man that getteth understanding."—*Proverbs*.

A BOOK, to be worth reading, must do more than amuse and interest. It must be instructive to be of real value to the reader. This book has a three-fold purpose:

First, It is an interesting romance.

Second, It teaches a moral lesson and proves the natural laws laid down in the Bible.

Third, It shows the value of science, foreknowledge and preparedness.

It has been well said that truth is stranger than fiction. This story is founded on facts and events, many of which have happened or will happen in the future.

The "Tunnel Thru the Air" is mysterious and contains a valuable secret, clothed in veiled language. Some will find it the first time they read it, others will see it in the second reading, but the greatest number will find the hidden secret when they read it the third time.

You will read it the first time because you are interested in the love story and for amusement. This will create a desire to read it a second time for instruction and knowledge. The second reading will unfold some of the hidden meanings and you will gain knowledge thru understanding which will stimulate an incentive to put knowledge gained into action. You will read it the third time because you want to make your dreams and ideals become real and find how to start knowledge into action.

When you read it the third time, a new light will dawn. You will find the hidden secret, the veiled meaning and will understand why the Bible says, "Seek and ye shall find, knock and it shall be opened unto you." You will want to understand more about the Bible. Then read the Bible three times and you will know why it is the greatest book ever written. It contains the key to the process by which you may know all there is to know and get all that you need to supply your demands and desires. You will appreciate why Solomon said, "Wisdom is the principal thing: therefore get wisdom and with all thy getting, get understanding." The future will become an open book. You will know that by following the laws laid down in the Bible, man's last great enemy, Death, will be overcome and will understand why Jesus rose on the third day and rested on the seventh day. Robert Gordon's seven days will no longer be a mystery because you will have gained understanding.

I believe this book will prove interesting and valuable to men and women in all walks of life. If it does, you will be thankful to the power that guided my hand in showing you the way to eternal Truth. My object will have been accomplished and I will have my reward.

W. D. GANN.

MAY 9, 1927.

THE TUNNEL THRU THE AIR

CHAPTER I

IN the extreme northeastern corner of the Lone Star State of Texas, about eight miles west of Texarkana, in a lonely farm-house on Sunday morning, June 10th, Amelia Gordon turned over in her bed and watched the sunlight streaming thru the window on the head of her new-born son. She had always hoped that this, her third son, would be born on Sunday, but he was born late Saturday night, June 9th, 1906. A few months before his birth, his mother had suffered a severe shock on account of the death of her oldest son in the San Francisco earthquake in April, and for a time it was feared that her third son might never be born to live. She was happy this Sunday morning when she looked at her bouncing baby boy, dreamed of his future, and thought of what his name should be.

Calvin Gordon, the baby's father, had been a Captain in the U. S. Army in Spain. He had won distinction for his cool courage and daring nerve, and after the close of the Spanish-American war, moved from Tennessee to Texas. Capt. Gordon had been very much depressed after the loss of his eldest son in the San Francisco earthquake, and was very much cheered up at the birth of this boy, and hoped that the youngest son might fulfill the ambitions he had for his first born.

It had always been the custom of Calvin and Amelia Gordon to go to the little country church every Sunday morning, but this morning Capt. Gordon remained with his wife so that they could talk over the naming of their son. Capt. Gordon suggested the name "Robert," which was the name of his father, and his wife quickly acquiesced, so the baby was named Robert.

Amelia Gordon was a great Bible student, and had always hoped that she would have a son born who would be a preacher, so she thought that little Robert might fulfill her hopes and ambitions.

Capt. Gordon was a farmer, growing mostly cotton crops on the Red River bottom lands. The following year, 1907, after the birth of little Robert, Capt. Gordon's crops were almost a failure. The Spring was late and overflows damaged cotton. This, together with unfavorable financial conditions, caused a panic in the United States in the Fall of 1907. Thus the first year of the boy's life started under unfavorable conditions.

When Robert was a little over two years old, his mother gave birth to a girl, the first born to her, but still she showed great interest in Robert; talked much of his future and took great interest in teaching him to live according to the Bible.

At about the age of five, his mother began to teach him the alphabet. He learned very quickly how to read and write, before he started to school. He was always willing and glad to go to Sunday School with his mother, took a great interest in the sermon, and what the Sunday School teacher had to say about the creation of the world, and about God's great plan.

Little Robert went to church one day and the preacher took his text from 1 Thes. 4:16-18, "For the Lord himself shall descend from Heaven with a shout, with the voice of the archangel and with the trump of God; and the dead in Christ shall rise first: Then we which are alive and remain, shall be caught up together with them in the clouds, to meet the Lord in the air: and so shall we ever be with the Lord. Wherefore comfort one another with these words."

Robert was very much interested in this sermon, and asked his mother to explain how the Lord could descend from Heaven and what kind of vehicle we would ride in if we were caught up in the clouds to meet the Lord in the air. His mind puzzled over this for weeks and months, and he was anxious to understand more about it. He said, "Mother, I should like to meet the Lord in the air."

His mother said, "You will be able to do so some day, Bobbie."

When in Sunday School one day, the teacher read from 2 Thes. 1:7-8, "And to you who are troubled rest with us; when the Lord Jesus shall be revealed from Heaven with his mighty angels, in flaming fire taking vengeance on them that know not God, and that obey not the gospel of our Lord Jesus Christ." The preacher said that the Lord had placed the rainbow in the sky as a testimony that he would never again destroy the world by water, but explained that God would come again in a flame of fire and thus take vengeance on those who did not believe and destroy the world by fire. Robert wanted to know if the good Lord who loves us so much would destroy the world and all of those in it. His mother explained that God would destroy those that were sinners and rebelled against him and had not accepted his word.

Bobbie was in Sunday School again and heard them read from 1 Tim. 2:11-14: "Let the woman learn in silence with all subjection. But I suffer not a woman to teach, nor to usurp authority over the man, but to be in silence. For Adam was first formed, then Eve. And Adam was not deceived; but the woman being deceived, was in the transgression." He asked the Sunday School teacher to explain what this meant,—by learning in silence and subjection. He also wanted an explanation of the statement that a woman should not teach, because he said that his mother had always taught him and loved him, and his father had paid no attention to him and had no desire to teach him. He wanted to know if it was wrong for his mother to teach him, and if God would punish her. The teacher replied that the Lord said, "Suffer the little children to come unto me, and forbid them not, for of such is the Kingdom of God." She explained that his mother set an example more by her love and devotion than by words; that a mother's actions would influence a child more than anything she could say, and this was the great silent teaching.

Robert often visited the colored mammies on the plantation and listened to the ghost stories they told, and the fear was created in his mind of the spirits that walked in the night. He was often afraid that the goblins would get him if he didn't watch out. One Sunday at church, the preacher took for his text Gen. 1:7, "For God has not given us the spirit of fear, but of power and of love and of a sound mind." When Robert heard this, he wanted to know how it was that we should fear things, if God had not given us the spirit of fear nor created the spirit of fear in us, but gave us a spirit of power and of love and of sound mind. His mother explained to him that the ghost and the fear of the dark which the old darkies told him about, were nothing but superstition, and he should banish it from his mind.

A few Sundays later, the minister took his text from 2 Tim. 3:1, "This know also, that in the last days perilous times shall come." Robert was anxious to know when the last days would come. His mother told him it would be at the time of the end of the world and God would again come to destroy the world by fire.

The minister continued to read from 2 Tim. 3:15, "And that from a child thou hast known the holy scriptures, which are able to make thee wise unto salvation through faith which is in Christ Jesus." Robert was desirous of knowing if children could teach more about the scriptures than grown people. His mother told him that the Bible said, "A little child shall lead them," and that anyone who would harm little children, can in no wise enter into the Kingdom of Heaven.

CHAPTER II

IN 1913, Robert suffered a severe illness in the Spring, and for a few months his life was despaired of, but he quickly recovered. Soon after his recovery, his father took him on a fishing trip to Spirit Lake. The old darky of slavery days went along, and while he was putting worms on Robert's hook, told the story about this lake and why it was named "Spirit Lake." The old darky said that the spirit of a beautiful lady walked on the waters of the lake at night and that was why they called it Spirit Lake.

Long, long years ago, the daughter of a wealthy planter fell in love with a poor but honest boy and after many years of courtship, in which they spent many moonlight nights rowing on the beautiful lake, the time came when they felt that they could no longer be separated. The young man pleaded with her father to consent to their marriage, but he stubbornly refused and threatened to kill the young man if he ever called at his home again. They then planned to elope one night, and as her sweetheart was placing a ladder under the window and helping her to get down, her father shot her lover and killed him. When she found that he was dead, she ran to the lake and drowned herself. They searched for days for her body and one moonlight night they saw her walking on the water. They rowed out

on the lake and found her body floating on the water.
He said that the fish would always bite better at full
moon, but the darkies were afraid to fish there because
the spirit of this beautiful young lady walked on the
water.

Bobbie came home very much interested and excited
and told his mother all about the fish they caught at
Spirit Lake and about the story old Moses told him
about the spirit walking on the water. He told his
mother that the Sunday School teacher had read in the
Bible where Christ walked on the water, and he wanted
her to explain how this could happen. She told him
that all of those things happened in the days of miracles
which had passed and no longer happened in these days.
Bobbie had a great desire to walk or ride upon the
water, and was enthusiastic about bicycles. He told
his mother that he intended to build a bicycle some day
that he could ride on the water.

In 1914, when war broke out, Capt. Gordon, who
had once served in the Spanish-American War, became
very much interested in the conflict and followed it very
closely, reading the papers daily and talking about it.
Robert soon began to take great interest in the war and
asked his father and mother many questions about the
foreign countries which were involved in the great strug-
gle. He would sit for hours, listening to his mother
read the Bible, from the Book of Revelation, the prophecies of the Great War, where it says that nation shall
rise against nation.

Robert's mother told him of his grandfather who distinguished himself in the Civil War, and the great hard-

ships her mother had to go thru during the war days; how her great-grandfather fought in the War of 1812. She talked of his grandfather, Colonel Robert Gordon, for whom he was named, and how he became famous during the Civil War, and how later Robert's own father went with Colonel Roosevelt and became a Captain in the Spanish-American War in 1898. Robert's oldest brother, Herbert, was born in 1894, and his second brother, Ralph, was born in 1898 after his father went to the war. His mother spent many anxious months and worried with the children while Capt. Gordon was away at war. She prayed that war would be ended for all time.

She said, "Bobbie, you come from a generation of fighters on both sides, but I hope that you will be a minister and preach against war. While the tragic death of your brother Herbert in San Francisco was a shock that I have never fully recovered from, yet I had rather know that he went that way than to have him go to war and lose his life. I remember well the many sleepless nights that I have passed thru while your father was away at war and how happy I was when he returned. I prayed to God then that war might be ended and that none of my sons would ever have to go to war."

"Mother," said Bobbie, "when I get to be a man, I will be a preacher and tell the people to be peaceful and stop fighting, but why doesn't God stop the war?"

"My son, war is the work of the devil, not of God, and the Bible tells us that the old dragon has to be loosed for a little season, but in the Book of Revelation, we read that Satan is bound for a thousand years. I hope I live to see that day and I feel sure you will. A few nights before you were born I had a very strange dream. I thought I saw San Francisco and Los Angeles destroyed in two days by some war machine, and that one of my sons came near losing his life there, but was saved and afterwards he saved his country and made peace with the world. I suppose I dreamed about San Francisco because Herbert lost his life there but, somehow, I feel that it was more than a dream, and that you are born to be a peacemaker."

Bobbie was greatly impressed with his mother's dream and her hopes and ambitions for him, but his brother would quarrel and try to fight with him. Bobbie would tell him that Dad wanted him to be peaceful and that his mother wanted him to be a peacemaker and that he would not fight. His brother called him "Cottonhead" because his hair was so white, and accused him of being a white-livered coward, but Bobbie was patient and did not lose his temper. His mother would commend him for this and tell him that the Bible said to control your temper and not let your angry passions rise.

About this time some of the prejudice which little Robert had inherited from his grandfather and from his father, began to show forth. Unfavorable conditions thruout the country and the low price of cotton left Capt. Gordon practically penniless, causing him and all of his children to labor hard in order to support themselves. He tried to force young Robert to work in the fields and help cultivate the cotton, but he stubbornly rebelled. He would play around the house, use his father's tools and talk about the great inventions that he was going to make. His mother was always in sympathy with Robert and tried to encourage him, but she could never get him to take an interest in working on a farm. He talked of being a preacher, talked of great inventions and discoveries, but would not work at hard labor.

In 1917, when the United States entered the World War, young Robert was eleven years old. He had great ambitions to join the Army and go to the war. His older brother Ralph joined the Army. Young Robert said that if he could not go and fight for his country he would stay at home and work on a patent which would help them to win the war. He did not agree or get along with his older brother and was glad when he had gone away to war. His parents were still in poor circumstances but they could not induce young Robert to do any work on the farm. He continued to tinker around and work with his father's tools, trying to make a bicycle which he could ride upon the water in the lake nearby. He tried various kinds of lumber to build wheels for the bicycle but none of them worked successfully. Finally his mother suggested that he use thin cedar boards because cedar was durable in the water, was light and would float easily. He finally succeeded in building the wheels out of cedar and after heating pine rosin hot and pouring it into the cracks, he was able to ride successfully across the lake, but in a short time the wheels sprung a leak and the bicycle sunk with him in the lake, but he swam out and brought the bicycle with him.

Bobbie was not the kind to be discouraged by obstacles and later his ingenuity overcame the difficulties. After trying to put inner tubes from bicycle tires on the inside of the wheels of his water bicycle and failing again, he finally got some inner tubes from an automobile and placed them inside his wooden wheels and pumped them up. When they were filled with air, they pushed against the wooden sides of the wheel, buoying up the wheel, and he was then able to ride his bicycle around over the lake without any trouble.

His mother was very proud of him and said "Bobbie, one day your dream of becoming a great inventor will be realized. You have not been wasting your time tinkering around with your father's tools trying to make things." His brother, Ralph, continued to call him "Fool Bobbie" and "Mother's dream"; said he would never amount to anything because he wouldn't work on the farm like the rest of them. Bobbie always found a willing listener in his mother. She helped him with his studies in school and encouraged him in every way and showed that she believed in him and had faith that one day he would be a great man. This encouraged him to do greater things.

The success with the water bicycle had kindled his ambition and created a desire to complete other inventions that he had in mind. He told his mother of a dream he had of a white-winged bird that flew across the ocean thru the air; that he was riding the bird and that he received a great triumph and reception when he visited the foreign countries, and how his own people received him in great glory when he returned. His father called these stories "pipe dreams," but his mother took great interest in them and always encouraged him. Robert talked very little to his father or brother but always went to his mother and talked over things and confided in her. She encouraged him because she felt that he was an answer to her prayer, after her eldest son had died,—that God might give her another son who would live and that she might have her desires and hopes realized which were lost thru the death of her eldest son.

Robert was entirely strange and different from other boys. He never seemed to want to play with them, but kept very much by himself; talked along different lines, and made a confidant of his mother only. She seemed to understand him as no one else did and he always came to her for an explanation of his problems, and for consolation in time of trouble.

Robert's mother ofter talked to Capt. Gordon about him—told him that he was a peculiar and most unusual child and that she thought that his refusal to work at manual labor was not because he was lazy but because she believed that he had a superior mind, and that if properly educated and trained, he would become a great man some day, an honor to his parents. She told him that Bobbie had advanced ideas fully a hundred years ahead of his time and that he should be educated and allowed to follow his own ideas. His father, failing to understand him, agreed with his mother and decided when Robert was about thirteen years of age, that there was no use trying to keep him on the farm, but that he should be sent away to Texarkana to school, to learn something and to become interested in the things along which his mind seemed to lead.

While in this school he met his first real boy chum, one who seemed to understand him and one who proved to be a help to him in school. Walter Kennelworth was the son of a wealthy lumberman. He had every advantage that money could bring and was far advanced in his studies, thus being able to render help to Robert, who had no interest in grammar but took a great interest in history and mathematics. Walter would help him with his work in grammar and geography. They became fast friends. Robert told Walter of his plans for the future; that he hoped to be a great inventor; wanted to get an education and travel around the world to see the country and learn about things and develop the ideas which he thought would help his country in time of war. He had heard so many stories about his grandfather's adventures in the Civil War and his father's experiences in the Spanish-American War that he had the desire to be a great soldier and serve his country. He spent nearly all of his time reading the newspapers and following the progress of the war. He was extremely interested in the victories of our boys overseas, and when they began to turn the tide against the Germans, he was greatly elated and told his mother that he knew that the Stars and Stripes would never trail the dust and that victory was sure as soon as the American boys went on the other side.

Walter Kennelworth also had ambitions of becoming a soldier and of making new discoveries and inventions along chemical lines. His hopes and aspirations were to one day become a great chemist. The vast difference in the environment and conditions under which these two boys had been brought up seemed to make no difference in their friendship. It ripened as the years went by. Robert and Walter were often together and Walter often invited Robert to his father's home. Walter's father and mother became very fond of Robert.

When the armistice came in 1918, Robert talked with his mother and father, asking them if that would be the last war. They, of course, expressed the hope that it would be, and Robert said that he had read the Bible and thought that the greatest war in history was yet to come. He began to express ideas about new inventions, years ahead of the times. He begged his father and mother to let him leave school and go to work in an automobile factory where he could learn about machinery and understand how to complete the inventions which he was always talking about.

School was over in the Summer of 1919, and Mr. J. H. Kennelworth, Walter's father, offered Robert a position in his office during the summer months. After business, Walter and Robert would often go out automobile riding. Along in July, he met with a serious accident. The automobile was overturned and Robert's arm was broken, and he suffered internal injuries. He was taken to the hospital where he lay for several weeks before recovery. His mother was very much worried and alarmed over this accident, and thought it was best

for Bobbie to return to the farm and not work in the city any more.

His brother Ralph had just returned from France, where he had met with many obstacles in the war but had received no serious injury. Robert went home for a rest after the accident. He had many disagreements and fights with his older brother, and it seemed to be impossible to get along. All of the trouble occurred over the fact that Robert would not work on the farm, or help his brother.

Bobbie prevailed upon his mother to let him go back to school in the Fall because he was making great progress and hoped to have a big position some day with Mr. Kennelworth's firm.

In the Fall of 1919, he returned to school, but made slow progress in his studies. His health was not good; he seemed unable to concentrate or make much progress. He barely passed his examinations at the end of the year, but continued to study hard and make progress in mathematics and history. In grammar, writing and geography he was always falling below his marks, and Walter Kennelworth had to help him out.

In the Spring of 1920, just before the close of school, Robert's father obtained help to cultivate the cotton plantation. He thought it best that Robert should come home that summer and help to work on the farm, but again the boy refused, and met with stubborn opposition and abuse from his brother, who called him "the fool inventor" and said that he would never amount to anything because he refused to work on the farm. He said that he wanted to be "Gentleman Robert," and called him the "white-collar boy." These disagreements and disputes with his brother were very annoying and disappointing to Robert's mother, because she wanted the children to get along in peace. Robert told his mother that on account of his brother he would never live at home again; that he would continue to stay in Texarkana and go to school until he had finished his education, and then he would go to work for Mr. Kennelworth. His mother had great faith in him and told him that she knew everything would come out all right for him, and that he should study hard, make the most of his opportunities, and prepare for the position Mr. Kennelworth was going to give him upon completing his studies.

Capt. Gordon had been very successful during the war growing cotton. Prices had gone very high and he had accumulated quite a little money. But in 1920 cotton prices declined rapidly and his cotton brought very little, which again reduced them to poor circumstances. Robert became very ill again from malaria during the Spring and Summer of 1920, so that he was unable to work even if he wanted to. Up to this time he had shown no ambition for any kind of work, except to try to make something with his father's tools; talk about inventions and some of the great things he was going to do in the years to come. His mother had always petted him because of his severe illnesses and accident, and his father often referred to him as his mother's burden or his mother's problem. But she had great faith in young Robert because he clung so strongly to religion, believing in the Bible. Robert would spend

days and hours reading the Bible and talking to his
mother and asking her questions about it and its meaning. He had a great desire to travel and see the world
and was always planning to visit strange places. While
he showed great affection for his mother, his desire was
to get away and see the world.

CHAPTER III

IN the Spring of 1921, Robert began to make greater progress in his studies, which greatly encouraged his chum, Walter Kennelworth. Robert would study and read early and late. Walter would often call on him in his room and find him there deeply engrossed reading the Bible and puzzling over the interpretation of the meaning of many parts of the Scriptures.

One Sunday in the early part of June, Robert and Walter went to church and the minister took for his text 1 Cor. 13:2, "And though I have the gift of prophecy, and understand all mysteries, and all knowledge; and though I have all faith, so that I could remove mountains, and have not charity, I am nothing." Then the minister read from the 7th verse, "Beareth all things, believeth all things, hopeth all things, endureth all things," and again from the 11th verse, "When I was a child, I spake as a child, I understood as a child, I thought as a child; but when I became a man, I put away childish things." The minister further read from the 13th verse, "And now abideth faith, hope, love, these three; but the greatest of these is love." Again he read from 2 Cor. 5:7, "For we walk by faith, not by sight," and concluded the reading of the text from Gal. 5:14, "For all the law is fulfilled in one word, even in this, Thou shalt love thy neighbor as thyself."

The minister preached a great sermon. Robert thought it one of the best he had ever heard and one which impressed him the most. The minister talked about the great work of faith and said that faith without works is dead; but that there could be no faith without love because love was the greatest of all things. That God was love, and that love was the fulfilling of the law, "For God so loved the world that he gave his only begotten son that whomsoever believeth on Him might not perish, but have everlasting life." He added that God loves children who honor and obey their parents, wives who love and obey their husbands, husbands who love and protect their wives, and admonished each man to love his neighbor as himself. Because love is the law of harmony, and the power that created the universe, it is the only power that can prevent destruction, war and human death, but with true love we can overcome the last great enemy, death.

When men love each other as God loves them, there will be no longer any strife or contention. Man will no longer covet what belongs to his neighbor. True love will deal justly and do unto others as we wish to have them do unto us. He preached about the ambitions, the love of country and patriotism which inspires men to go to battle and give their lives for the protection of their home and country. He said, "Greater love hath no man than this, that he lay down his life for his friend," and that a great reward was sure to come to those who love and obey God. He talked of God's great command, "If you love me, keep my commandments."

This sermon stirred Robert's ambition as nothing else

had ever done before. It made him realize the love that he owed to his mother, whose great faith and love had helped to lay the foundation for his future career. He thought about what the preacher said—that a man deserts father and mother to cleave unto his wife, and that this was as it should be. He had always felt his greatest love for his mother, but now for the first time in his life he began to think of love for another woman.

His mind turned toward the many beautiful girls that he used to meet in Sunday School and those who were in his class. Robert's chum, Walter, had already had a puppy love affair in school with a girl by the name of Caroline Oglethorpe. Robert had laughed at Walter about this and thought it was all foolishness. But now he began to think that maybe there was something more to love than what he had heretofore believed it to be. Walter Kennelworth's family being one of the most wealthy and prominent in Texarkana, they were at all the social functions, at which Robert met all the younger set in the city.

A few weeks after the minister had preached this sermon on charity and love, Robert was in church one morning, and after Sunday School, was talking with Caroline Oglethorpe, and with her was her chum, Marie Stanton. Walter introduced Robert to Marie. Marie was the daughter of a wealthy and prominent family. Her father, Colonel Stanton, had made a fortune in building railroads. He was now a big lumberman, and one of the most prominent in Texarkana. Marie was a beautiful young girl of about thirteen years of age when Robert met her. She was of the true brunette type, with glossy black hair and dark eyes that sparkled like diamonds.

About this time, Robert began to read novels and love stories and became very much interested in them, always taking strong sides with the hero and becoming very much agitated and aroused against the villain. He saw Marie frequently after this, as she attended the same school as Robert and Walter. Every time that Robert saw Marie, she looked more beautiful to him. Robert soon began to lose sleep thinking about Marie, and realized that love was the greatest thing in the world. He confided his secret to his friend, Walter.

Being very bashful, he had never said anything about his love to Marie. Finally he made up his mind one night that he would write her about it, so this is what he wrote:

Wednesday Eve.

DEAR MARIE,

You probably remember several weeks ago, when I was introduced to you in church, the sermon that the minister preached and his text from St. Paul where he said, "The greatest thing in the world is love." I agree with St. Paul; that is why I am writing to you.

I liked you the first time I met you, and every time I have seen you since, I have liked you more. Now that I know I love you so much, I feel that I must tell you. I hope that you are going to love me some day.

Your friend,

ROBERT.

Marie replied to the letter as follows:

DEAR ROBERT,

I received your nice note. This is the first time that anyone has ever written to me about love and I am all excited over it.

I never thought that you liked me, Bobbie. I always thought that you were making eyes at Kitty Anderson in school. I do like you and think that you are a nice boy.

Yours,

MARIE.

When Robert read the last line, he felt his heart jump right up in his throat. His hopes and ambitions soared higher than they had ever before. He began to dream of the future with Marie as his wife. He talked of his plans to Walter, and his hope of being a great inventor some day and making a lot of money so that he could marry a wealthy girl like Marie.

The following Sunday, he went home to the country to see his mother, and told her the story of the new love affair. "Bobbie," said his mother, "you are little over fifteen years old, and this is only puppy love, or what they call school-boy and school-girl love. It will soon pass away, but there is no harm in it. Love is a great thing and some day you will meet the right girl, but there is no use being in any hurry about it."

Bobbie told his mother that Marie was the only girl in the world for him, and that he would live and work for her; that if he couldn't marry Marie he never wanted any other girl. His mother laughed at this and told him that they all thought that way over the first love affair, but that after a while, as the years went by and he met the real one, this would all pass away. However, she did tell Bobbie that she had never forgotten her first love, as there is something different about the first love, even tho it doesn't last.

"Stick to your studies," said she, "and do not let your love for Marie interfere with your progress."

She saw that this love was a great stimulator for Robert and that his ambitions were greater than ever. He told his mother that he was going to Sunday School every Sunday and that he was studying hard, reading the Bible and learning a lot, and that he was preparing to be a great man. His mother said, "Bobbie, I have always had great faith in you, and I know that one day my dream will come true, and you will do something that will make me very proud of you."

In June, 1921, Robert Gordon and Walter Kennelworth were in the graduating class. Altho Walter was one year younger than Robert, his early advantages enabled him to graduate at fourteen, while Robert was graduating at the age of fifteen, and would not have been able to pass all of his examinations except for the help and assistance rendered him by Walter. Marie Stanton, who was then thirteen years of age, graduated the following year.

After Robert graduated, he at first decided to secure a position and go to work, but after consulting with Walter, he decided that it would be best to enter High School and get thru as soon as possible. So in the Fall of 1921, he and Walter began High School. Here is where his greatest work began to show forth. He took a great interest in physics and higher mathematics, studied day and night, making very high marks in these studies. Also took an interest in chemistry, which Walter was specializing in, because he knew that it would be useful to him with his invention, which he was still talking so much about, and his plans.

The time passed by quickly and in 1924 Robert Gordon and Walter Kennelworth graduated from High School in Texarkana with high honors. In the meantime, the love affair between Robert and Marie had continued with the usual interruptions, obstacles and petty quarrels existing between young people of their age.

In the Fall of 1924, it was finally decided that Walter should go to Columbia College in New York to begin his course. Robert's parents were unable to finance him through College, and it was decided that he should go to work for Mr. Kennelworth in his office. Robert hated to part with his old friend, Walter, but they thought it was for the best and talked of the future in New York, hoping that one day Robert could join Walter there.

In the following year, 1925, Marie Stanton graduated from High School with the highest of honors. Robert was at the graduation exercises and thought that Marie had grown more beautiful every year, and was anxious for the day to come when he could claim her for his wife. Soon after her graduation from High School, there was much talk about the College Marie should enter. Her father and mother finally decided that she should go to the Kidd-Key College at Sherman, Texas, as this was nearby and Marie could go home occasionally.

As the time neared for Marie to go away, Robert became more anxious. He thought Marie would fall in love with someone else. He talked with her about the future, and for the first time, spoke of marriage. He talked to her of the difference in their station in life, and said that his mother thought that a marriage between a wealthy girl and boy of poor circumstances could never result in harmony and happiness. He told Marie the story that the old darky had related on the fishing trip, about the love affair between the poor country boy and the wealthy planter's daughter, and their tragic death. Marie thought her father would never consent to their marriage, but she said she really loved Robert and when the time came, she would elope with him if necessary. This greatly cheered Robert and made it easier for him after Marie went away to College.

Love letters passed between them during the first year she was at college, and all went well. Robert worked hard in his new position in Mr. Kennelworth's office. He was a willing worker, an expert stenographer and secretary. Robert continued to show expert mechanical ability and could fix anything that was wrong with an automobile.

Walter corresponded often with Robert and also wrote to his father asking how Robert was getting along. Mr. Kennelworth replied that Robert was making great progress, that he was a very brilliant boy and he was going to help him all he could for he thought Robert had a great future.

1926 was to be one of the most eventful years in the life of Robert Gordon. In the Spring his father died suddenly, and after a consultation with his mother, it was decided that he should leave his position, return to the farm and help them to get things straightened out. He encountered the usual obstacles and opposition from his brother, because he knew nothing about farming and of course did not like it. The result was that he put all of his savings into helping to make the crop. While it turned out to be a good crop, the low prices of cotton in the Fall of 1926 left them in debt.

While on the farm, he contracted malaria fever and a severe spell of illness followed, during which time he received many consoling letters from Marie. Soon after he was able to return to his position with Mr. Kennelworth, he met with another severe automobile accident, this time breaking his right arm. This necessitated six weeks in the hospital before he was able to return to work again. One disappointment followed another, but Robert had learned to practice patience. He read the Bible, especially the story of Job, continued to go to church, and while he was suffering many trials and tribulations, his mind was expanding. He could not accept the theory preached and taught by preachers, because he knew that the things they taught were wrong.

Marie returned home for her vacation. She was now eighteen years old, and had grown more beautiful and began to attract more attention from young men. As the Kennelworths and Stantons had been friends for years, Walter suggested to his parents that they give a party in honor of Marie Stanton. A young man by the name of Edward Mason, the son of a very wealthy northern family, was there, and showed marked attention to Marie. Robert became very jealous and after the party had a quarrel with her. Then followed long weeks of agony.   Many letters passed between Robert and Marie.

When the end of August drew near and Robert knew that Marie was to return to school soon, he was anxious to make up before she went away and wrote the following letter:

DEAREST MARIE,

I am very sad.   I feel the reason you refuse to make up with me is because you are in love with Edward Mason.   I have never loved anyone but you and never will.   If we are not reconciled before you go back to school, I fear we never will be.   I am sending you two poems, "Parting" and "Yesterday," which express how I feel.

Sorrowfully,

ROBERT.

PARTING

Kiss me!   The spell is broken,
　　The dream we dreamed is gone;
Nothing remains but memory—
　　Memory, and dawn.

Kiss me!—and then your hand, dear,
　　Do you not feel the beat,
The rhythm of our pulses?
　　It does not spell defeat.

It spells the song that life sings,—
　　The message of the heart—
Pathways meet but to widen
　　And lips meet but to part.

YESTERDAY

Dreams—just dreams of yesterday,
    When love to me was sweet,
Romance has now gone astray,
    No other love will I greet.

It was short—my little romance,
    Short—but God—how good!
Went along as smooth as a dance,
    Part us? It seemed no one could.

But someone did—tho' I forgive,
    He loved her as did I,
For her only—did I live,
    And now—for her I'd die!

When Marie received the letter, she replied:

DEAR ROBERT,

    Your letter and poems received. You are again accusing me wrongfully. You are all in the wrong and until you can see your mistake, I will never think of making up.

                Sincerely,

                      MARIE.

In September, 1926, Marie returned to school at Sherman, Texas, leaving Robert very much broken-hearted because she refused to make up. She told Robert his jealousy was wholly unfounded, but he persisted in accusing her of being in love with Edward Mason. Feeling this way, she was unable to reconcile herself and make up, so she went away, disappointed herself and leaving Robert in the same fix.

Following her return to school, Robert spent many

long weeks of anxiety, becoming very blue and dejected. Many letters passed between them. He wrote much poetry to Marie, all without avail. Finally, he wrote a letter and told her that it would be the last; that he knew she was in love with Edward Mason, and that there was no use going on.

DEAR MARIE,

This is to be my farewell letter to you, for I have given up hope. Ever since I first met you, you have been my ideal and my one inspiration. I have lived for you, worked for you, thought of nothing else but you. Your love has given me great encouragement to go on, and now I realize that I have lost you and that your love has been given to another. I shall always love you and hope that you will some day change your mind, and your heart turn to me.

Sorrowfully, your own

ROBERT.

With this letter he sent the poems "Loved and Lost" and "Good-bye."

DEDICATED TO MARIE:

LOVED AND LOST

It isn't failure to have lost
A girl of whom you have nobly thought,
If buffeted and tempest tossed,
You fail to win the girl you sought.
It isn't failure, though the prize
In another's hand is placed;
A hero very often dies
If dying keeps him undisgraced.

To bow unto a better man
Is not the worst thing I could do,
Success is not in the things we scan,
But in the heart forever true,
It takes more courage for to fail
Than win a girl undeserved.
To bear the taunts of those who rail
Than from your purpose to be swerved.

When a girl frowns darkly
And hope is on the wane
Be constant, true and patient
Defeat will blossom into gain.
If your aim is high and honest
In victory it will tell,
For before the pearl is gotten
There must be a broken shell.

ROBERT.

TO MARIE,

GOOD BYE

And now I fly to bear my wound away,
    Haply the future heals me of this hurt,
Since, sorely wounded, I still keep today
    Mine honor as an armor around me girt.

But these last words, fair lady, bear in mind:
    Ere for your sport another heart you break,
Forbear the triumph dear to womankind
    And spare your victim, even for my sake.

When Robert had finished this letter, he wrote to his
old chum, Walter Kennelworth, in New York, that he
had written a farewell letter to Marie and that it was
all over.   Walter replied:

DEAR ROBERT,

I have received your letter filled with gloom. Now, cheer up, old pal, the sun will shine again and Marie or some other girl just as good will smile on you. You are too young to let a girl wreck you. Stick to business and keep up your studies.

I enclose a poem which I think about fits your case, and it will probably work out about that way.

With all good wishes,

Your friend,

WALTER.

A BROKEN VOW

It was a broken hearted boy who vowed a solemn vow,
I will not write a letter to that pretty little Editoress anyhow;
I will not do that fearsome thing, I will not pen a jest,
About the beautiful Hostess who mocks the staying guest.

He made a postscript to his vow, he made a codicil,
He was serious as tho he formed his will,
And then he sat down and smiled with all his might
About all the love letters he did not have to write.

But in a day or two he felt exceedingly queer and strange,
A restless something filled his mind, he longed for a change;
He asked the doctor what was wrong, the doctor gave a pill,
And made a memorandum to add twenty to his bill.

Then the pictures of all the girls he knew,
Came flocking to his brain;
Marie's lovely angel face marched sternly in the train,
And each of them and all of them compelled him to think
Just as a man thinks when he quits smoke or drink.

At last a little disappointing note came—then he said:
Just one more farewell love note I'll write;
It shall not be serious, something fancy and light.

He wrote a love letter,
Just as a man who says he has sworn off; \
Takes Rock and Rye or some such thing to stop a cough.

But why pursue this sorry tale,
Why tell of what he did;
'Twas like the one more smoke or drink
That throws away the lid.

He wrote of the things she'd wrote and said,
Of memories of sweet caresses that haunted the heart and head;
He wrote of how much better she was than the other girl of
    the South,
Of her beautiful eyes and ruby mouth.

He wrote of love for her,
And how well she had served cocoa and consomme;
He wrote of love lost and debauched,
Until the break of day.

And when they came and found him ill
And sought to nurse him thru,
They said, "Here taste this chicken soup
She made, it will be good for you."

Robert became very despondent. He no longer took
an interest in his work. Mr. Kennelworth finally wrote
to Walter in New York, telling him of Robert's lack of
interest in business, and that he wondered what had
brought such a change in him. Walter, of course, had
received letters from Robert about his break with Marie,
so he wrote his father frankly and told him to have
patience with Robert, that when this love affair passed
away, he was sure he would be all right again.

Upon receiving Robert's letter, Marie wrote:

MY DEAR ROBERT,

This is to be my farewell letter to you. I quote from Solomon, 2:5, "Stay me with flagons, comfort me with apples; for I am sick of love." Robert, I would rather have green apples and a stomach-ache, like Solomon says, for I am sick of what you call love. I want you to read St. Paul again, and see if the way you are acting is the way love acts. Paul says that "Love suffereth long, and is kind; love envieth not, doth not behave itself unseemly, seeketh not her own, is not easily provoked, thinketh no evil." Robert, if love is founded on faith and trust, it cannot be jealous. Love is the foundation of understanding, and if you understood me and if I thoroughly understood you, we would be in love yet, and be happy.

> "Love seeketh not its own to please
> Nor for itself hath any care,
> But for another gives its ease
> And builds a heaven in hell's despair."

So long as you persist in jealousy and accuse me falsely, how can I go on loving, because you are not the old Robert who first loved me and taught me to love all of these years, and was never jealous before. Love that has been founded on years of confidence cannot change in a moment for another, and my love has not changed to Edward Mason, as you think. I still love you, but you have been wrong in your accusations.

I am sending you a little article, "Love," and hope that you may some day see how wrong you have been, and when you do, if you feel that way, write and tell me so.

Regretfully,

MARIE.

LOVE

The spark of love gives more light than the universe of truth; yet truth is in love, and in order to act the truth, you must make love the truth, for remember that the handshake of friendship, or the kiss and love of an innocent child, will do more to lift a soul to the light than the strongest and wisest argument even when rightly understood.

Beyond the boundaries of love no thought ever passed for love is everywhere. Love is a prophecy of freedom, and its song of melody is heard in the rhythmic motion of the ocean.

Each "fowl of the air, each fish of the sea, and every living thing that moveth upon the earth" is the manifestation of love, for in their subsistence love has said, "As I CREATE SO I PROVIDE." Thus in every conceivable thing with form or without, with harmony or with discord—there love is manifested.

Love is the life of every plant, of every sunset, of every soul. It is the inspiration in the happy mind, and the voice that speaks to us in the time of temptation.

Love is the foundation of all understanding, it transcends all reasoning, for it is the fulfillment of the greatest.

Love gives faith to all things, for love believeth in its own.

Love symbolizes the everlasting, for it is the spirit of the beginning, and its wonderful radiance of color decks each sunrise and sunset.

Love is the breeze that blows away the clouds of doubt making the landscape of the soul radiant with joy and gladness. Each heart keeps time in unison to the rhythmic harmonies of love, for each is LOVE in ALL.

Love has thrown into the shapeless void the breath that has given life to worlds and this vital spark or the life of man, illuminates the picture that love has painted.

CHAPTER IV

WHEN Robert received Marie's letter, he began to see himself in a different light. He read again the Book of Job, and realized what Job meant when he said, "I had a great fear, and it has come upon me." Robert realized that he had been fearful of losing Marie, and that as soon as there seemed to be a possibility of someone else being attracted to her, that that fear had come upon him and caused him to become jealous without cause, and that he had lost or was about to lose, Marie, who had been more than life to him. So he replied to Marie as follows:

DEAREST MARIE:

Your sweet letter received. It has opened my heart to understanding and made me see myself as I am. I have read St. Paul on the greatest thing in the world and find that I have not been patient, have not been kind or generous. Above all, I have been jealous without cause. All of these things are not a part of true love. Paul says, "Faith, Hope and Love, but the greatest of these is Love." If I had had that great faith which never faileth and which is founded on love I would not have been jealous. I have been selfish; have sought myself to please, and have not thought enough about you.

I am sending a little poem that I have written, entitled "The Garden of Love," which I think will express to you fully just how I feel and how I see things now. I have tried to enter the Garden of Love through the wrong gate, and now I want to enter it through the right gate. I will be happy and trusting, loving and thinking only of you.

No more doubts or jealousy will ever be in my mind again, because love will be there, and these foul weeds can never remain where love is.

I want you, Marie, and only you. Please forgive and forget and make me happy again.

With all the love my heart can send, I am

Hopefully,

Your own ROBERT.

DEDICATED TO MARIE STANTON, WHO INSPIRED IT.

THE GARDEN OF LOVE

Many enter the Garden of Love thru the wrong gate while there really is only one perfect gate. Imagination often leads us into the wrong path.

SELFISHNESS

We enter thru the gate of Selfishness and immediately find ourselves in the dark Valley of Doubt where the foul weeds of deceit, lack of confidence, malice, greed and jealousy abound. Just on the other side of the Valley of Doubt lies the Mountain of Jealousy, which springs from lack of faith, understanding and forgetfulness. From the Mountain of Jealousy flows the river of Hate which has its source in the Valley of Doubt. This river leads to the Sea of Unhappiness, Sorrow, Despair and Death.

UNSELFISHNESS

We now enter the right gate to the Garden of Love, where we see a golden sign "Unselfishness" which can only lead to Love. We enter the Garden thru the Gate of Understanding where a beautiful bed of white lilies grow in all their fragrance. Grasp one quickly and carry it thru life, for these are the lilies of faith which smother out all the foul weeds in the garden.

Next you will see a fountain of pure water. Touch your lips to it for it is the Water of Forgetfulness and it feeds the Lily of Faith. After this you are ready to pass on thru the Garden and enjoy the flowers which blossom forth nurtured by the Water of Love. Among these are Self-sacrifice, which is the basis of real love. Then you will find a beautiful flower that many never see at all, Confidence. It is beautiful and fragrant and stands near the Flower of Happiness.

You will find the flower of Kindness in full bloom beside the Rose of Charity, then near the end of the Garden there is a tiny flower blooming all alone. It is pale and delicate and few appreciate it until late in life,—*it* is Unrewarded Kindness. But we do reach it just before we pass into the Vale of Content, and we realize that the path which leads to Love and Happiness is only found by helping to lead our fellow travelers thru the Field of Content.

When we have progressed thus far we look for the other entrance to the Garden and find that the Gate of Selfishness has disappeared and the Valley of Doubt is now covered with the Lily of Faith, and the Mountain of Jealousy has been melted into a Valley of Self-sacrifice. Where the River of Hate flowed we now find a Sea of Kindness flowing into the Ocean of Happiness. When we reach the end of the Garden we find the flower of all flowers, its beauty and radiance far outshining the noon-day Sun. Seek no further—it is the Flower of Love. Place the Lily of Faith beside it, nurture it with the Water of Kindness and you will have it always.

ROBERT.

This was the letter that won Marie, because she agreed with St. Paul that love was the greatest thing in the world. She did not wait to write, but telegraphed Robert:

YOUR SWEET LETTER RECEIVED—YOU ARE MY OLD ROBERT AND
I AM YOUR MARIE AND ALWAYS WILL BE

MARIE.

Marie then wrote the following letter:

DEAR ROBERT,

I have just wired you because I am happier now than I
have ever been and I know that we are always going to be
happy. You are going to be my ideal Robert, the way that
I want you to be, and I am going to love you and make you
so happy that you'll always be that way.

I knew all along that it was useless for us to make up until
you saw things in the right light and realized that there was
no cause for jealousy and that my long years of devotion
should have proven my love. Until you could see it that way
and make up under those conditions, it would only invite more
trouble later.

There is really nothing more to say, but to let bygones be
bygones, live and love each other and make the future everything we want it to be, because love creates everything and
made the world. God is love.

The little poem you sent, "Loved and Lost," seems very
appropriate now for in it you said that before the pearl is
gotten, there must be a broken shell. You did have the broken
shell, Robert, and now we are going to mend it. I believe that
your aim has been high and honest, and now in future it
will tell.

I can hardly wait to see you, Robert. I want you to come
over next Saturday afternoon, and spend Saturday evening
and Sunday with me. I want to look into your trusting eyes
again and know that you still love me in the same old way.
I want to make you know that I have never loved Edward
Mason or anyone else, but have always loved and trusted you.

With all the love my heart can give, I am

Your

MARIE.

P.S.   I am enclosing a poem, "The Land of Beginning Again." We are really going to begin again, aren't we, Robert, and be more happy than ever?

THE LAND OF BEGINNING AGAIN

I wish that there were some wonderful place
    Called the Land of Beginning Again,
Where all our mistakes and all our heartaches
    And all of our poor, selfish grief
Could be dropped, like a shabby old coat, at the door,
    And never put on again.

I wish we could come on it all unaware,
    Like the hunter who finds a lost trail;
And I wish that the one whom our blindness had done
    The greatest injustice of all
Could be at the gates, like an old friend that waits
    For the comrade he's gladdest to hail.

We would find all the things we intended to do
    But forgot and remembered—too late,
Little praises unspoken, little promises broken,
    And all of the thousand and one
Little duties neglected that might have perfected
    The day for one less fortunate.

It wouldn't be possible not to be kind,
    In the Land of Beginning Again;
And the ones we misjudged and the ones whom we grudged
    Their moments of victory here
Would find in the grasp of our loving handclasp
    More than penitent lips could explain.

For what had been hardest we'd know had been best,
　And what had seemed loss would be gain;
For there isn't a sting that will not take wing
　When we've faced it and laughed it away;
And I think that the laughter is most what we're after
　In the Land of Beginning Again!

So I wish that there were some wonderful place
　Called the Land of Beginning Again,
Where all our mistakes and all our heartaches
　And all of our poor, selfish grief
Could be dropped, like a shabby old coat, at the door,
　And never put on again.

LOUISA FLETCHER TARKINGTON.

On a beautiful sunshiny Saturday afternoon on the 23rd of October, 1926, as the train wended its way across the prairies for Sherman, Texas, Robert kept watching out of the car window, his face beaming with smiles as he thought of his meeting with Marie. He counted every turn of the wheels because he knew they were bringing him closer to her.

When he arrived in Sherman that night, Marie welcomed him with open arms. They spent Saturday and Sunday together and were happier than they had ever been before. He confided to Marie his future plans. Told her that he was working on an invention, and also planning to make some money speculating in Stocks and Commodities. That he hoped to make a lot of money and prove himself worthy of her, so that her father would consent to their marriage. That he would return with all the hope and faith a man could have in a woman, and with that faith and her love failure was impossible, as there wasn't anything in the world he

couldn't do. Marie assured him of her faith and confidence. So long as he had that faith and her love,
she knew he could do great things. Said she would
willingly wait until he made a success.

After Robert returned, he began to study the Bible
more than ever, and work out things according to
science. He read the Book of Ezekiel, and planned on
building an airplane along the lines outlined by Ezekiel.
Figured that there must be a way to build a plane of
this kind which would be the greatest ever, and felt that
the day was coming when his country would need the
protection of the greatest invention of the age. From
reading of the Bible, war seemed inevitable, and Robert
believed that the next war would be in the air.

He began to read all the magazines along the lines of
science and invention and studied the Bible in order to
understand natural law and know how to apply it.

Robert wrote to Walter telling him that he had been
to Sherman to see Marie, that they had made up and
that he was supremely happy. He confided to Walter
his hopes of a great discovery and told him that with
the love of Marie and her faith in him there was nothing
he could not do.

He had figured out from the Bible that a time of
trouble such as the world had never seen would begin in
1927, and would continue until 1932. There would be
war, famine and pestilence all over the earth, and that
except the time be shortened every human being on the
face of the earth would be destroyed according to the
Bible. He was anxious to make money to complete his
invention to protect his own country because he knew

that the United States was yet to face the greatest war in history, and every nation would rise against us. The great gold supply that was gathered by the United States from the beginning of the great World War had caused commercial jealousy of all other nations and it would only be a short time before we were at war. Unless we were prepared with modern inventions we were going to lose the next war. He knew what was coming and wanted to prepare to meet the emergency that was to come.

Many letters passed between Robert and Marie during the latter part of 1926. Her letters of love and encouragement helped Robert to make progress in his work. He saved his money and planned for their future.

Christmas, 1926, was the happiest that Robert had ever known and wanting Marie to share it with him he sent her a beautiful ring, wrote her that he had saved his money and was now in position to buy it. The diamond, he said, represented purity, firmness and faith and symbolized all those things in her and his great trust in her. He told her that he was anxious to get in shape to go to New York to continue his studies, and work and make money and be near his old chum, Walter, who had always been a great comfort to him and encouraged him in so many ways.

In thanking Robert for the ring, Marie wrote that so long as she lived, she would wear it in honor of him, and as an emblem of faith and trust in the greatest man in the world. That she knew there was nothing he could not do. The little poem entitled, "It Can Be

Done,'' which she sent along was a great inspiration
to Robert when trials, troubles and obstacles arose in
the years that followed.

IT CAN BE DONE

Somebody said that it couldn't be done,
　　But he, with a chuckle, replied
That maybe it couldn't, but he would be one
　　Who wouldn't say so till he tried.
So he buckled right in, with the trace of a grin
　　On his face. If he worried, he hid it,
He started to sing as he tackled the thing
　　That couldn't be done, and he did it.

Somebody scoffed: "Oh, you'll never do that:
　　At least it has never been done,"
But he took off his coat and he took off his hat,
　　And the first thing we knew he'd begun it,
With the lift of his chin, and a bit of a grin,
　　Without any doubting or quiddit,
He started to sing as he tackled the thing
　　That couldn't be done, and he did it.

There are thousands to tell you it cannot be done,
　　There are thousands to prophesy failure;
There are thousands to point out to you, one by one,
　　The dangers that wait to assail you;
But just buckle in with a bit of a grin,
　　Then take off your coat and go to it;
Just start in to sing as you tackle the thing,
　　That cannot be done and you'll do it.

On the 1st day of January, 1927, Robert received a
beautiful letter of commendation from his employer,

Mr. Kennelworth, in which was enclosed a check for $500 as a bonus, and also notice of an advance in his salary of $50 a month. This was very gratifying to Robert, because he felt that he was making progress, and that a man who had made the great success that Mr. Kennelworth had, must have been watching him closer than he thought. He thought that Mr. Kennelworth had seen something in him worthy of advancement, so he only worked harder to show his appreciation. He wrote a letter to his friend Walter in New York telling him of his father's generosity and how much he appreciated it now that he was working, planning and saving his money, hoping to be with Walter in New York soon where he could start speculating and make a lot of money so that he could complete his great invention and do something to benefit the world.

Robert wrote Marie of this good fortune which had come to him in the new year and how it had stimulated his hopes to greater things in the future. He was sure that with her love, he would continue and accomplish every desire that he had hoped for. Marie wrote him beautiful letters of encouragement, filled with love and admiration for the man that she was living for,—her ideal. She told him that she was making great progress with her studies and hoped to graduate in a few years and be an honor to him and assist him in his work. She sent a little poem, entitled: "Act the Man and Face It Out."

ACT THE MAN AND FACE IT OUT

Should life's storms be blowing gusty, or the road be hot and
    dusty,
  Don't give up and pull a face all glum and blue;
Cheer up, man, and tackle trouble. If your efforts you re-
    double
  There'll be brighter days ahead awaiting you.

Where's the use of whining, moaning, or of wasting time in
    droning
  Never yet have such things pulled a fellow thru,
When you've trouble you must meet it, that's the proper way
    to treat it,
  Always bear in mind results depend on you.

Never heed the whiner's chatter, 'tis right deeds that matter,
  That will pierce the clouds—the roughest pathway span,
Every trouble is made lighter, and you'll find your outlook
    brighter
  If you tackle things and face them like a man.

If you mean to conquer trouble, you must take it at the double.
  You must act the man and face the matter out;
Tackle trouble, gamely fight it. Shirking it will never right it,
  Face it bravely, and your trouble you will rout.

                      Tid Bits.

Marie wrote of her plans for the future. How she
hoped to live to see him the greatest man in the world;
how she wanted to one day bring him before her father
and show him what her love and confidence in a poor
boy had done for him. She wanted her father to be
proud of Robert as she was. After all the success she

wanted them to be able to enjoy the closing years of
their lives in peace and quiet together, where they could
reminisce over the trials, troubles and obstacles overcome which had led to the victory which is always the
fruit of true and lasting love.   Here follows a poem—
"After the Years—Quiet."

AFTER THE YEARS—QUIET

At last—after the years have wrought their will,
Go build a house of solace for thyself;
With things that pleasure thee its rooms upfill—
Turn thy soft light; a rosejar on thy shelf.

Have there the books thou wilt not read again,
So well thou knowest all of their magic old;
Have there the lute that silent shall remain,
Thy heart all music from its tones of gold.

And dream beside thy fire; dream of the guest
That cometh now no more—yet he is there,
If so thy soul would shape him, and thy rest
And dream—within a dream with thee will share.

Have there all things thou countest as thine own;
And what thou wouldst have had—there let it be.
But what thou wouldst not let it pass unknown,
After the years have wrought their will on thee.

And take no more a burden on thy heart,
Wrestling—if this be good—if that be ill;
And strive no more to better what thou art;
With consolation thy whole being fill.

And so with quiet lapping thee around,
A presence like a God's thy house shall fill,
But question not thereof nor even pray,
For importuning words such joy might mill.

Build thee that house of solace—out of sight;
A charm above the door and on the sill,
And trouble shall go by thee. 'Tis thy right—
At last—after the years have wrought their will.

                              EDITH M. THOMAS.

Robert sent Marie an article entitled, "A Standard" by Christian D. Larson. He told her that this was going to be his standard for the future, and that following this standard with her love and faith he would accomplish everything that she hoped for him to.

A STANDARD

To be so strong that nothing can disturb your peace of mind.

To make all your friends see that there is something in them.

To look at the funny side of everything and make your optimism come true.

To think only of the best, to work only for the best, and to expect only the best.

To be just as enthusiastic about the success of others as you are about your own.

To forget the mistakes of the past and press on to the greater achievements of the future.

To wear a cheerful countenance at all times and give every living creature you meet a smile.

To give so much time to the improvement of yourself that you have no time to criticize others.

To be too large for worry, too noble for anger, too strong for fear; and too happy to permit the presence of trouble.

To think well of yourself and to proclaim this face to the
world, not in loud words but in great deeds.
To live in the faith that the whole world is on your side so
long as you are true to the best that is in you.

CHRISTIAN D. LARSON.

Marie continued to write him encouraging letters
from time to time.   Their love affair continued smooth
with no troubles or interruptions.   Marie was a great
reader and was studying carefully, always collecting
poems and articles which she thought would help and
encourage Robert.   One was entitled:

"WHY THE SAINTS WERE SAINTS"

Because they were cheerful when it was hard to be cheerful;
And patient when it was hard to be patient;
And because they pushed on when they wanted to stand still;
And kept silent when they wanted to talk,
And were agreeable when they wanted to be disagreeable.

AUTHOR UNKNOWN.

and also another one by Herbert Kaufman, reading
as follows:

Don't let busy-bodies turn you from the path you have se-
lected,
Incredulity and unbelief are quite to be expected,
What if butters-in do scold you?
What if fools try to remold you?
If you aren't streaked with yellow such
Discouragement won't hold you.
Some will doubt you.
Lots will flout you.

More than one will lie about you.
They'll deride you
And decide you.
Need an "Older" hand to guide you.
Do not listen to the croakers—fight it out once you have commenced it.
If you meet with opposition simply run your head against it.
All big things that we know about were won by self-believers.
Quitters, never have been, nor can they be, achievers.

HERBERT KAUFMAN.

CHAPTER V

MARIE'S love and devotion for Robert were bearing fruit. He studied the Bible day and night, worked on his plans for the future and continued his investigation of science, for he believed that the Bible was the key to the process by which man may know all there is to know. He realized that by studying it he might be able to forecast the future and benefit himself thereby. Above all things he was interested in airplanes, inventing and improving an airplane that would be useful in the future wars. He had found the plan for a great airplane in Ezekiel 1:4-16:

And I looked, and behold, a whirlwind came out of the north, a great cloud, and a fire infolding itself, and a brightness was about it, and out of the midst thereof as the colour of amber, out of the midst of the fire.

Also out of the midst thereof came the likeness of four living creatures. And this was their appearance; they had the likeness of a man.

And one had four faces, and every one had four wings.

And their feet were straight feet; and the sole of their feet was like the sole of a calf's foot; and they sparkled like the colour of burnished brass.

And they had the hands of a man under their wings on their four sides; and they four had their faces and their wings.

Their wings were joined one to another; they turned not when they went; they went every one straight forward.

As for the likeness of their faces, they four had the face

of a man, and the face of a lion on the right side; and they four had the face of an ox on the left side; they four also had the face of an eagle.

Thus were their faces; and their wings were stretched upward; two wings of every one were joined one to another; and two covered their bodies.

And they went every one straight forward; whither the spirit was to go; they went; and they turned not when they went.

As for the likeness of the living creatures, their appearance was like burning coals of fire, and like the appearance of lamps: it went up and down among the living creatures; and the fire was bright, and out of the fire went forth lightning.

And the living creatures ran and returned as the appearance of a flash of lightning.

Now, as I beheld the living creatures, behold, one wheel upon the earth by the living creatures, with his four faces.

The appearance of the wheels and their work was like unto the colour of a beryl; and they four had one likeness: and their appearance and their work was as it were a wheel in the middle of a wheel.

Robert felt sure that this was the prediction and description of an airplane that Ezekiel was talking about. He thought that an airplane could be built with four wings, which would be more powerful and useful than any of the airplanes yet built. It was his great desire to build an airplane of this kind.

Robert read Ezekiel 5:2 and 12:

Thou shalt burn with fire a third part in the midst of the city, when the days of the siege are fulfilled; and thou shalt take a third part, and smite about it with a knife; and a third part thou shalt scatter in the wind; and I will draw but a sword after them.

A third part of thee shall die with the pestilence, and with

famine shall they be consumed in the midst of thee; and a
third part shall fall by the sword round about thee; and I
will scatter a third part into all the winds, and I will draw
out a sword after them.

Also Ezekiel 7:2 and 12:

Also, thou son of man, thus saith the Lord God unto the
land of Israel. An end, the end is come upon the four corners
of the land.

The time is come, the day draweth near; let not the buyer
rejoice, nor the seller mourn; for wrath is upon all the multitude thereof.

Robert thought he saw in this the coming war and
famine on the earth from the cycle, that a greater
portion of the earth would be destroyed by war and
famine, and that the end was near. Ezekiel 7:13:

For the seller shall not return to that which is sold, although
they were yet alive; for the vision is touching the whole multitude thereof, which shall not return; neither shall any
strengthen himself in the iniquity of his life.

Ezekiel 8:1 and 14:

And it came to pass in the sixth year, in the sixth month,
in the fifth day of the month, as I sat in mine house, and
the elders of Judah sat before me, that the hand of the Lord
God fell there upon me.

Then he brought me to the door of the gate of the Lord's
house which was toward the north; and behold, there sat
women weeping for Tammuz.

Ezekiel 10:9-11:

And when I looked, behold, the four wheels by the cherubims, one wheel by one cherub, and another wheel by another

cherub: and the appearance of the wheels was as of the colour of a beryl stone.

And as for their appearances, they four had one likeness, as if a wheel had been in the midst of a wheel.

When they went, they went upon their four sides; they turned not as they went, but to the place whither the head looked they followed it; they turned not as they went.

Robert felt sure that it was an airplane which Ezekiel was talking about and which was going to be made in the future. He thought the one referred to with "the face of an eagle" referred to the United States Government. He hoped to build some day and help win the great war in the air and make peace when the days of the "End" come and the great air battles would be fought. Ezekiel 10:19 and 21:

And the cherubims lifted up their wings, and mounted up from the earth in my sight; when they went out, the wheels also were beside them; and every one stood at the door of the east gate of the Lord's house; and the glory of the God of Israel was over them above.

Every one had four faces apiece, and every one four wings; and the likeness of the hands of a man was under their wings.

Ezekiel 12:22:

Son of man, what is that proverb that ye have in the land of Israel, saying, The days are prolonged, and every vision faileth?

Ezekiel 14:14, 16 and 21:

Though these three men, Noah, Daniel and Job, were in it, they should deliver but their own souls by their righteousness, saith the Lord God.

Though these three men were in it, as I live, saith the Lord

God, they shall deliver neither sons nor daughters; they only shall be delivered, but the land shall be desolate.

For thus saith the Lord God. How much more when I send my four judgments upon Jerusalem, the sword, and the famine, and the noisome beast, and the pestilence, to cut off from it man and beast.

Ezekiel 16:1 and 44:

Again the word of the Lord came unto me, saying,

Behold, every one that useth proverbs shall use this proverb against thee, saying, As is the mother, so is her daughter.

Ezekiel 17:3 and 7:

And say, Thus saith the Lord God, A great eagle with great wings, long-winged, full of feathers, which had divers colours, came unto Lebanon, and took the highest branch of the cedar:

There was also another great eagle with great wings and many feathers; and, behold, this vine did bend her roots toward him, and shot forth her branches toward him, that he might water it by the furrows of her plantation.

Ezekiel 20:46:

Son of man set thy face toward the south, and drop thy word toward the south, and prophesy against the forest of the south field:

Robert interpreted this to mean that the day was coming when there would be a great air fight from the southern part of the United States. Ezekiel 20:47:

And say to the forest of the south, Hear the word of the Lord, Thus saith the Lord God, Behold, I will kindle a fire in thee, and it shall devour every green tree in thee, and every dry tree; the flaming flame shall not be quenched, and all faces from the south to the north shall be burned therein.

He thought this meant the South would be destroyed by airplanes with liquid fire and poisonous chemicals when the war would take place.

Robert read Ezekiel 21:14, 26 and 30:

Thou, therefore, son of man, prophesy, and smite thine hands together, and let the sword be doubled the third time, the sword of the slain; it is the sword of the great men that are slain, which entereth into their privy chambers.

Thus saith the Lord God, Remove the diadem, and take off the crown; this shall not be the same; exalt him that is low, and abase him that is high.

Shall I cause it to return into his sheath? I will judge thee in the place where thou wast created, in the land of the nativity.

Ezekiel 28:3:

Behold thou art wiser than Daniel; there is no secret that they can hide from thee:

Robert had great faith in the prophecies of Ezekiel because the Lord said: "Behold, thou art wiser than Daniel. There is no secret that they can hide from thee." He understood from Ezekiel's prophecies that a great war was coming and that it would be fought in the air by the great airplanes as described by Ezekiel 32:1 and 2:

And it came to pass in the twelfth year, in the twelfth month, in the first day of the month, that the word of the Lord came unto me, saying,

Son of man, take up a lamentation for Pharaoh king of Egypt, and say unto him, Thou art like a young lion of the nations, and thou art as a whale in the seas; and thou camest forth with thy rivers, and troubledst the waters with thy feet, and fouledst their rivers.

From these predictions of Ezekiel and others in the Bible which Robert believed was a repetition of previous battles, he interpreted it to mean that there was to be a great flood during the year 1927. He predicted terrible floods along the Mississippi Valley, which would destroy the cotton crops and would lay waste vast acres of fertile land. He wrote that it would be one of the greatest floods in history. Ezekiel 32:7:

And when I shall put thee out, I will cover the heaven, and make the stars thereof dark; I will cover the sun with a cloud, and the moon shall not give her light.

· Robert understood this to mean the two great eclipses that would occur in June, 1927.
Ezekiel 33:21 and 33:

And it came to pass in the twelfth year of our captivity, in the tenth month, in the fifth day of the month, that one that had escaped out of Jerusalem came unto me, saying, The City is smitten.
And when this cometh to pass, (lo, it will come) then shall they know that a prophet hath been among them.

Robert felt that he knew the Scriptures and was prepared to prophesy the future and warn the people of the famine, pestilence and the coming war.
Ezekiel 35:1 and 8:

Moreover, the word of the Lord came unto me, saying,
And I will fill his mountains with his slain men: in thy hills, and in thy valleys, and in all thy rivers, shall they fall that are slain with the sword.

Ezekiel 36:1 and 34:

Also, thou son of man, prophesy unto the mountains of

Israel, and say, Ye mountains of Israel, hear the word of the Lord.

And the desolate land shall be tilled, whereas it lay desolate in the sight of all that passed by.

Ezekiel 37:9, 16, 17, 19 and 22:

Then said he unto me, Prophesy unto the wind, prophesy, son of man, and say to the wind, Thus saith the Lord God, Come from the four winds, O Breath, and breathe upon these slain, that they may live,

Moreover, thou son of man, take thee one stick, and write upon it, For Judah, and for the children of Israel his companions: then take another stick and write upon it, For Joseph, the stick of Ephraim, and for all the house of Israel his companions:

And join them one to another into one stick; and they shall become one in thine hand.

Say unto them, Thus saith the Lord God, Behold, I will take the stick of Joseph, which is in the hand of Ephraim, and the tribes of Israel his fellows, and will put them with him, even with the stick of Judah, and make them one stick, and they shall be one in mine hand.

And I will make them one nation in the land upon the mountains of Israel; and one king shall be king to them all; and they shall be no more two nations, neither shall they be divided into two kingdoms, any more at all.

Robert interpreted this to mean the coming of the great war when the United States should be the one great nation that would rule the world; that there would be no more divided kingdoms and no more divided countries, that it would be the United States of the World, which would be the land of liberty where freedom exists.

Ezekiel 38:19:

For in my jealousy and in the fire of my wrath, have I spoken, Surely in that day there shall be a great shaking in the land of Israel.

Robert understood—"the jealousy in the fire of wrath"—to mean chemical elements which would be used in the coming war and the use of airplanes.
Ezekiel 39:2:

And I will turn thee back, and leave but the sixth part of thee, and will cause thee to come up from the north parts, and will bring thee upon the mountains of Israel.

Robert's interpretation of this was that the last great battle of the war was to be fought in the northern part of the United States.
Ezekiel 39:8 and 9:

Behold, it is come, and it is done, saith the Lord God; this is the day whereof I have spoken.
And they that dwell in the cities of Israel shall go forth, and shall set on fire and burn the weapons, both the shields and the bucklers, the bows and the arrows, and the handstaves and the spears, and they shall burn them with fire seven years.

He thought the 9th verse where it says that everything should be burnt with fire seven years, meant either seven years of war, or seven days. He had read where it says, "I will appoint a day for a year and a year for a day."
Ezekiel 39:11, 12 and 14:

And it shall come to pass in that day, that I will give unto Gog a place there of graves in Israel, the valley of the passengers of the east of the sea; and it shall stop the noses of the passengers; and there shall they bury Gog, and all his multitude; and they shall call it, The Valley of Hamon-gog.

And seven months shall the house of Israel be burying of them, that they may cleanse the land.

And they shall sever out men of continual employment, passing through the land to bury with the passengers those that remain upon the face of the earth, to cleanse it; after the end of seven months shall they search.

Robert thought all this referred to the war yet to come, in which the United States was to play the final and principal part, and the use of the airplanes should reach its greatest perfection.

Ezekiel 43:1, 2, 3, 4 and 10:

Afterward he brought me to the gate, even the gate that looketh toward the east:

And, behold, the glory of the God of Israel came from the way of the east, and his voice was like a noise of many waters: and the earth shined with his glory.

And it was according to the appearance of the vision that I saw when I came to destroy the city; and the visions were like the vision that I saw by the river Chebar: and I fell upon my face.

And the glory of the Lord came into the house, by the way of the gate whose prospect is toward the east.

Thou son of man, shew the house to the house of Israel, that they may be ashamed of their iniquities; and let them measure the pattern.

Ezekiel 44:1, 4, 5 and 26:

Then he brought me back the way of the gate of the outward sanctuary, which looketh toward the east, and it was shut.

Then brought he me the way of the north gate before the house; and I looked, and, behold, the glory of the Lord filled the house of the Lord; and fell upon my face.

And the Lord said unto me, Son of man, mark well, and behold with thine eyes, and hear with thine ears, all that I say unto thee concerning all the ordinances of the house of the Lord, and all the laws thereof; and mark well the entering in of the house, with every going forth of the sanctuary.

And after he is cleansed they shall reckon unto him seven days.

Robert thought this referred to the last seven days at the end of the Great War in the Air.
Ezekiel 45:25:

In the seventh month, in the fifteenth day of the month, shall he do the like in the feast of the seven days, according to the sin offering, and according to the meat offering, and according to the oil.

Robert thought this referred to the 15th day of July, 1932.
Ezekiel 46:1, 2 and 17:

Thus saith the Lord God, The gate of the inner court that looketh toward the east shall be shut the six working days; but on the sabbath it shall be opened, and in the day of the new moon it shall be opened.

And the prince shall enter by way of the porch of that gate without, and shall stand by the post of the gate, and the priests shall prepare his burnt offering and his peace offerings, and he shall worship at the threshold of the gate: then he shall go forth; but the gate shall not be shut until the evening.

But if he give a gift of his inheritance to one of his servants, then it shall be his to the year of liberty; after it shall return to the prince; but his inheritance shall be his son's for them.

Ezekiel 47:5, 6, 8 and 9:

Afterward he measured a thousand; and it was a river that

I could not pass over: for the waters were risen, waters to swim in, a river that could not be passed over.

And he said unto me, Son of man, hast thou seen this? then he brought me, and caused me to return to the brink of the river.

Then said he unto me, These waters issue out toward the east country, and go down into the desert, and go into the sea: which being brought forth into the sea, the waters shall be healed.

And it shall come to pass, that everything that liveth, which moveth, whithersoever, the rivers shall come, shall live: and there shall be a very great multitude of fish, because these waters shall come thither: for they shall be healed; and everything shall live whither the river cometh.

Ezekiel 48:14 and 15:

And they shall not sell of it, neither exchange, nor alienate the first fruits of the land: for it is holy unto the Lord.

And the five thousand that are left in the breadth, over against the five and twenty thousand, shall be a profane place for the city, for dwelling, and for suburbs; and the city shall be in the midst thereof.

CHAPTER VI

ROBERT wrote to Walter in New York and told him about his plans for the future; how well he was getting along, about his new discoveries and how he had worked out the future from the Bible. He asked Walter's advice about sending an article to Walter's father in regard to his future predictions based on the Bible. Walter thought it the opportune time, in view of the fact that his father had confidence in Robert.

After he had worked out his cycle theory according to the Bible, and decided that he could forecast the markets and make money, he wrote to Mr. Kennelworth, his employer.

Texarkana, Texas.
January 15, 1927.

Mr. J. H. Kennelworth,
Texarkana,
Texas.

MY DEAR MR. KENNELWORTH:

I want you to know how much I appreciate the bonus you gave me on the 1st of the year. While I want to use it wisely, together with a little other money I have saved, I feel it is my duty to tell you what I intend to do with it.

I have been studying the Bible night and day for many years, and I believe that I have found in it the key to all prophecy,—the rules fortelling the events in the history of the country, the progress in invention, and also rules for forecasting the future of stocks and commodities. I have been reading some books and studying commodities and stocks and have applied the rules as I understand them from the Bible. I feel sure that I am able to foretell what is going to happen in stocks and commodities, and I am very anxious to make some money out of it so that I can go to New York and join Walter there, where I will have greater advantages and can study and experiment with some inventions which I have in mind.

From the teachings of the Bible and the methods which I have worked out, I feel confident that the price of cotton is going very high this Spring. I figure that there are going to be some heavy floods along the Mississippi River, and that there will be a late, wet Spring, and that the demand for cotton will greatly increase, helping to put prices very high. Therefore, I have decided to use the $500.00 which you gave me and another $500.00 which I have saved up, to buy cotton to hold for the Spring and Summer. I would like to have your opinion of this venture.

Assuring you of my appreciation of your advice, I am

Sincerely yours,

ROBERT GORDON.

About this time Mr. J. H. Kennelworth received the following letter from his son, Walter, in New York:

New York City,
January 12, 1927.

DEAR FATHER:

I have just received a letter from my good friend, Robert, and he tells me that he is anxious to join me in New York in a few months, that he has figured out some new discoveries and inventions from the Bible, and that he wants to do some speculating in order to make some money. He asked my opinion of putting before you some of his discoveries and getting your opinion on them. I wrote him that I was sure he would find a sympathetic listener in you and advised him to put his plans frankly before you.

Father, I hope that you will give Robert your best advice and co-operation because I have great faith in him. He is a brilliant boy and is going to have a great future. He is loyal and honest, you know, and a hard worker, and I would hate to see him leave your employ. At the same time I would like to see him in New York as soon as possible.

I am getting along nicely with my studies, and hope to graduate in a couple of years.

Give my love to mother, and all,

Your son,

WALTER.

When Mr. Kennelworth received Robert's letter, he dictated the following reply to his stenographer:

MY DEAR ROBERT:

Your very interesting letter received. I have the greatest faith in your ability and believe that if anyone can work out anything valuable from the Bible, you can do it. I have watched very carefully your persistency, and am much impressed with your loyalty and determination. It is admirable the confidence and faith that you have in yourself, as well as having great confidence in the greatest book of all, The Holy Bible.

But when it comes to speculation, Robert, I want to give you some advice from my experience. It is a very dangerous game. It may be inviting, but it is not a business, Robert. It is a gamble. Of course I know that some men make it a business. Most men cannot control themselves when they get into it, the result—they gamble, and in the end, lose all.

I will give you a little experience that I had. I went to New York many years ago, and on advice and information from some friends of mine, was induced to buy some oil stock. This was in the Fall of 1919. Oil stocks advanced rapidly, and along in October, my friends advised me to buy more. I had some handsome profits and did buy more. I confess that I knew nothing about oil stocks or any other stocks, but simply followed my friends' advice in buying them. In November, 1919, the market smashed all to pieces, and the oil stocks declined 50 to 100 points. I had big profits at the top, but before the break was over, I not only lost all of my profits, but about $50,000 or $60,000 of my capital.

This taught me a lesson. I had made my money in the lumber business and in railroading. I had now gone into something that I knew nothing about and suffered a heavy loss. My friends and brokers tried to induce me to hold on and put up more margin; said that I would eventually come out all right, but I took the loss and charged it up to experience. Had I held on to these stocks, I would have lost my entire fortune, because they continued to go down during 1920 and 1921, and were 50 to 60 points lower than where I sold out. So you can see, Robert, what a costly experience this would have been and how wise I was to stop in time.

The best advice that I can give you is, to stop before you start. You will save time and worry, aside from the loss of what little money you have saved up. I want to encourage and help you in every way possible, and I feel that I am helping you in giving you advice of this kind.

Wishing you all success in your studies, I am

Yours very truly,

J. H. KENNELWORTH.

Robert's second letter to Mr. Kennelworth:

January 24, 1927.

MY DEAR MR. KENNELWORTH:

I have read your letter with a great deal of interest. I appreciate your fatherly advice and know that you have my interest at heart. I appreciate your telling me of your experience in speculation and know that this can be the only result where people only guess at the market, or follow tips. I have secured some books from New York and read a great deal about the market, and I feel that I already know that there are many pitfalls in the game of speculation, but if it can be made a science and followed according to the rules laid down in the Bible, success and profits are sure.

Sir William Crookes said: "To stop short in any research which bids fair to widen the gates of knowledge, to recoil from fear of difficulties or adverse criticism, is to bring reproach upon science." I feel that I have my own life to live; that I must have faith in myself and above all, have the faith which is instilled in me through the study of the Bible. I must neither fear difficulties nor criticism. I must put my theories and my discoveries to the test. The only way that I can do that, is to follow what I think is right.

I have already made arrangements and sent my money to a broker in New York, and have today bought 200 bales of July cotton at 13.80. I am going to hold this cotton. If it goes up, as I am sure it will this Spring and Summer, as my profits accumulate, I am going to buy more on the way up.

I believe in what the Bible says:

"Prove all things and hold fast to that which is good."

Jacob said:

"I have read in the tables of heaven whatsoever things shall befall both of you and your children."

I believe in the stars, I believe in astrology, and I have figured out my destiny. The Bible makes it plain that the stars do rule. 147th Psalm, 4th verse:

"He tellest the number of the stars, he callest them all by name."

Dante said:

"Follow thy star—thou shalt see at last a glorious haven."

Napoleon and many other great leaders of olden times followed their stars, and believed in them.

Mr. Kennelworth, I have gained a great deal of knowledge by following the Bible. I have gone into secret places to pray, and have kept my discoveries to myself. I believe in the saying:

> "In silence, by silence, through silence were all things made."

Daniel makes it clear that the stars influence:

> "And he changeth the times and the seasons: he removeth kings, and setteth up kings: he giveth wisdom unto the wise, and knowledge to them that know understanding."

> "He revealeth the deep and secret things: he knoweth what is in the darkness, and the light dwelleth with him."

I have followed the teachings and admonitions of Solomon, and realize that knowledge is the greatest of all things. I have tried to get understanding and believe that I have received it from the Bible, and that I must use it.

I refer to Daniel:

> "And in the days of these kings shall the God of heaven set up a kingdom which shall never be destroyed: and the kingdom shall not be left to other people, but it shall break in pieces and consume all these kingdoms, and it shall stand forever."

Mr. Kennelworth, I believe this prophesy is yet to be fulfilled. I believe that the United States is the kingdom which is never to be destroyed; that we will eventually see the United States of the World, and that this country, which is the land of love and liberty, will rule wisely all other nations.

I quote from Daniel:

> "And whereas they commanded to leave the stump of the tree roots; thy kingdom shall be sure unto thee, after that thou shalt have known that the heavens do rule."

I have demonstrated this to mean that the planets rule our destinies. It is right for us to understand them as Daniel did and interpret the secret and hidden things.

I believe the wise men of the East, the astrologists before the birth of Jesus Christ, knew where and when he would be born by the study of the stars. St. Matthew, Chapter 2: 2—

> "Saying, Where is he that is born King of the Jews?
> for we have seen his star in the east, and are come
> to worship him."

This shows to me that the wise men believed that certain stars
arising would indicate a great man would be born, a savior
of the world. St. Matthew, Chapter 6: 6 and 8—

> "But thou, when thou prayest, enter into thy closet, and
> when thou hast shut the door, pray to thy Father,
> which is in secret; and thy Father, which seeth in
> secret, shall reward thee openly."

> "Be not ye therefore like unto them: for your Father
> knoweth what things ye have need of before ye ask
> him."

I have prayed and studied in secret, and I believe I am going
to receive my reward. I believe that our heavenly Father,
the ruler and maker of this universe, does know our needs,
and that he gives us understanding according to the way we
would receive it.

I was much impressed when I read St. Matthew 6:33—

> "But seek ye first the kingdom of God, and his righteous-
> ness; and all these things shall be added unto you."

I have sought that kingdom and I have found it where the
good book says it is: "The kingdom of heaven is within you."
Again the good book says:

> "If ye believe in me, greater things than these shall
> ye do."

I believe that I can and will do great things.

Ever since I was a small boy, and used to kneel at my
mother's knee, and she taught me first to pray, I have believed
in that great book and in God's power to guide me right and
give me understanding of all things. My own father never
understood me or had any sympathy with me or my ideas,
which I feel were far advanced. My own brother was my
worst enemy, and I find that the Bible bears me out in this

> "And a man's foes shall be they of his own household."

My father and brother opposed me because they did not understand me.

I firmly believe that the Bible and the Scriptures contain the key to all knowledge, and that all a man has to do is to seek and he shall find, knock and it shall be opened unto him. I believe it is best for me to go away to New York as soon as I can, away from my own people, for the good book says:

> "A prophet is not without honor, save in his own country, and in his own house."

The Bible points the way to read the signs and the stars. St. Matthew 12: 38, 39 and 40—

> "Then certain of the scribes and Pharisees answered, saying, Master, we would see a sign from thee."

> "But he answered and said unto them, An evil and adulterous generation seeketh after a sign; and there shall no sign be given to it, but the sign of the prophet Jonas:"

> "For as Jonas was three days and three nights in the whale's belly; so shall the Son of man be three days and three nights in the heart of the earth."

I have read the Book of Jonah thru very carefully, and I believe that I understand what the Saviour meant when he said:

> "No sign shall be given, but the sign of the prophet Jonas."

I believe there was a secret meaning in what he said; that the Son of man be three days and three nights in the heart of the earth. I believe that a man who understands the meaning of that has all the power under heaven and earth, as the Bible says he shall have. I believe that that is the key to the interpretation of the future. I am sure I have found it and know how to apply it.

I do not wish to burden you further with this long letter, Mr. Kennelworth. I am very much interested in my work on future cycles, and if you are interested in what I can work out on the future cycles, I will be glad to send them to you and let you watch them. I have figured out the repetition of each cycle when wars will come. I believe that the wheat prices forecast coming wars. Through my study of the Bible, I have determined the major and minor time factors which repeat in the history of nations, men and markets.

I trust that you will understand me and not feel that I do not appreciate your advice when I started speculating. If my new discoveries work, as I hope they will, I look forward to the day when you can join me in a great campaign for making money.

Assuring you of my deep appreciation of all your kind advice, I am

Sincerely yours,

ROBERT GORDON.

On the same night, January 24th, after Robert had received a telegram from his broker in New York, stating that he had bought 200 bales of July cotton at 13.80, Robert figured that this would margin him to 12.80. He was sure from his study that July cotton would never decline to 13.25.

He sat down and wrote:

MY DARLING MARIE:

Love is the greatest thing in the world. It is all powerful, and your love for me is going to make me the greatest man in the world. Today I have started on the road to fame and fortune. When we were together last, I told you about my discoveries of the cycles from the Bible and said I was sure that I could figure out what the stock, cotton and grain markets were going to do; that I was going to start speculating as soon as I got the money.

You discouraged me. Recently I wrote to Mr. Kennelworth about the matter, and he also discouraged me. He told me what a hazardous and dangerous business it is. I hope that you won't scold me, because I have already bought 200 bales of July cotton at 13.80 and put up $1000 as margin. I am sure that I am going to make money, and that it is going to be the means of bringing us a great deal of happiness. If I can make money, I can complete my invention and discoveries, go to New York where I will have all the advantages, and we can soon be married and realize our dream.

Ever since we made up last Fall, and I was sure of you and your love, I have been very ambitious and have not wasted a minute, have studied day and night. Wanted to prove to you that your faith in me was not to go unrewarded. I believe that the great success of many men has been because some good little woman placed a hand upon their shoulder and said: "I trust you and love you." I have read a great deal of the history of the men of great achievement, and every time I found back of the success the love of some good woman. It is the love of my mother and the love of you which has inspired me to greater things. I am sure that success is going to crown my efforts. Won't you give me your good wishes in my start on the road to success?

.With all my love, I am

As ever,

ROBERT.

Sherman, Texas.
January 26, 1927.

MY OWN DEAR ROBERT:

Your sweet letter just received. No, Robert, I am not going to scold you, because I believe in you. I know you are doing what you think is right, regardless of what anyone else thinks. I love you all the more because you have confidence in yourself, and above all, confidence in the Holy Bible. I want you to know, Robert, that should you lose your money and should things go wrong, disappointment befall you, my love will never waiver. My confidence in you is supreme, and I look forward to the day when I may bring you before my father and show to him that my confidence was not misplaced and that you have sustained my faith and hope.

I love you and will always love you, Robert, if you never make a dollar. It is not the money that counts with me, but it does count with my father and mother, and I want you to prove to them that without the help of anyone you can make as much money as father has. I know you can, and I will always love you and stand by you.

Devotedly,

Your MARIE.

On January 27th Mr. Kennelworth wrote to Robert:

MY DEAR ROBERT:

I have read your letter with a great deal of interest and understanding. You are a deep thinker and a great reader. Success is bound to come to a mind which interprets the meaning of things. I shall be very happy to have you write me about the future cycles as you interpret them, and shall watch them with a great deal of interest.

Now that you have taken the step, Robert, and started in speculating, I want to wish you success. I admire your courage in following your convictions and the faith you have in yourself, and if it is possible for you to win, I believe and hope you will.

Sincerely yours,

J. H. KENNELWORTH.

Robert's reply:

MY DEAR MR. KENNELWORTH:

My great desire to make money, I want you to understand, is to do some good with it and benefit my country, when she will need the benefit most. Please read Ezekiel very carefully, for I believe that Ezekiel is the greatest of all prophets. He aptly describes an airplane which I can make that will be a great aid in time of war. I believe that Ezekiel plainly foretold the war yet to come which will be fought in the air, and that the United States will be in great jeopardy, but will finally win out. So you see, my object in speculating is not a selfish motive altogether, but to help others and to help my country.

The following verses show that Ezekiel was predicting something to happen in the future and was carrying out God's instructions. Ezekiel 13:2 and 3—

> "Son of man, prophesy against the prophets of Israel that prophesy, and say thou unto them that prophesy out of their own hearts, Hear ye the word of the Lord";

Ezekiel 14:14, 16, 18 and 21—

> "Though these three men, Noah, Daniel and Job, were in it, they should deliver but their own souls by their righteousness, saith the Lord God."

> "Though these three men were in it, as I live, saith the Lord God, they shall deliver neither sons nor daughters; they only shall be delivered, but the land shall be desolate."

> "Though these three men were in it, as I live, saith the Lord God, they shall deliver neither sons nor daughters, but they only shall be delivered themselves."

> "For thus saith the Lord God, How much more when I send my four sore judgments upon Jerusalem, the sword, and the famine, and the noisome beast, and the pestilence, to cut off from it man and beast?"

Ezekiel 17:3—

> "And say, thus saith the Lord God, A great eagle with great wings, long-winged, full of feathers, which had divers colours, came unto Lebanon, and took the highest branch of the cedar":

Ezekiel 21:30—

> "Shall I cause it to return unto his sheath? I will judge thee in the place where thou wast created, in the land of thy nativity."

From this, I believe that more famines, earthquakes, pestilence and wars are yet to come and that the noisome beast referred to is the airplane. If we make calculations from the date and place of birth, I think we can determine what our future is to be, and in this way live according to cause and effect, which is God's divine law.

When I stated that I believed Ezekiel the greatest prophet of all, my authority is found in Ezekiel 28: 3—

> "Behold, thou art wiser than Daniel. There is no secret they can hide from thee."

Daniel was known to be a great prophet and astrologer. In his prophecies, he foretold war, pestilence and famine to come upon this earth, and by a proper study of the repetition of cycles we can determine the time when important events will take place in the future.

I am enclosing an article which I have written on Future Cycles, and also one on the Cycles of Transportation.

Thanking you for your interest in my work, I am

Sincerely yours,

ROBERT GORDON.

CHAPTER VII

FUTURE CYCLES

January 28, 1927.

IN making my predictions I use geometry and mathematics, just as the astronomer does, based on immutable laws.

I am a believer in the Bible. It is the most wonderful book ever written, a book of science, philosophy and religion. I claim that all scientific laws are laid down in the Bible if a person knows where to find them. Refer to St. Matthew 7:7, which says:

> "Ask and it shall be given you, seek and ye shall find, knock and it shall be opened unto you."

1 hold that the Bible contains the key to the process by which man may know all there is to know of the future, if he will only seek diligently for the rules laid down in the Holy Book.

My calculations are based on the cycle theory and on mathematical sequences. History repeats itself. That is what I have always contended,—that in order to know and predict the future of anything you only have to look up what has happened in the past and get a correct base or starting point. My authority for stating that the future is but a repetition of the past is found in the Bible.

Read Eccl. 1:9:

> "The thing that hath been, it is that which shall be;
> and that which is done, is that which shall be done:
> and there is no new thing under the sun."

Again

> "That which has been is now and that which is to be
> hath already been."

This makes it plain that everything works according to past cycles, and that history repeats itself in the lives of men, nations and the stock market.

We are told that the great continent of Atlantis, for centuries submerged under the Atlantic Ocean, possessed a civilization greater than ours of today. The people of Atlantis had their telephones, wireless, radios and airplanes. There is considerable truth in that statement. According to mathematical sequence, the wonderful inventions that brought comfort and convenience to the Atlantians are due to appear again, and we are now only on the threshold of another great age.

Remember, everything in this universe is elliptical or circular in motion; that applies both to the abstract and the concrete, the mental, physical and spiritual. Every thought you think makes a circle, and it comes back to you. It may take years but you will get the effects, good or evil, according as the thought was either good or evil. That is a truth we should learn, and the world will be the better for it.

In making my calculations on the stock market, or any future event, I get the past history and find out what cycle we are in and then predict the curve for the future, which is a repetition of past market movements. The great law of vibration is based on like producing like. Like causes produce like effects. Wireless telegraphy, the phonograph and the radio are based on this law. The limit of future predictions based on exact mathematical law is only restricted by lack of knowledge of correct data on past history to work from. It is just as easy to figure 100 years or 1000 years in the future as one or two years ahead, if you have the correct starting point and know the cycle which is going to be repeated.

A few years ago even scientific men, not alone the public, would have laughed at such a thing and refused to believe it. But mathematical science, which is the only real science that the entire civilized world has agreed upon, furnishes unmistakable proof of history repeating itself and shows that the cycle theory, or harmonic analysis, is the only thing that we can rely upon to ascertain the future.

Sometime ago an article appeared in the *New York American* commenting on the writings of Sir Arthur Evans, foremost English archeologist, who published "The Palace of Minos," a book concerning the ancient City of Minotaur. He described the excavation on the Isle of Crete in the Mediterranean Sea, in which they found modern apartment houses, bath tubs and corsets, the same as used today. The plumbing that they found was so excellent that it is still working after thousands of years. It is estimated that the ancient city was destroyed over 5000 years ago, or about 3500 B.C. The fact that a long time elapsed before apartment houses became popular again is another proof of history repeating itself and shows

"There is no new thing under the sun,"

but that we simply resurrect the old ones.

"How do I forecast future cycles?" you may ask. In order to forecast future cycles, the most important thing is to begin right, for if we have the right beginning, we will get the right ending. If we know the cause of the effect, then there can be no doubt about predicting the future event or effect.

I have always looked for causes and when once I determine a cause I can always be sure of the effect or future event which I predict. IT IS NOT MY AIM TO EXPLAIN THE CAUSE OF CYCLES. The general public is not yet ready for it and probably would not understand or believe it if I explained it.

In every law of nature there is a major and a minor; a positive, a negative, and a neutral. Therefore, in cycles there must be a lesser, a greater and intermediate cycle, or cycles within cycles. Like Ezekiel says: "Wheel within a wheel."

Time is the great factor that proves all things. The measurement of time first originated and is based on the earth's motion upon its axis. One of the smallest cycles, or time factors, which repeats regularly in things that are very active and have a high vibration, is the four-minute cycle. The reason for this is that the earth moves one degree every four minutes. The next cycle is 24 hours, the complete time required for the earth to make one revolution upon its axis. That is how man

measured his cycle of a day. The next important cycle
is one year, the time required for the earth to move
around the sun. This brings about the four seasons
of the year. These are the minor cycles.

The major cycles run in 100 and 5000 years with
variations based on minor cycles. In order to be sure
of world events and important changes, it is necessary
to go back at least 1000 years and prove up the cycles.
We find ample proof of the 1000-year cycle in the Bible:

> "A little one shall become a thousand and a small one
> a strong nation; I the Lord, will hasten it in his time."

Also

> "One day is with the Lord as a thousand years, and
> a thousand years as one day."

Another evidence of the 1000-year cycle:

> "And he laid hold on the dragon, that old serpent, which
> is the Devil, and Satan, and bound him a thousand
> years."

If we go back 1000 years, we can find ample proof
of how history has been repeating itself in the past few
years. From about A.D. 916 to 923 Europe went thru
about the same conditions that prevailed 1000 years
later or around 1914 to 1920. During the first period
referred to, Europe experienced wars, panics and crop
failures. History shows that in 916 agriculture in
the British Isles was at its lowest ebb and that there
was great scarcity of wheat and corn. Very few people
were engaged in tilling the soil on account of wars. The

same conditions prevailed 1000 years later in 1916 and 1917, when this country was called on to furnish food to starving Europe and send men and money to save their armies from defeat. In 917, Constantinople was besieged by the Bulgarians and war continued to 919. We know that war prevailed in Turkey and all over Europe between 1914 and 1919. In 923 there was Civil War in France and 1000 years later, or in 1923, France again had her troubles and is still having them.

Another proof of the 1000- and 2000-year cycle is evidenced by a lecture given by Prof. Hans Delbruck of the University of Berlin at the University College of London, just before the outbreak of the World War in 1914. He said:

> "One of his first observations in comparing the phe-
> nomena of the history of wars in the different ages
> was the likeness between the battles in which the Swiss
> conquered Duke Charles the Bold, and the battles in
> which the Greeks overcame the Persians. They had in
> an interval of 2000 years exactly the same arms and the
> same political institutions fighting against each other."

What proof of the 100-year cycle do we get from 100 years ago of what has happened in the past few years? In the United States, between 1814 and 1822, we had crop failures, war and yellow fever, especially from 1819 to 1822. In 1821 Persia was visited with Asiatic cholera. In 1823 cholera broke out in several ports along the Mediterranean. During the same period, corresponding to 100 years ago, the United States had the terrible epidemic of influenza and in Europe, Russia was visited with famine, cholera and all kinds of diseases, killing millions. In 1822 there was a famine in Ireland and 100 years later they were winding up their troubles and trying to make settlement and peace with England. In 1922 China and Russia were both suffering from famines, another proof of the 100-year cycle. Some more important evidence of this cycle is found by going back 100 years in history, in which we find that in 1819 the first steamship crossed the Atlantic Ocean. In 1919, 100 years later, the British dirigible R-34 made a successful flight from Scotland to Mineola, Long Island.

Where do we find proof in the Bible that the great World War was coming?

The proof that it is possible to make predictions of wars, famines, pestilences and general world events thousands of years in advance, is plainly substantiated by the Bible. The great World War was prophesied in the Book of Revelation.

What proof do we find in the Bible of what events or conditions will follow wars? What does the Bible say of the great World War which St. John the Divine foretold in the Book of Revelation?

> "For nation shall rise against nation, and kingdom against kingdom; and there shall be famines, and pestilences, and earthquakes in divers places."

Again the Bible says:

> "Immediately after the tribulation of these days shall the sun be darkened, and the moon shall not give light, and the stars shall fall from heaven, and the powers of the heavens shall be shaken."

Again, it says:

> "The Lord hath called for a famine; and it shall also come upon the land seven years."

And seven years from the close of the World War, Europe had the terrible crop failures, strikes, business depression and calamities, which occurred in 1923 to 1926.

Some evidence of long-range predictions which have been fulfilled, that has attracted attention, appeared in the *New York American,* January 29, 1922. The article refers to an amazing prophecy of the twelfth century made by Malachy, a priest, in A.D. 1139, in which he foretold accurately the personality of the Papal succession by means of mottoes and numbers. He foretold the long struggles which Ireland would have to go thru and the eventual peace, which has been recently signed. His prophecy on the future Pope is No. 266. Fides Intrepida, which means—"Unwavering Faith, unshaken belief in the face of danger; unfaltering devotion." To those who understand numbers, "266" reveals some remarkable events that are to follow the election of the new Pope. It shows that wars are not yet over and that Europe will have troublesome conditions, and in fact, the entire world must yet pass thru a very evil period between 1926 and 1932. It also confirms both the major and minor cycles which indicate that the years 1928 and 1930 to 1932 are to be years of famine, depressing business conditions and panic, not only in Europe, but in the United States. The maximum evil of the great 1000-year cycle, which will not be completed until 1932 to 1934, will bring serious troubles to the United States. Another bad period for the United States will be 1940 to 1944.

The question arises:—If we can know the future, is it of value to us? It has been well said: "Forewarned is forearmed," but I prefer to look to the Bible for authority and proof. When Pharaoh had his wonderful dream, he went to Joseph to have it interpreted. Joseph said:

> "And the seven thin and ill favored kine that came up after them are seven years; and the seven empty years, blasted with the east wind, shall be seven years of famine."

Listen to the advice Joseph gave him:

> "Let them gather all the food of those good years that come, and lay up corn under the hand of Pharaoh, and let them keep food in the cities. The people throughout the land should take warning and prepare for the unfavorable years to follow."

The Bible is the BOOK of all books, and if we only study it and understand it, we can gain a proper knowledge of all things. I believe it the duty of any man who understands science and mathematics and the cycle theory, and knows what is coming, to warn the people in order that they may prepare for trouble ahead. Many will scoff and laugh and refuse to believe until it is too late. The Bible is full of references where God has given us signs by which we may know what is coming, if we will only believe them. He says:

> "O, ye hypocrites, ye can discern the face of the sky; but can ye not discern the signs of the times?"

Again the Bible says:

> "And God said, Let there be lights in the firmament,
> of the heaven to divide the day from the night, and
> let them be for signs, and for seasons, and for days,
> and years."

How few people are willing to study the Bible in order
to understand the signs and discern the future and profit
by it.

CHAPTER VIII

CYCLES OF TRANSPORTATION

THE coming mode of transportation will be by air-plane and I feel sure they will be used in the great war to come. The Bible tells us that Enoch, who was the seventh from Adam—a number generally referred to as divine—was translated to heaven for his faith at the age of 365 years. This event took place about 3017 B.C. I believe that at that time they had all modern inventions and that Enoch went up in an airplane. The writer of the book, probably not having seen an airplane before and seeing Enoch go into the sky, thought that he had gone to heaven. We are now in the 5000-year cycle, from the time that Enoch was transferred to heaven, and this indicates the progress of the airplane at this time. Elijah was also translated to heaven in a cloud of fire, in 896 B.C. I believe this, too, was an airplane. Since the chariot was seen blazing with some kind of fire or gas, the recorder thought it was just something to take Elijah to heaven.

Man first traveled by land, then conquered the water and last, the greatest feat of all, is conquering the air, which was plainly foretold in the Bible.

In 1602 there was a railway built in New Castle, England, operated by horsepower. In 1776, the first iron rails were laid, the first important step leading to railways. In July, 1801, there was a completed tram road from Croyden to Wandsworth, England. In 1802, the first high-pressure locomotive was invented. In 1813, William Hedley built a locomotive. In 1824, the first locomotive, by George Stephenson, traveled six miles per hour. In 1829, the Rocket made a speed of fifteen miles per hour. In 1834, the Firefly Locomotive made a speed of twenty miles an hour, and in 1839, the North Star made a speed of thirty-seven miles per hour.

Man used the air as power for sailing vessels long years before he ever dreamed that it could be used to travel thru by airplane. The first idea of steam navigation was patented by Jonathan in 1713, and later in 1783, a steamboat by Fitch. In 1793, the first real steamboat by Fulton. On August 9, 1803, Fulton's steamboat, "The Claremont," made its first trip up the Hudson. In 1807, Fulton started a steamboat line on the Hudson. On July 15, 1819, the first steamship made a trip from New York to Liverpool in twenty-six days. In October, 1829, a locomotive by steam carriages started in Liverpool. In June, 1838, the "Great Western" made a trip from Bristol, arrived in New York, making the voyage in eighteen days. The next record for ocean travel was made in 1851 when the "Pacific" crossed the Atlantic in 9 days, 19 hours and 25 minutes. In 1917, a German submarine boat made a successful trip from Germany to Baltimore.

The advent of automobiles, or gas engines, began in 1877, when the first gas engine was invented by Otto.

In 1879, a gasoline motor was invented by Selden. In 1892, the first automobile was operated by C. A. Duryea. Note that this was repeating the 500-year cycle, and 100 years before the first attempt was made to start an iron railway, and in 1783, the first time a balloon went up which carried a passenger.

In our modern times the first attempt by man to conquer the air by means of plane or balloon was in June, 1783, when Joseph and Stephen Montgolfier built the first balloon, but it carried no passengers. In November, 1783, for the first time man went up in a balloon that sailed over Paris. In 1859, John Wise sailed in a balloon from St. Louis to Henderson, N. Y., in twenty hours; the greatest distance accomplished up to that time. In 1900, Count Zeppelin flew the first dirigible. In November, 1903, Wilbur and Orville Wright made their first flight in an airplane which rose under its own power. Note that his was 100 years after Fulton's first steamboat went up the Hudson, again repeating the 100-year cycle. In July, 1908, Glenn H. Curtiss flew his first airplane. In July, 1909, Charles K. Hamilton flew from New York to Philadelphia—seventy-four miles. Note 100 years before this, in 1807, Fulton started the first steamship line up the Hudson.

From 1914 to 1918, airplanes were used in the great World War; 100 years before steamers began crossing the Atlantic Ocean for the first time. In June, 1919, first non-stop flight from St. John's, Newfoundland, to Ireland. In July, 1919, the R-34 made a successful flight from Scotland to Mineola, Long Island. The R-34 made the trip in 64 hours and 13 minutes. One hundred years previous to this the first fast steamship crossed the Atlantic.

In May, 1923, Lieut. Macready and Kelly made a non-stop flight from New York to San Diego, California. In July, 1923, sunrise to sunset flight from New York to San Francisco. The flight was made by Russell L. Maughan. March 17th to September 28, 1924, L. H. Smith and Lee Wade flew around the world the first time. May, 1926, Richard E. Byrd circled the North Pole with the dirigible. May 21, 1927, Charles A. Lindbergh made the first successful flight across the Atlantic from New York to Paris.

Note how the airplane followed 100 years later after the fast steamer across the Atlantic. As railroad and ocean transportation made rapid progress from 1807 to 1838, so is airplane transportation making rapid progress and I predict that in 1938, airplanes will be traveling at the rate of 1000 miles an hour to all parts of the earth, carrying passengers and freight. My interpretation of the cycles to repeat in future indicates that from 1928 to 1932, one of the greatest battles of all history will be fought in the air. In the next few years airplanes will be making successful trips around the world and carrying passengers.

Man has succeeded in traveling on the earth by steam, gas and electricity. The automobile solved the problem of motor transportation without rail. The water was first conquered in a crude canoe, next with a sailing vessel, then the fast steamers and later the submarine by which man can travel secretly under the water. The next and last great conquest was the air, and as nations have fought battles on the land, on the water and used the submarine for successful warfare under the water, the next and last great step in transportation will be in the air. It is but natural to expect that the greatest battle of all will take place in the air when all modern inventions will be used to destroy human life. As stated in the Bible, unless the time be shortened, no human being will be left on this earth, but the Good Book has promised that the time will be shortened. Nations will try this new mode to conquer each other before the United Kingdom, spoken of in the Bible, can be realized.

CHAPTER IX

SUPPLEMENTING his former letter, Robert Gordon wrote:

DEAR MR. KENNELWORTH:

I am anxious to make some money in my cotton deals and get into wheat for the big advance that I figure is coming this Spring and Summer. Then I want to be in position to buy some Right Aeroplane and Sell Major Motors and other stocks short, because I believe that in the next few years I can make a fortune buying Right Aeroplane stock and selling short Major Motors.

Just as the railroad locomotive attained great speed from 1834 to 1839, and the big steamers cut down the time between New York and Europe, so will airplanes 100 years later cut the time around the world and to all points of the world. Just as the automobile has supplanted the railway passenger trains in carrying passengers across the country, so will the airplane take the place of railroads and automobiles in transportation through the air, because it will be much faster and safer. I believe that the airplane described by Ezekiel is going to be the model of a great plane in the future and I would like to make money enough to be the man to build the first plane according to the plans laid down in the Bible.

Mr. Kennelworth, I want to help you and show my appreciation for all your kindness to me. I would like to help you make back the money that you lost in the big slump in stocks in the Fall of 1919, and believe that if you will buy some July or October cotton right now, and hold it, you will make a lot of money. To show your faith in me, buy at least 100 bales. Then along about the 5th of April, we will have a lot of big profits made and can buy some wheat and corn as I figure that wheat and corn are going to start up the early part of April and advance twenty-five to thirty cents per bushel. Haven't you faith enough in me and faith enough in the Bible to risk a few hundred dollars and make back all the money you have lost? Of course you don't need it, Mr. Kennelworth, but it would make me very happy to see you make some money, anyway.

Sincerely,

ROBERT.

After reading over Robert's letters and explanation of the cycles, Mr. Kennelworth answered:

February 1, 1927.

MY DEAR ROBERT:

Your amazing letter and forecast of the future cycles, received. I am surprised to find one so young possessed of so much knowledge. It shows that you are a deep student and have been searching for the hidden mysteries. You will receive your reward.

I have faith in the Bible and in you, Robert. In 1919, I followed tips and lost a lot of money. Now I must have enough faith in you to risk a little money on your predictions, based on the Bible, so I telegraphed my brokers in New York today and bought 500 bales of July cotton at 13.70. If it goes up, I am going to hold it and the money I make on it, I am going to give to you and Marie when you are married as a wedding present, or if you need the money to promote your invention, I will let you have it to use for that purpose.

Please keep me posted on your studies and on your new discoveries. Always feel free to come and talk your matters over with me. I am always interested in anything that you have to write or talk to me about. Have faith in you and believe you are right about the great war to come.

It is plain that the nations in Europe are rapidly getting ready for war, and, of course, it will be with airplanes. While

I hate to think the United States will again be called into war, at the same time I realize that all of the foreign countries are jealous of us, because we have such enormous gold supply and have grown so prosperous. The United States is now the banker of the world, and while it was no fault of ours that the great World War occurred, which resulted to our benefit by transfer of gold from other nations to us, at the same time they are jealous and have a real hatred for America.

So you are probably right in preparing to build a great airplane to be used in defending your country. Such noble intentions, my boy, fill my heart with pride. I am going to drive out to the farm to see your mother next Sunday if I can get time. Want to have a talk with her and tell her of your brilliant achievement. It makes every mother's heart glad to know that her boy is trying to accomplish something. I feel sure that you are going to accomplish your aims, Robert, and I am with you always.

Sincerely yours,
J. H. KENNELWORTH.

After hearing from Mr. Kennelworth, Robert was very happy, and of course, had to share his happiness with Marie.

February 5, 1927.

SWEET MARIE:

I am very happy on this Saturday night, and nothing could make me happier than to be with you. I feel that I have won a great victory. I have put my theories up to Mr. Kennelworth, explained all that I could about my discoveries of the cycles in the Bible, and urged him to buy some cotton and make back the money that he lost in 1919. He said that he had faith in me and the Bible so he bought 500 bales of July cotton at 13.70 as I suggested.

While the market hasn't gone up much since I bought mine, at the same time it is holding steady and I am sure that it is going up. I believe Mr. Kennelworth is going to make a lot of money on his cotton and I want to see him make it because he is an honest, whole-hearted man and has done everything he could to help me. The $500 bonus he gave me in January enabled me to have margin enough to buy the cotton, and if I make a great success I will feel that I owe him a great debt of gratitude, because he has really helped me get a start.

Don't think I fail to appreciate all you are doing, my little sweetheart, and the faith that you have in me. I am looking forward to the day when I will make Wall Street hum with you standing by my side. Nothing would be left for me to work for if it wasn't the hope of having you, and the happiness that you can bring. Money will not mean anything except to accomplish my purpose, help my country and buy the things that will make you happy.

Love is indeed the greatest thing in the world and you are the greatest woman in the world. With your love, there is nothing that I cannot do. You are my last thought when I go to sleep at night and the first when I wake in the morning. Everything I do, I always think is for you. Your sweet little letters are always so encouraging and your supreme faith in me urges me on to greater things.

With all the love that my heart can send, I am as ever
Your loving

ROBERT.

Monday, February 7, 1927.

MY OWN DEAR ROBERT:

Your letter received this A.M. It is the happiest Monday morning that I have ever had. Am glad to know that Mr. Kennelworth is backing up your judgment. If I had some money I certainly would send it to you to buy some cotton for me. Maybe I will have some in a few months, because I am saving something every week from my allowance which Papa sends me

Every night when I kneel to pray, I ask God to give you strength and confidence, Robert, and I know that he can and will help you. It makes me very happy to know in all of your plans for the future, you think of me, and I am going to try to prove worthy of that great love. You are so noble, pure and unselfish; always thinking of others and thinking of what you can do to help protect your country in time of war.

I do hope and pray as your mother does, that the days of wars may pass away; that man may cease to fight and may know and understand each other, setting their differences on the basis of love. I will welcome that day, and hope that I may stand by your side, when there will be no more wars and our loved ones will not be taken away to war.

Write me often, Robert, and know that you have all the love that the heart of one little woman can send.

Your own

MARIE.

The month of February slowly passed away. Cotton was very slow and inactive, but on February 23rd, it started up and went up fast. On March 2nd, July cotton had advanced to 14.80, and Robert had a profit of $1,000.00 and Mr. Kennelworth had a profit of $2,500.00. Robert was very much elated over his progress and the profit for Mr. Kennelworth. He wrote Marie how the market was working out according to his prediction; how the money was piling up; and that he would soon have money to start on his invention and new discovery. Marie was very happy over Robert's success and wrote encouraging letters. Mr. Kennelworth was also very happy and congratulated Robert on being able to buy cotton very close to the low level in January.

March was the month to bring disappointment to Robert. Cotton started to decline and by the middle of the month had declined to around 13.75 wiping out all Robert's and Mr. Kennelworth's profits, but still leaving their capital intact. Robert was not discouraged. He told Mr. Kennelworth that the flood was sure to come in the Mississippi Valley during April and May, the Spring would be late, and the price would be sure to advance. He had no thought of selling out his cotton and urged Mr. Kennelworth to hold his, which he did.

Marie had become very much interested in the market and was reading the paper every day and watching the prices. She saw the price decline to around 13.75 and knew that Robert's profits would now be wiped out. She felt very sorry for him and wrote him:

March 15th, 1927.

MY DEAR ROBERT:

I have not heard from you in several days. I see that the market has declined to where you now have no profit left on your deal. Do not get discouraged; I have great faith in you and believe that you are yet going to come out all right and make a lot of money. Why don't you hold your cotton, and tell Mr. Kennelworth to hold his, because my intuition tells me that you are certainly right?

I have been saving money every week from my allowance. A few weeks ago I wrote Papa and told him that I had to have some extra money and asked him if he could let me have $300.00. He sent the money at once, so I now have $400.00 and I am sending it to you. I want you to buy me 100 bales of July cotton. I was talking with a broker from Dallas a few days ago, and he says that he believes cotton will go up even tho it may be slow for a while. Take the money, and if you can get the broker to buy a hundred for me, do so. This is my faith in you, and in the Bible. So don't be afraid to buy for me, Robert. I am just as game as you are.

With all love and wishing you luck,

As ever, your own

MARIE.

This letter was a great consolation and encouragement to Robert. He had begun to feel a little blue because cotton had declined. Not that he thought it wouldn't go up again, but he was sorry that he had failed to get the profits.

He took Marie's money and on March 17th bought 100 bales of July cotton at 13.90. The cotton market was slow during the balance of March, but it did not decline, and Robert was greatly encouraged. The market was slow again during April, but prices were holding steady and Robert felt encouraged that they did not decline. On April 20th a flood started in the Mississippi Valley. The Spring was late and planting delayed. Cotton started to advance and went up fast, July reaching 15.40 by April 25th. Robert's profits were now piling up fast, and Marie had a profit of over $700.00 on her 100 bales. Mr. Kennelworth had held his cotton and profits were accumulating fast for him. He congratulated Robert on his wonderful prediction that the flood came as he forecast. Marie was watching the papers so she wired Robert as follows:

YOU ARE A WONDER   THE MARKET IS MAKING GOOD AND WE ARE GOING TO WIN   I AM WITH YOU ALWAYS   LOVE

MARIE.

Robert now began to see possibilities of his dream being realized, and thought in a few months he could resign his position and go to New York and continue to speculate in order to make money enough to build his airplane and work out ideas for his other discoveries. So he wrote Marie this letter:

April 30th, 1927.

MY DARLING MARIE,

The Lord has been good to us. Fortune is smiling on us. Cotton is on its way up. In a few weeks will be up around 17c a pound, and we will have a lot of money made. I bought another 100 bales today and Mr. Kennelworth bought 500 bales more. It won't be long until I have money enough to go to New York. When I go, I want you to go with me, because I cannot go there and succeed alone without you. I need your love and encouragement, and want you to marry me and start to New York together. Of course I don't like to have you leave school before you graduate, but I feel it is best for you to go with me.

Write and let me know what you think about it.

With all my love,

Your ROBERT.

Marie's reply:

Sunday, May 1st, 1927.

MY DEAR ROBERT,

I have just received your letter, and I am happy to know that the cotton is moving your way. I know that you love and trust me and I want you to know that I love and trust you, so please try to understand me. While I have the greatest faith in you and know that you will succeed, I feel that marrying you just now might handicap you and prevent your success. When once I am yours, Robert, you will have realized your fondest hope, and possibly your ambition may wane. You will fight harder to win if you still cling to the hope of winning me. They say that hope and anticipation are greater than realization, Robert. Never cease to hope for I am with you. Even when I am not with you, trust me as I trust you, for I love only you.

I am going to tell you a dream that I had a few nights ago. I saw you a great success. Fortune was smiling on you. The world was at your feet, but I seemed to see a great tragedy follow this. It seemed I left you in a mysterious way and then came back to you just as mysteriously. Now, don't think that I do not want to go with you, Robert, and don't think that I believe in dreams, but somehow it has made a great impression on me.

Of course you know that father would never consent to me leaving school to marry you, and if we married, we would have to run away. Would it not be best for you to go to New York, as you have planned, work on your invention, and let my love and faith guide you to success? You could live for my love, which you have always said was the greatest thing in the world. You have all my love and will always have it.

I could continue in school and later, if you became despondent and could not get along without me, remember that I would have faith and love enough to give up father, mother, and everything else and come to you. I want to do what I feel is best for your future, Robert, and I hope that you will believe me and see it that way. I want you to come over to see me next Sunday, so we can talk over all your future plans.

With all of my love for you always,

Your MARIE.

When Robert received Marie's letter, he was disappointed, but felt that when he saw her and talked matters over, he could get her to change her mind, give up school, if necessary, marry him and go to New York with him. He had heard and read much of the pitfalls of the great City of New York and felt that he did not care to venture there alone without Marie with him as his wife. While his old school-mate and chum, Walter Kennelworth, was in New York and could work with him and be a great help and comfort, he felt that Marie, his one great inspiration, was absolutely necessary to his success and that he must persuade her to go with him to New York.

On Sunday, May 1st, Robert went to visit his mother in the country. He found that Mr. Kennelworth had been there and told her of Robert's success and his faith in him. Robert's mother was very happy when he told her that cotton was advancing and he was making money rapidly and Mr. Kennelworth was making money; that Marie had such great faith in him that she had put up her only $400.00 and bought 100 bales of cotton and now had a profit of about $1,000.00.

Robert told his mother of his plans. That he expected within a few months to go to New York, establish himself there, and speculate in order to make money so that he could build his great airplane according to Ezekiel's plan and prepare to help his country in time of war. Mrs. Gordon was very happy to learn of her boy's success. She was sad when he began to talk about war. Robert assured her that the Bible plainly foretold the great war which was to be fought in the air and that it was his duty to help protect his country. While his mother admired his patriotism, she again referred to the dream that she had had years before, about a great war which would come and in which she thought that Robert lost his life in San Francisco.

She talked to Robert of his future and told him she hoped he would be a preacher. Robert confided to her that he could never be an orthodox minister, for he could not preach and teach the things which the orthodox ministers were teaching. He did not believe in a personal devil or believe in Hell, but believed in a God of Love and Justice. He did not believe that God would inflict upon any of his children eternal punishment but thought that whatsoever a man soweth, that shall he also reap and that we receive our reward here upon earth.

He told her that the Bible plainly said that the kingdom of heaven is within us and he believed it. If we kept our conscience clear and did unto others as we would like to have them do unto us, he believed we would find our heaven and our reward here upon earth. Said that times and conditions were changing rapidly; that the new inventions and discoveries caused men to think differently than in the old days; that the old religious ideas would pass away and give place to more liberal, advanced ideas. He hoped to live to see the day when men would not only be too proud to fight, but would be too full of love for their fellowmen to settle disputes with the sword. This was God's plan and it would come to pass this way, and he believed that he could be a great power for peace and hoped to live to see a world of peace with all nations united under one kingdom and one God, the God of Love and Justice.

Mrs. Gordon felt that her faith in Robert had been justified and that she understood him better than his father and brother. He told his mother of his hopes for an early marriage with Marie and that when he went to New York, he wanted to take Marie with him as his wife. His mother was not in favor of an elopement. She wanted him to make good, act in an honorable way and ask the consent of Mr. Stanton to his marriage with Marie, but she felt at this time Mr. Stanton would not give his consent because he wanted Marie to complete her education and it was right and proper she should. His mother asked him if he didn't think it would be best to continue his position with Mr. Kennelworth for a few years longer, after he saw that he was making a success before going to New York where he might fail in a strange city. Robert was filled with a great determination to go. He wished to make a success and knew he would, because he read the Bible and had learned how.

The week ending May 7th was the greatest week in Robert Gordon's life up to that time. Cotton advanced rapidly about $4.00 per bale, and by May 7th Robert's profits were about $2,500.00. Marie had a profit of over $1,000.00 on her 100 bales which Robert bought for her, and Mr. Kennelworth now had a profit of about $7,000.00.

On Saturday morning, May 7th, Mr. Kennelworth called Robert into his private office and asked him if he knew what the cotton market was doing that morning. Robert said he hadn't heard what the price was. Mr. Kennelworth told him that July was now selling around 16 cents per pound, and that while he had some nice profits, the money was not the thing that counted with him, but the fact that Robert was right on the market made him happy that he had faith in him and encouraged him.

Robert then confided to Mr. Kennelworth that he was very anxious to go to New York just as soon as possible. He had been reading about the contemplated flights of the airplanes from New York across the Atlantic, and he wanted to be in New York by his birthday in June, 1927, because he figured by that time the airplanes would have crossed the Atlantic and there would be great excitement in New York. He wished to be there and get all the information he could about airplanes, because he wanted to start building his own just as soon as he had money enough and felt that he could do so. He asked Mr. Kennelworth what he thought about him resigning in a short time to go to New York. Mr. Kennelworth told him that he would regret very much to lose his services, but that he had great faith in Robert's study of the Bible and what he thought he could do, and that if he wanted to do so, he would let him go and not only that, but would aid him financially. Robert confided his hope and desire to take Marie with him. Mr. Kennelworth didn't exactly agree with this but told him that this was a problem he would have to solve for himself; that if Marie had faith enough in him to take the step, he was sure it would work out all right; and that he could always have his old position back any time that he wanted to return, and could have any help that he could render him in New York.

After his conference with Mr. Kennelworth, Robert wired Marie as follows:

EXPECT TO BE WITH YOU SUNDAY WILL COME OVER ON AFTERNOON TRAIN TODAY.

Robert arrived in Sherman, Texas, Saturday evening, and Marie met him at the train. She was overjoyed at Robert's success. They spent Saturday evening and Sunday together. It seemed to them the happiest days of their lives. Robert talked over his plans and Marie was enthusiastic about his future. He told her that if the market worked as he expected, he intended to trade in wheat and corn in the near future; that he hoped to go to New York by the early part of June, as he was very enthusiastic about the air flights from New York across the Atlantic to Paris, and get started on his studies and invention. Marie was willing to give him all the money she had made to help him out but he told her that the one thing he wanted was her and her love, and that he wanted her to go with him to New York.

She knew her father would never consent to their marriage and the only way would be to elope. While she thought it best to finish her studies in school and join him in New York later, said if he insisted, she would go with him. Robert left for Texarkana on Sunday afternoon, May 8th, with Marie's promise that if he decided to go to New York within a few weeks, they would make arrangements to elope and be married in St. Louis on their arrival there. Robert had his Bible with him and on his way back home Sunday night, spent several hours reading it and going over the predictions by Ezekiel and the plans outlined by Ezekiel for an airplane, which Robert hoped and expected to build in the near future.

During the next ten days, cotton was slow and reacted 40 to 50 points. But this in no wise discouraged Robert, as he felt sure that a big advance was coming the latter part of May and during the early June.

On May 19th, July cotton was again up around the 16 cent level. Robert felt that now was the time to start buying wheat and corn. He wired his broker in New York to buy 10,000 July wheat and 10,000 July corn, and to raise the stop loss order on his cotton and also place a stop loss order on the wheat and corn, to protect the broker and himself. The broker wired that he had bought 10,000 July wheat at 1.38½ and 10,000 July corn at 92 cents. On May 20th Robert bought 10,000 July corn at 92½ cents for Marie's account. He told Mr. Kennelworth that he figured wheat and corn were now going to have a big advance, and advised him to buy some, which he did.

CHAPTER X

MAY 21st was a red-letter day in the life of Robert Gordon. Wheat, corn and cotton all advanced to the highest levels of the season. Robert had read reports in the paper that Charles A. Lindbergh had started on his lone flight from New York to Paris. He went down to the telegraph office in the afternoon to inquire if there was any news about the success of Lindbergh's flight. The operator said that nothing had come over the wire yet, but there had been a report that Lindbergh had passed over Ireland early that morning. Robert waited in the telegraph office until about 5 P.M. when a flash came over the wire that Lindbergh had landed in Paris. This fired Robert's enthusiasm, and he was very much excited. Right then and there decided that he was going to New York in the very near future and start to build an airplane according to his own plans. He went immediately to the home of Mr. Kennelworth and told him about his plans and desire to go to New York just as soon as possible.

Mr. Kennelworth was also very enthusiastic about Lindbergh's flight across the Atlantic, and told Robert that he contemplated going to New York to be there for the reception when Lindbergh returned, and that he wanted to visit Walter and see how he was getting along anyway. So Robert tendered his resignation to Mr.

Kennelworth to take place on May 31, 1927. Mr. Kennelworth accepted the resignation with the understanding and promise from Robert that if anything went wrong or he should lose his money or meet with disappointments in New York, he would immediately return and assume his old position. Robert thanked him for his kindness and told him that he would feel free to call on him but that he felt he would never have to return to take up the position again. In view of his discoveries of the cycles in the Bible, he could make money in the market, but his object was not alone to make money for selfish purposes, but to use it to benefit others and for the protection of his country at the time of the coming great war which would be fought in the air.

On Sunday, May 22nd, Robert wrote to Marie:

My dearest Marie,

The past week has been a great one for us, and yesterday, the 21st, was the greatest day in history. Lindbergh, the lone aviator, crossed the Atlantic and landed safely in Paris. Wheat, corn and cotton went up and we made more money. Profits are piling up fast, and I will soon have plenty of money to build my airplane.

I had a long talk with Mr. Kennelworth yesterday afternoon after we received the news of Lindbergh's flight, and resigned my position, to take place on May 31st. Expect to go to New York some time in the early part of June, and of course I want to take you with me as my wife. With the profits we now have made in the market, there will be no trouble about us getting along all right in New York and I am sure that I am going to make a lot more money.

Cotton is going away up in the early part of June and wheat is going very high in the latter part of May and early June. I will sell out and take some of my profits so we can get started in good shape. Will see you next Sunday and talk the matter over and plan the best way.

Your love and faith has sustained me thus far and helped to make me the success that I am, and with that love, there is no height which I cannot reach.

I love you more than ever. You are all and everything to me.

Lovingly,

ROBERT.

During the week ending May 28th, Robert watched the markets very closely because he figured that wheat and corn would be top around May 28th to June 1st. He wanted to sell out and get the profits so that he could go to New York. Cotton advanced to the highest level that week and on Saturday, July was up to 16.40. Robert had a profit of over $3,000.00 in his cotton. He sold out his July wheat on May 28th at $1.50 and sold the corn at $1.03½, making about $2,300.00 profit. This, together with his stock profits, gave him about $6,000.00. He sold out Marie's corn at $1.03½, making a profit of about $1,100.00 there. She also had a profit of about $1,200.00 on the cotton which she was still holding because he believed it was going higher. Marie's profit now amounted to about $2,300.00.

Robert was going to Sherman, Texas, on Saturday afternoon, and Monday being Decoration Day, he would not return until Monday night. He had a talk with Mr. Kennelworth before leaving and Mr. Kennelworth told him that he had been buying more corn on the way up and more cotton; that he now had a profit of about $25,000.00, all of which was due to Robert's advice.

Robert said that he was going away to see Marie and

confided that he was going to try to get her to elope with
him and go to New York. Mr. Kennelworth told him
that he could take the good news to Marie that he was
going to give them a wedding present of $10,000.00,
which was less than half of the profits he had made.
He was going to continue to hold the cotton until Robert
thought it was time to sell.

On the afternoon of May 28th, Robert boarded a train
for Sherman, Texas, with the lightest heart that he had
ever experienced in his life. Now that his dream was
really going to be realized, he was never so happy. He
figured that with the money he had made and with
Marie's money, and the $10,000.00 which Mr. Kennel-
worth was going to give them, he would have about
$18,000.00 which would give him capital to continue
to speculate in the market and money for his plans on
his great airplane.

As the train rolled across the plains of Texas and
Robert watched the sun setting across the prairies on
that Saturday afternoon, he dreamed of the day when
he, like Lindbergh, would cross the country in his great
airplane. He could think of nothing else but Lindbergh's great flight and what it meant to the world. He
realized that Ezekiel's prophecy of that war which was
to come and be fought in the air, was coming true, and
the great plane described by Ezekiel, the eagle with
wheel within a wheel, would one day become a reality.
He could now see the possibilities of his dream being
fulfilled and he was sure of success.

Marie welcomed him with enthusiasm and open arms.
She was so proud of him and so happy that he made

good in the market. He had been so thoughtful to buy cotton and corn for her and sold out the corn with $1,100.00 profit. She told Robert that he was a wonder; that he was one of the greatest young men in the world and a genius, and that he would be a greater man than Lindbergh when he was as old as Lindbergh.

Robert said that on June 9th, he would be 21 years of age, and on that day he wanted to be married and start on his career as a real man. He wanted to go back to Texarkana after the holidays, wind up his affairs and get ready to go to New York. Wanted her to go with him, starting Saturday, June 4th, so they would arrive on Sunday, June 5th, in St. Louis, be married, and proceed immediately to New York. He asked Marie what she thought about going to her father, telling him he had now made good and had enough money to start out, and ask his consent to their marriage. Marie said that it was useless; that her father would never consent to her leaving school and being married, no matter how much money the man she was going to marry had to take care of her. Her father was bent on her finishing her education and she knew it would be a hopeless case. There was no use talking about it.

She asked Robert if he didn't think it would be better for her to remain in school for another year or two, to finish her education, and then she could join him in New York and be married. She thought it possible that he might get along better for a while without her. But Robert would not listen to this and told her that he would never go without her. His future happiness and success depended upon her love and encouragement.

Her love had guided him safely thus far and would lead him on to greater things. He had dreamed of the time when he would come home at night from his work or study, to find her there and see her beautiful eyes, the lights that would guide him on to success. She could either make him the most miserable man in the world or the happiest. His entire future and fate were in her hands and she could do with him as she willed. Marie agreed to keep her promise she had made to him long before,—that regardless of money or conditions, she would leave father, mother, brothers and sisters, and go with him anywhere, even unto the ends of the earth, and that if he insisted, she would elope because she knew that was the only way since her father would not give his consent.

On Sunday, May 29th, Robert and Marie went to Dallas, Texas. They had planned when they were ready to elope, that Marie would leave from Dallas on the "Sunshine Special" in the afternoon of June 4th. She was to keep her plans absolutely secret and Robert was to board the same train that night at Texarkana, and after the train was out of Texarkana, he was to find her, go on to St. Louis together, be married there on Sunday morning, and leave Sunday noon for New York. Robert was extremely happy and talked of nothing but the success that was to come to them; of his great plane that he was to build and the part it would take in protecting the country in the great air battle which he was sure was yet to come, when foreign countries thru their jealousy, would attack the United States from the air and do great damage to this country. He told her that in the end Uncle Sam would win; that the Stars and Stripes would proudly float from the great buildings in New York, and that they would live to see that day and he wanted her there with him when his great "ship" would help win the victory for his country. Walter Kennelworth was in the city and they were going to work together on inventions and discoveries that would help win the war which he knew was sure to come.

It was the most interesting and pleasant Sunday that they had ever spent together. They drove around Dallas and talked over their future plans. Sunday afternoon they returned to Sherman, and Monday forenoon Robert spent with Marie. They went out to the cemetery and placed some flowers upon the graves of soldiers who had lost their lives in defense of their country.

Robert talked of the great feat of Lindbergh and of the honors that he would receive from the foreign countries, and told Marie what a great time they would have, as Mr. Kennelworth was going to New York and they would all be there at the great reception when Lindbergh returned. He said good-bye to her on Monday afternoon and started back for Texarkana, knowing that the next time he would meet her, would be on board the train for St. Louis, where she would become his wife.

From that time on, Robert counted the minutes, in anticipation of the great happiness of the following Sunday when they would be married in St. Louis. He was strongly attracted to St. Louis because Lindbergh had left from there in the "Spirit of St. Louis," on his successful flight. He thought it would be good luck to marry in St. Louis and start from there to New York to spend their honeymoon.

On Tuesday morning, May 31st, Robert started early to Mr. Kennelworth's office as that was to be his last day in the office and he was anxious to clean up all the business necessary and render Mr. Kennelworth all the service possible before he went away. He confided to Mr. Kennelworth the arrangements of eloping with Marie. Mr. Kennelworth told him that he would arrange to go to New York about the 11th of June and was sorry that he couldn't make the trip with Marie and Robert and see them married in St. Louis. But he said to Robert, "That is the time when two young people like to be alone, and I am afraid that I wouldn't be a very good chaperon on the trip. So it is all for the best and you will get along all right without me."

Robert told Mr. Kennelworth that he figured according to his cycle theory, cotton should be sold out about June 1st or 2nd, that there would be a reaction. He had also figured that it was time to sell wheat and corn for a reaction.

On June 1st, Robert sold out his July cotton at 16.80 and also sold out Marie's cotton. Robert's profits and capital together now amounted to $7,000.00. Robert sold 25,000 July wheat at 1.48½ and 25,000 July corn at 1.06½ on June 1st. He went down to the broker's office to watch the market for that week, because he knew the next few days would be very important and anxious days for him. He was thinking every minute of the day when he would start to New York and would make Marie his wife. This would be the greatest start of all his life, as he was starting it under favorable conditions and with plenty of money. He knew that success was certain and was never more hopeful.

On Saturday, June 4th, he closed his short contract in July wheat at 1.43 and his corn contract at 1.02. He had made a profit of over $2,000.00 on wheat which brought his capital up to $9,000.00. Mr. Kennelworth had taken Robert's advice and gone short of wheat and corn on June 1st, after selling out his cotton. Cotton declined from June 1st as Robert figured it would. He told Mr. Kennelworth on Saturday morning that he was going to buy in his wheat and corn, because he was getting ready to go away that afternoon and was not going to make any more trades until he had arrived in New York. He would have everything in cash and ready to make a new start after the honeymoon.

Mr. Kennelworth had sold wheat and corn heavily and had made over $50,000.00 since he started to follow Robert's advice. He made back all the money he had lost in the slump in oil stocks in 1919 and was very grateful to Robert. He handed Robert New York exchange for $10,000.00 as a wedding present. Told him that he could call on him for any additional help that he wanted in financing the building of his airplane or for any other purpose. Robert assured him that he would not need any more help; that he could make all the money he wanted and that his success was assured.

Robert told Mr. Kennelworth that he made over $4,000.00 for Marie on her little capital of $400.00 with which she had started. Mr. Kennelworth was very much elated over this. This was the first time he had heard about Marie putting up $400.00 to buy cotton. He told Robert she was the kind of a woman to marry, the one who believed in him and would back him with her money and everything else. He believed it was love of the right kind—that success was sure to follow. Robert was so happy that afternoon that he called Marie on the long-distance 'phone, and told her of his great success in the market in wheat and the money Mr. Kennelworth had made; told her that they had now a working capital of around $25,000.00 and with that much money, in New York it would be only a question of a few years when he would be a millionaire. The main thing, however, was not money but the use he wanted to put it to in completing his invention. Marie was very happy and told him that she was making arrangements to go to Dallas and would leave there that afternoon on the "Sunshine Special," and after the train pulled out of Texarkana, he would find her on board. He was to keep everything quiet and not let anybody know anything about the elopement, as her father might try to stop her. No one in Texarkana but Robert's mother and Mr. Kennelworth knew about the secret elopement. Robert kept everything quiet about his resigning from Mr. Kennelworth's and going to New York, because he thought that there might be some leak somewhere and that Mr. Stanton might find out about Marie's elopement and stop it.

CHAPTER XI

AT 7 P.M. June 4th, 1927, Robert walked into the Railroad Station at Texarkana and bought a ticket for St. Louis, with a reservation on the "Sunshine Special." This was the greatest and happiest moment of his life. He knew that Marie was already on her way and that in a couple of hours the train would arrive and he would go aboard for St. Louis, where he was to make her his wife. After buying his ticket, he went over to the Huckins Hotel and met Mr. Kennelworth for a final conference and to say good-bye. He told Mr. Kennelworth that he figured it would be time to buy cotton on a little reaction Monday morning, and also time to buy wheat again. Mr. Kennelworth assured him that he was going to plunge on his profits, and if he lost money now, it would be out of profits. He was going to get into the market and try to make a lot more money before he went to New York. Robert said that he intended to wire his broker from St. Louis to buy cotton and wheat for him on Monday morning.

Mr. Kennelworth bid Robert good-bye with all good wishes for success and said he was sure he was going to succeed, but that if failure and disappointment should come, he should always remember that he could rely upon him; that a young man often had trouble and disappointment and made many mistakes before he reached his goal and that if anything went wrong in the market, he could always come to him and ask for any aid possible and he would gladly grant it. He thought as much of Robert as he did of his own son, Walter, and wanted them to work together in New York, and was sure that they could be a great success. He wanted Robert to encourage Walter to continue his studies along chemical lines, because he believed that Walter would be able to make some great discoveries and they could work together to good advantage.

The "Sunshine Special" was a little late on Saturday night, June 4th, and Robert's heart was in his throat. He was anxious for that train to roll in. Finally, when the whistle blew and the signal light in the yard of the Texas Pacific showed the "Sunshine Special" was rolling in, the glare of the headlights on the train was the most welcome sight that Robert had ever witnessed thru all the days of his life. He boarded the train as quickly as possible and sat down nervous and anxious awaiting the moment when the train would get about 20 miles out of Texarkana, so that he might go back and look for Marie.

The minutes passed slowly away and it seemed like years before the train crossed the Red River and Robert decided that it was safe to go back to the car where Marie was and see her. He found Marie all anxious and nervously awaiting his arrival. She flew into his arms and seemed the happiest woman in the world and Robert was too happy for words. They sat there and talked of their future plans until after midnight.

Marie told Robert that she knew if her father found out she was eloping, he would make every effort to stop

her and prevent their marriage, as she was not of age; and he was anxious that she complete her education. Robert asked her if she had any regrets in the steps she was taking, and she told him she did not, that if she did have, she would never have started. She thought it was wonderful that Robert had been able to make money so rapidly and was very happy that he had stuck to the Bible and studied so hard, and now was getting his reward for his faith and hard work. She expressed her supreme confidence in him and the work that he intended to do. Robert hoped it would be a beautiful sunshiny Sunday morning when they arrived in St. Louis, so that they could be married and then proceed to New York.

Marie seemed very enthusiastic over the prospect of getting to St. Louis. Robert had a little surprise for her, and she asked him to tell her what it was. But he said, she must wait until they arrived in St. Louis. "Robert, just suppose the train should be wrecked and I should be killed, or something should happen that I would never see you again, don't you think you had better tell me about the surprise now?" He said, "No, there is not going to be any wreck. Good luck is following us, and the surprise will keep until tomorrow morning." She said, "Robert, I may not be able to sleep. I don't think I can sleep anyway, after all this excitement and happiness and everything that is to come in the future." Robert knew that he couldn't sleep either, but he would go up to his car, lie down and try to get some rest before they arrived in St. Louis the next morning. They agreed to meet early in the morn-

ing and go back into the dining car for breakfast before
they arrived in St. Louis.

Robert returned to his berth and tried to rest, but
found that he couldn't sleep. He thought over what
Marie had said about—"suppose the train should be
wrecked, or something should happen that you should
never see me again." He thought that nothing could
happen to separate Marie from him, but just the same
it was the thought that she said something might happen. He felt lonesome being separated from Marie.
She was two cars back, but he felt that the good God
who had endowed him with faith would protect Marie,
and that no harm would come to her; that there was no
danger of a wreck on the "Sunshine Special" and that
there was sunshine waiting for Marie and himself. In
the wee small hours of the morning, Robert dozed off
and had a few hours of sound sleep. He arose early
and dressed. About 8 o'clock, he hurried back to
Marie's car, to take her to breakfast. When he arrived
at her berth, he found it empty. He went back to the
dining-car to look for Marie, but couldn't find her there,
and then went on thru to the end of the train, but was
unable to locate Marie. The Pullman porter told him
that he hadn't seen her that morning and the last he
saw of her was when Robert was talking to her in the
berth late that night. Robert then searched the train
again from one end to the other and become uneasy and
anxious about Marie. He returned again to her car
and had the porter look for her baggage, and after looking thru the car, found that it was gone. Robert
was now almost frantic and could not imagine what

could have happened to her, because her baggage was gone. The porter assured him that there had been no hold-up of the train that night and that nothing unusual had happened. He had been up all night helping people get on and off at different stations but had seen nothing of Marie at any time. The train conductor was notified and the Pullman-car conductor was told. Both of them searched the train from one end to the other, and nowhere could Marie be found.

Robert did not explain to the conductor or the porter that they were to be married in St. Louis that morning. The conductor told him that it seemed plain that in some way during the night, she must have left the train because her baggage was gone. Robert was now almost in a state of collapse. He imagined all kinds of things which might have happened to Marie. Thought that she might have become insane during the night, and had thrown her baggage out of the window, and jumped out. Thought her father might in some way have found out about her plans and had some officer or someone secreted on the train who had taken Marie off at some point enroute. But no matter what he thought or imagined, it was no relief to his mind because he did not know where Marie was. All his future happiness was blasted in a moment.

By the time the search was over, the train was nearing St. Louis. Robert began to think of all the things he could and must do to try and find Marie. The first thing he thought of was to wire Mr. Kennelworth, and have him make a search and ascertain whether her father or mother knew anything about what had happened. The railroad conductor and Pullman conductor had tried to cheer Robert up and assure him that nothing seriously wrong could have happened to her, and that for some unknown reason she must have left the train at some station during the night without anyone knowing it, because they were sure that she could not have jumped out or fallen from the window without someone knowing about it and they thought there was nothing to worry about. Robert had decided on sending telegrams and making every search possible to locate her. He put his hand in his inside pocket to find a pencil and draw out a wallet. In the pocket was an envelope addressed to him in Marie's handwriting. He did not know where it had come from or how it could have gotten into his pocket, but he hurriedly tore the envelope open and this is what he read:

June 5, 1927—3 A.M.

DEAREST ROBERT:

According to your faith, be I unto you. Love will always have faith, understand and wait. Time proves all things. You will get everything you want. I will come to you when I mean the most and your need for love is the greatest.

Lovingly always,

MARIE.

When Robert finished reading this little note, tears were streaming down his face. He was frantic. He knew that the mysterious letter was written by Marie's own hand and must have been written on the train and for some unknown reason she was leaving him. He at once thought of his great faith in her, and his faith in God and the future as he read. He wondered what this could mean: "According to your faith be I unto you—love will always have faith, understand and wait." Robert thought, "How can I understand, how can I wait, when I left her only a few hours ago supremely happy anticipating being married a few hours later in St. Louis, and going on to New York to spend our future lives together. What in the world can she mean by, 'time proves all things.'" Time had proved his faith and love for her. She had had faith in him and had encouraged him; had put up the $400.00 she had saved, not to make money for herself but to try to help him. She told him that she didn't want the money, but wanted him to use it in any way that would help him. Then he pondered the next line where she said: "You will get everything you want." He thought, "My God, there is only one thing that I do want, there is only one thing in this world that means anything to me and that is my Marie, and where will I find her." Reading the next line over and over, "I will come to you when I mean the most and your need for love is the greatest."

He almost exclaimed aloud, "My God, my God, now is the time that I need her the most. I will never need her more. How can I go on? Life will be a blank. I will be a dismal failure without her." He wondered if there ever could be a time in the future when he would need her more, when she would mean more to him, than she meant at this moment.

He could imagine no unfriendly circumstances, no break of any kind that would cause Marie to change in a few hours and decide to turn back from the step she had taken. He could not understand how she could have slipped to his berth in the wee small hours of the morning and placed this note in his inside coat pocket. It was her handwriting, and he knew that Marie had written it. But why! why! why!

As the train rolled into the Union Station at St. Louis he stood in the car dazed, with her letter crumpled in his hand. With a heavy heart he made his way to the station and sat down to think what he could or should do. Finally, he decided to send a telegram and lay the circumstances of Marie's disappearance before Mr. Kennelworth and ask his advice before making any move.

Robert realized that he must have time to collect his thoughts, if he ever could think again. His thoughts turned back to the dream Marie had told him she had, where some terrible tragedy had overtaken him and she had gone out of his life in a mysterious way and came back into it in the same way. He wondered if at that time Marie had had any doubt that she might not want to continue to carry out the plans agreed on. Then he thought of what she said just before bidding good-night in the train, when she had asked him to tell her what the surprise was he had for her and said to him that the train might wreck and kill her or that something might happen to separate them. He wondered then if she had something in her mind which she thought might separate them during the night, or if she intended to hide from him in some way.

But he must get all that out of his mind—must have faith in Marie, must understand and wait. Then like a flash he became contented. Thought it was all a joke that Marie had played on him, that she was hiding somewhere in the train and in a few minutes would show up, so he decided not to send a telegram to Mr. Kennelworth but simply stay in the station and wait. He opened his suit case and took out the Bible, and there began to read from St. Paul, who said that love suffers long and is kind, seeks not its own, is not easily provoked and thinks no evil. Robert resolved to have patience, to have faith in Marie, and never doubt her, and never to think any evil of her no matter what happened. His mind was relieved. He felt happy and more cheerful, and was hopeful.

He waited a short time in the station, hoping Marie would join him. The seconds drifted away like weeks, the minutes seemed like months, and when an hour had gone by, to Robert it seemed like years. He waited and hoped; watched in every direction for Marie's beautiful eyes, the eyes he told her he loved so much and always wanted them to greet him when he came home from his work because they were an inspiration. Slowly the hands on the great clock in the Union Station showed it was nearly 12 o'clock noon. Robert listened attentively as the old clock tolled twelve times for 12 o'clock and each time it seemed that the blood from his heart was slowly trickling away. Hope was fast giving away to despair. Robert found his patience waning, but that was not to be. He must trust to the word of God which said: "O, ye of little faith, saith the Lord," and must try to find Marie who meant everything to him.

As the last stroke of the clock died slowly away, Robert started to think again. He finally decided that he would stay in the Union Station and have patience to wait one more hour for Marie. He thought that she was really playing a joke on him and would surely come by 1 o'clock. While he waited he continued to read the Bible: "The heavenly Shepherd is leading you in the right way to his own blessed fold. Leave all to him, to his faithfulness, his love, his power, his watchful, sleepless care." Robert decided to trust, to have faith and leave it all to God that He might protect Marie and bring her safely back to him.

Then he read the poem by Gerhart:

> "The prison where thou art
> Thy God will break it soon,
> And flood with light thy heart
> In his own blessed noon."

Robert thought how happy he would have been, as he expected by this time to be married to Marie and happily on their way to New York to celebrate their honeymoon. The hour had drifted slowly away and it was now a quarter to one. Robert was troubled and discouraged, but had not lost hope. He opened his Bible and read—Job 6: 8:

> "Oh that I might have my request, and that God would grant me the thing that I long for!"

Robert knew that he longed for Marie and believed that if he had faith God would answer his prayers. He read again—Job 6:11-13:

> "What is my strength, that I should hope? and what is mine end, that I should prolong my life?
>
> Is not my help in me? and is wisdom driven quite from me?"

This was a great consolation to Robert. He realized that at last in desperation like Job he must hope and have faith; that his wisdom and strength was in himself and that if he had faith in God and trusted him that he would find Marie; that he would be able to overcome trials and tribulations and would have wisdom and faith to hold on and hope until he realized his dream and again found Marie. Robert remembered reading in the Bible where it said:

"Whom God loveth he chastiseth."

He thought that Marie was chastising him to try his faith and decided that he would not lose patience no matter what happened, that he would seek her to the ends of the earth.

Robert watched the movement of every woman who passed thru the gates of the Union Station for Marie, but each minute brought bitter disappointment. His heart, which but a few hours ago was filled with love and happiness, was sad. Robert looked up as the hands on the clock in the Union Station pointed to 1 o'clock, —the time that he had appointed unto himself to wait without taking some action to try to find Marie. No Marie was in sight. He walked over to the news stand and bought a paper and decided to sit down for a few minutes and try to read. As he slowly turned the pages of the paper looking for something he knew not what, suddenly his eyes fell upon the heading; "The Best Thing on Earth" by R. L. Cole. The first thought that entered Robert's mind was that the best thing on earth was Marie and that the greatest thing in the world was love. He read the entire article.

CHAPTER XII

The Best Thing On Earth

By R. L. Cole

JOHN WANAMAKER said: "I have for the government, and in my own business, made contracts involving millions of dollars. I have signed checks for millions of dollars, but the greatest purchase I ever made in my life was when I was 11 years old. I saved every penny of my hard-earned money and bought a Bible that cost $2.75. That was my best investment and has had most to do with the rest of the riches of my life. Every other investment I have ever made holds a secondary place to the first and greatest one of them all."

Lord Bacon, the literary genius and philosopher, lifted the Bible one day above his head, and said: "There God speaks."

God speaks in the first verse, saying: "In the beginning God!" And all through the Book we find expressions as "Thus saith the Lord," "the word of the Lord came," "God said," "the Lord commanded," etc.

These expressions are used four thousand times in the Bible, thus indelibly stamping the divine mark.

"All scripture is given by inspiration of God." Inspiration means breathed into. God breathed his thoughts into the Book. The Book contains the breath of God, and lives because God lives.

Jesus said: "Heaven and earth shall pass away but my word shall not pass away."

The Bible tells us things we get nowhere else. It tells us of the beginning, for only God was in the beginning. It tells of the beginning of creation, the beginning of the human race, the beginning of the human family; the beginning of sin, the beginning of redemption; the beginning of the arts, sciences, music, agriculture, of nations and languages. Of the Hebrews, of law, etc.

Much of ancient history of the earliest times is borrowed from the Bible.

The Bible tells of things that are to occur thousands of years in the future. The destruction of Babylon, Nineveh, Tyre and Jerusalem was foretold in detail and has come to pass exactly as was predicted.

The first coming of Jesus Christ was foretold—that He would come to the tribe of Judah, would be born of a virgin, would be born in Bethlehem, would come out of Egypt and would grow up in Nazareth, would be despised and rejected of men, would work miracles, would be betrayed by one of his own followers, would be falsely accused, crucified. That they would gamble for his garment; would be buried in another man's tomb, would rise again; that His gospel would be preached to all nations; that to Him would be given a name greater than any name. All these prophecies have been fulfilled. The prophecies of the Bible are yet being fulfilled, and will all be fulfilled.

In Naomi we are told that in the day of His preparation the rivers shall be opened, the palace shall be dissolved and chariots shall be flaming torches, shall run like the lightning and rage in the street. Notice this prophecy: the bridges shall be opened. The suspension bridge opens our rivers. The palaces shall be dissolved. They have been.

Russia and Germany are notable examples. We are living in an era of democracy. The flaming chariots running like the lightning so much like the automobile.

In Isaiah we are told that with the coming in of the Gentiles to the brightness of His rising they shall fly as doves to their windows. That sounds like the airships.

The Bible is a priceless book because it makes promises no other book can make. It promises pardon, salvation, eternal life, soul rest, peace, comfort, strength and succor; victory over trials and temptations; strength in the dying hour, and heaven for all eternity.

The Bible is priceless because it is indestructible. For two thousand years the critics have hurled against it their anathemas, and it still lives. Time and again it has been gathered up and burned, and its advocates for ages were persecuted and put to death, but it has survived fires and floods.

A popular author of fiction boasts 9,000,000 copies of his book published in eight years. 240,000,000 copies of the Bible have been sold in the same eight years.

Another publisher boasts that his book has been

printed in 23 languages. The Bible is published in 770 different languages and dialects.

> Last we passed beside a blacksmith's door,
> And heard the anvil ring the vesper chime,
> Then looking in, I saw upon the floor
> Old hammers worn with beating years of time.
>
> "How many anvils have you had," said I,
> "To wear and batter all your hammers so?"
> "Just one," said he, then with a twinkling eye,
> "The anvil wears the hammers out you know."
>
> And so thought I, the anvil of God's word,
> For ages skeptics' blows have beat upon,
> Yet thru the noise of falling blows was heard.
> The anvil was unharmed—the hammers gone.
>
> Last we passed beside, *etc.*

Hume gone, Voltaire gone, Tom Paine gone, Bob Ingersoll gone. The present-day enemies in the church and out of the church will wear their hammers out. God's word that has for two thousand years endured the test, will endure and stand forever.

The individual or nation that believes the Book, and lives according to its teaching, will live as long as the Book lives, and the individual or nation that spurns it will go down.

Martin Luther gave the Bible to Germany and for generations Germany respected and loved the Book, and lived. Then Germany began in her schools to criticise and spurn the Book and brought on the World War. Germany by turning away from the Book, committed suicide, and so shall it be with any nation.

God forbid that America should ever turn away from the Bible!

> "Lord God of hosts be with us yet
> Let we forget, lest we forget.
>
> We've traveled together, my Bible and I,
> Thru all kinds of weather, with smile or with sigh.
> In sorrow or sunshine, in tempest or calm,
> Thy friendship unchanging; my lamp and my psalm.
>
> We've traveled together, my Bible and I,
> When life has grown weary, and death e'en was nigh;
> But all thru the darkness of mist and of wrong,
> I found thee a solace, a prayer and a song.
>
> So now who shall part us, my Bible and I.
> Shall isms or schism or new lights who shall try?
> Shall shadow for substance, or stone for good bread
> Supplant its sound wisdom, give folly instead?
> Ah no, my dear Bible, revealer of light,
> Thou sword of the spirit, put error to flight;
> And still thru life's journey, until the last sigh;
> We'll travel together, my Bible and I."

*   *   *   *   *

These statements agreed exactly with Robert's views. He had found his greatest help in the Bible and knew John Wanamaker was right when he said that the greatest purchase he ever made in his life was when he was 11 years old and bought the Bible for $2.75. As Robert read:

> "Heaven and earth shall pass away but my word shall not pass away,"

he remembered that the Bible said that whenever you

pray, believe that you have it and you shall. As he knew that all things are possible with the Lord, he determined to pray believing that Marie would soon return to him. Robert was much impressed with the statement that all the prophecies of the Bible are being fulfilled and will be fulfilled. He knew that every promise that God had ever made to man, he had kept. This renewed Robert's faith and again he read Marie's note where it said: "According to your faith, be I unto you," and Robert thought that if faith would bring Marie back to him she would surely come. He knew that time would never change his love and that there was no other woman but Marie for him. He would live, work and hope for Marie until he found her, but if she had gone from him forever and such bad news should come to him, he knew that he would bury all life and that hope would depart from him and life would not be worth living.

At the end of the article he read the poem on the Bible and was much impressed with these lines:

"Ah no, my dear Bible, revealer of light,
Thou sword of the spirit, put error to flight;
And still thru life's journey, until the last sigh;
We'll travel together, my Bible and I."

Robert felt that this article had been written especially for him when he needed it most, making him realize the value of his Bible and the trust he should put in it, applying its wisdom to his present problem and troubles.

By the time Robert had finished reading this article, it was after 1:30 P.M. and he decided that it was hopeless to wait longer for Marie, that something radically wrong had happened and she had either gone away or an accident had befallen her. He must make some plans for locating her. Decided to go to a hotel and call Mr. Kennelworth on long-distance 'phone at Texarkana. With this plan in mind, he made his way to the hotel, registered and as soon as he was assigned to his room, put in a long-distance call for Mr. Kennelworth. Mr. Kennelworth was at his residence and it was only a question of a few minutes until he had him on the 'phone. Between sobs, he told his sad story to Mr. Kennelworth about Marie's disappearance and asked his advice. Mr. Kennelworth told him that he thought for some reason Marie may have decided to return to school and complete her education, and probably was at that time on her way back to Sherman. The best plan would be to wait until the next night to see if she returned, altho it was possible that she might get back late that night. Mr. Kennelworth told Robert that he would go to see her father and find out any information he could for him. Robert was to remain at the hotel and if he got any information, he would telephone him. He advised Robert to notify the railroad authorities, and have them make a search and inquire at all of the stations where the train stopped that night on the way from Texarkana to St. Louis, in order to get a clue to Marie's disappearance.

After talking with Mr. Kennelworth, Robert got in touch over the 'phone with the railroad officials in St. Louis and notified them of Marie's disappearance from the train. They promised to send telegrams to all the station agents, to have all the trains watched and try to secure some information for him. They were to communicate with him just as soon as they had anything definite one way or the other.

Robert now realized that he must go thru the greatest ordeal yet—that of waiting hourly for some news of Marie. He knew the hours would pass slowly and decided to formulate a plan in case Marie did not return to school or to her home, and if no news came from her the next day what would be his next move and what he should do to try to locate her.

The next time Robert noticed the time of day, it was after 6 P.M. and he realized that he had had no breakfast, lunch or dinner, but his heart was heavy and he felt that he could not eat anything. The shock had been so great and had come so suddenly that Robert found it hard to adjust himself to it or to realize what it all meant or what it might mean in case Marie should pass out of his life forever. It would mean every hope blasted, every sweet dream gone and would leave him with an uncertainty of life, like a ship without a rudder. He decided to pass the time by reading and seeking consolation in the Bible.

Robert had always been a great admirer of the poet, S. E. Kiser; always read his poems in the daily newspapers and a few months previous to this time, had bought a little book entitled, "Poems That Have Helped Me," collected by S. E. Kiser. He remembered that he had this little book that he liked so much in his suit-case so he unpacked it to look for the book and as he did, he came across the present, the surprise that he had for Marie, that he had told her about before and refused to give to her or tell her more about it until they arrived in St. Louis.   The present was a wedding ring set with diamonds and a beautiful brooch made of two hearts woven together and tied with a cluster of diamonds and pearls.   This was to be the great surprise for Marie and he was going to present it to Marie after they were married, as a token of the two hearts that now beat as one.   Robert looked at this and thought of how the diamonds represented Marie in all of her beauty and that she was a pearl of great price.

It was too much for him.   He broke down completely and wept like a baby.   Alone he was—the most alone he had ever been in his life before—away from friends, away from mother, and above all, separated from Marie, who meant more than life to him.   He sobbed for hours.   His heart was breaking, but with a wondering mind, he realized that he must have strength, and that he must have faith and hope on—hope and believe that Marie was alive and he knew that if she were alive, there was hope.

He picked up his favorite little book, "Poems That Helped Me," and started to read.   The first one that caught his eye was, "Faith" by Tennyson:

> "We have but faith; we cannot know;
> For knowledge is of things we see;
> And yet we trust it comes from thee,
> A beam of darkness: let it grow.
>
> Let knowledge grow from more to more,
> But more of reverence in us dwell;
> That mind and soul, according well,
> May make one music as before,

> But vaster. We are fools and slight;
> We mock thee when we do not fear;
> But help thy foolish ones to bear;
> Help thy vain worlds to bear thy light.
>
> Forgive what seemed my sin in me;
> What seem'd my worth since I began;
> For merit lies from man to man,
> And not from man, O Lord, to thee."

This cheered Robert and he resolved to have more faith, realizing that while he could not see or understand Marie's action he must have faith and love and trust her, and trust that time would bring understanding and solve the problem.

He read another poem by Aubrey de Vere, and these words seemed to sink into his heart as he read them:

> "Hid it; dropt it on the moors!
> Lost it, and you cannot find it"—
> My own heart I want, not yours
> You have bound and must unbound it.
> Set it free then from your net,
> We will love, sweet—but not yet!
> Fling it from you—we are strong
> Love is trouble, love is folly;
> Love, that makes an old heart young,
> Makes a young heart melancholy."

Robert felt that love might be trouble, but that love was the greatest and sweetest thing in the world and that he would go thru any troubles in the world, suffer anything, only to regain Marie and her love. As Robert slowly turned the pages of the little book, his eyes fell upon another poem, "Courage" by Thos. F. Porter:

"What if the morn no joy to you shall bring,
No gleam of sunbeam shine across your way;
What if no bird one joyous note shall sing
Into your listening ear thru all the day!

What if no word of comfort you shall hear
As thru the hours long you toil and strive;
What if to you no vision bright appear
To keep your hungry heart and soul alive!

What if the blest companionship men crave
Come not to you thru all the day's long length,
But, bound and fettered even as a slave,
Within yourself you have to find your strength!

And if, when you have toiled and wrought alone,
The sweet reward you sought you do not gain,
And find the hoped-for bread is but stone,
In that sad hour for grief, should you compalin?

Ah no! It matters not if shade or sun,
Or good or ill, your efforts shall attend;
In doing you have but your duty done
As best you knew—and should do to the end."

He eagerly devoured the words one by one, because
he was looking for something to give him courage to
go thru this terrible ordeal. He thought that this poem
would do. It surely had been written for him in this
very hour of trouble and realized with Job he must find
his strength within himself and have courage, hope and
faith.

He then read another little poem from the book; "Not
in Vain" by Emily Dickinson:

"If I can stop one heart from breaking,
I shall not live in vain:
If I can ease one life the aching,

Or cool one pain,
Or help one fainting robin
Unto his nest again,
I shall not live in vain."

Robert felt that he had tried always to be kind and considerate and charitable towards others, and knew that he must go on regardless of what happened, and live his life hoping to find Marie. About this time, Robert, tired, hungry and worn out fell asleep. The next time that he remembered anything, he awoke on Monday morning with the sun streaming in thru the window of his hotel and realized that he had fallen asleep. The little book, "Poems That Have Helped Me," lay on the bed beside him. Because the sun was coming in the east window he knew that he must have slept thru some part of the night, and it was now morning. His first thought was of Marie, and of any news that might have come. Picking up the little book, the first thing that struck his eye was the poem, "Press On" by Park Benjamin:

"Press on! Surmount the rocky steps,
Climb boldly o'er the torrent's arch;
He fails alone who feebly creeps,
He wins who dares the hero's march.
Be thou a hero! Let thy might
Tramp on eternal snows its way,
And thru the ebon walls of night
Hew down a passage unto day.

Press on! If once and twice thy feet
Slip back and stumble, harder try;
From him who never dreads to meet
Danger and death they're sure to fly.

To coward ranks the bullet speeds,
While on their breasts who never quail,
Gleams, guardian of chivalric deeds,
Bright courage like a coat of mail.

Press on! If Fortune play thee false
To day, tomorrow she'll be true;
Whom now she sinks she now exalts,
Taking old gifts and granting new,
The wisdom of the present hour
Makes up the follies past and gone;
To weakness strength succeeds, and power
From frailty springs! Press on, press on!

Robert hastily read this poem and found some consolation in it. He resolved that he would press on, and hastened down stairs to the hotel desk to inquire if any telegrams had been received for him, or if any long-distance call had come during the night when he had fallen asleep, but again he met with disappointment. There were no telegrams and there had been no 'phone calls.

Robert felt very faint and weak because he was hungry. He had not eaten all day Sunday, and now realized that he must get something to eat, and strengthen himself for the ordeal to follow. He went to the dining-room and ordered a light breakfast but when the food was served, he found it hard to eat because he thought of the breakfast the Sunday morning before that he had intended to have eaten with Marie on the dining-car. Everything he saw reminded him of her. Her smile was in the glittering sunshine which played upon the windows in front of him or appeared in the clear crystal water in the glass and the sweet odor

from the flowers on the table brought memories of sweet
kisses and soft caresses which haunted him. Finally,
Robert managed to eat a little, because he knew he must
if he expected to keep up and have strength to fight
on and find Marie.

When he had finished his breakfast, he returned to
his room and decided to call the railroad office again and
ascertain if they had any information for him. The
general passenger agent was there, and was very courte-
ous over the 'phone to Robert. He had taken a great
interest in the case and they had received reports from
every station along the line, but nowhere had any trace
been found of Marie. He assured Robert that the railway company would use every effort to continue the
search and report to him promptly any information that
they received.

Robert decided to call Mr. Kennelworth on the long-
distance 'phone at his office in Texarkana and soon got
him on the wire. Mr. Kennelworth said that he had
gone to see Marie's father, Mr. Stanton, soon after
Robert's telephone message Sunday afternoon and had
told Mr. Stanton of Robert's success since he had been
with his firm; how hard Robert had studied and planned
and how he had figured out the cotton and grain markets
and the large amount of money that he had made on
such a small capital. He confided to Mr. Stanton the
secret of how Marie had saved up her money and how
much money Robert had made on the $400.00 which he
had invested for her. Mr. Stanton and his wife were much
impressed with the story and felt that they had been
wrong in opposing Marie's love for Robert and their

marriage. They told Mr. Kennelworth that when Marie returned they would give her their consent to marry Robert then or any time later. They felt that they might be to blame for any harm that would come to Marie or for the sorrows that Robert was suffering. However, they were hopeful that Marie was either returning home or was on her way back to Sherman, Texas, to complete her education, and, therefore, were not greatly alarmed and intended to wait until Monday afternoon to find out if Marie had gone back to Sherman. Mr. Kennelworth stated that Mr. and Mrs. Stanton wished him to convey their sympathy to Robert and to tell him that they had great faith in him and wanted to help make him and Marie happy.

This message was great consolation to Robert because he felt that it was going to solve the problem, that no matter what had prompted Marie's decision to leave the train and not to go ahead and marry him when she found that her father and mother had changed their attitude, she would be only too glad to return to Robert. They could then be married and continue on to New York where he could take up his studies and complete the building of his airship as soon as he had made enough money to do so.

Mr. Kennelworth told Robert that he would call him on the 'phone about 8 o'clock that night and let him know if any word had been received from Marie or if news was received sooner, he would call immediately, but at any rate would call at 8 o'clock. Mr. Kennelworth praised Robert and told him not to lose hope but take a philosophical view of the matter. He felt sure that no harm had come to Marie, for had there been any accident it certainly would have been discovered by this time by the railway company. The fact that Marie's baggage had disappeared was convincing evidence to him that in some way, at some station during the night, she had left the train and had probably concealed herself and was waiting to return on another train, later. He believed before the day was over they would have some good news in regard to Marie, and advised Robert to get busy and go right ahead with his trading in the market and continue to make money, as he was sure that everything was going to come out all right.

After Robert received this telephone message he was more hopeful. He secured a morning newspaper and found the headlines filled with Lindbergh. Read about the preparations for Captain Lindbergh's return to Washington and New York and the plans for his reception. Of course, Robert had looked forward to being there at that time and have Marie with him as his wife. He had been looking forward to the day when his own dream would be realized and he would build one of the greatest airships of the age.

Returning to his room, he fell upon his knees and breathed a prayer; a prayer that only a man whose heart is filled with love for a good woman can pray. He prayed to the Universal Power that created the Universe, the master of land and sea, who rides on the winds and walks upon the water, to whom all power was given over heaven and earth. Prayed for strength and for guidance to do only that which was right and

that the good God of the Universe would return Marie
to him in safety. Prayed not only for himself, or the
strength to come to him, but for Marie, for her happiness, for her safety. It was an unselfish prayer; the
kind of a prayer that a mother prays when her child
is lost, when she thinks nothing of herself but only of
the child that she loves.

When Robert arose from the prayer he felt better;
felt that some of the strength of that unseen guiding
hand, which is ever a comfort and in great demand in
time of trouble, had come to him. In God and his word
alone he found comfort and consolation. He realized
the significance of money and how little it meant;
thought how quickly he had made money on a thousand
dollars in the market and now how he would give every
cent of it for just a message from Marie; just to know
that she was alive. He had never tried to make the
money for a selfish purpose, but thought of the things
that it could buy to make Marie happy and give her comfort, and what he might be able to do for his country
in time of war when they would need service and inventions which would protect them against the enemy.

After he had time to collect his thoughts, he decided
to call his old pal, Walter Kennelworth, in New York
on the long-distance telephone and tell him all that had
happened in such a short time.

Robert had not informed Walter that he was coming
to New York at this time. He intended to telegraph
him from St. Louis on Sunday morning after he and
Marie had been married, and, of course, he knew that
Walter would be at the train to meet them on their

arrival. After some delay he got Walter on the long-distance 'phone and told him as quickly as possible all that had happened. Walter was more amused than shocked at the news and said: "Robert, Marie is just a little devil and full of fun. She is only testing your love. There is nothing to worry about. I know her ways better than you do." He was sure that everything would be all right. But Robert felt that too much time had already elapsed for it to be a joke and that Marie was not waiting around St. Louis or hiding somewhere playing a joke that long. It was too serious a matter for Robert to feel that Marie would punish him in this way so long. Walter begged Robert to come right on to New York, but Robert told him he would never leave St. Louis until he had some definite news, one way or the other, as to what had happened to Marie.

After his talk with Walter, Robert felt better because he was his closest friend and it was always a pleasure to talk with him. He hoped that Walter was right and that Marie would show up soon. At the same time, he feared that something might have gone wrong, but every time this thought occurred he would read Marie's letter again and this would give him hope and courage because it plainly said she would come to him when he needed her most. Of course, he realized that she could not know just how badly he needed her now and felt that he would never need her more than he did at that very moment.

When Robert was troubled and blue it had always been his practice to read either the Bible or some other good book. He had a scrap book where he had collected

poems and he took this book out and began to look
thru it.   He noticed a clipping that he had pasted in
only a short time before headed: "Tomorrow's Chance,"
by his favorite modern poet, S. E. Kiser:

I may not reach my goal today
Nor move one step ahead;
No effort that I make may pay,
I may lose ground, instead;
But I can try no matter what
Obstructions I shall find,
And let no thought
Of turning from the path I've sought
Take root within my mind.

There may be many reasons why
No effort I can make
Shall send my fancies soaring high
Or clear the course I take;
Mischances I could not foresee
May check me everywhere,
But I can be
Determined bravely, faithfully,
To keep my purpose fair.

It may be that at every turn
Discouragement shall lurk;
My lessons may be hard to learn.
Men may condemn my work;
My trust may be betrayed by those
Whom I have thought my friends,
But I can close
My mind against imagined woes,
And strive for worthy ends.

No matter how my hopes shall fail,
Or how I fall behind,
I'll not sit down tonight to wail
That God has been unkind.
But, with a duty to fulfil,
And with a proud, defiant glance,
I'll prove that still
I have the courage and the will,
And gird me for tomorrow's chance.

This poem seemed to fit his case and he read it over carefully. He resolved that regardless of discouragement or disappointment, blasted hopes, lost ideals or shattered dreams, he would still have the courage to exert himself for "Tomorrow's Chance."

After reading this poem he began to think about the future and his plans. He knew that he had intended to go into the market again on Monday or Tuesday, but the thought came to him—What good would money do now, without Marie? However, he remembered her letter saying, "According to your faith, be I unto you." Therefore, braced himself and again determined to have faith to go on, watching and waiting for Marie.

Robert bought the evening paper and looked over the financial page and noted that cotton had gone down as he had figured it would. The following day was the time that his forecast indicated that it would strike bottom so he must pull himself together and buy some cotton, both for his own account and for Marie's. Wheat had also declined and he felt that it was time to buy wheat for another advance as his cycle indicated an up-trend to run for the next ten days. Robert looked over the stock page and noticed the heading; "Major Motors advances above 200, a new high level." Robert had figured out that Major Motors would not advance much above 200 before it would be a short sale for big profits. He figured out from the cycle of Major Motors that it would hold until along in June and July and that it would decline to a very low level in 1928, so he decided he was going to go short to hold for a long campaign and make a fortune.

Robert was still holding his Right Aeroplane stock, which he had bought at 31 on May 21st, the day that Captain Lindbergh completed his successful flight to Paris. He figured that he could make a great fortune by buying Right Aeroplane stock and holding it for years and at the same time selling Major Motors short. The markets in Wheat, Cotton, Major Motors and Right Aeroplane were all doing just exactly as he had calculated they would. The fact that he was making money on Right Aeroplane stock encouraged him to continue his work on his own plane.

Robert did not forget sweet Marie or what she meant to him. At the same time he realized what the study of the Bible had brought him and felt that thru the aid of that book and the knowledge and wisdom he had gained through its teaching, there would be a way to find Marie if she were alive. He believed she was and he would hope and wait. But in the meantime he would try to make some money in order to provide all the luxuries and comforts for her when he found her. Since Marie's father and mother had agreed to withdraw all their opposition to their marriage, he thought that as soon as Marie heard this she would certainly come to him or communicate with him.

On June 7th, Robert sent a telegram to his broker to buy 500 bales of October Cotton and 500 bales of December Cotton at the Opening on Tuesday morning. He also ordered him to buy 100,000 bushels of July Wheat and gave an order to sell 500 shares of Major Motors when it reached 203. After sending these telegrams he returned to the hotel feeling some better and hoping that when he heard from Mr. Kennelworth on the long-distance 'phone he would have some good news. So he ate his dinner and returned to his room to wait for a message. Later he inquired for telegrams and 'phone calls and was informed that none had been received. He settled himself down in the room and concluded to wait for the long-distance call, hoping that it would bring good news.

At about 8:15 the telephone rang and Mr. Kennelworth was on the wire. Robert knew from Mr. Kennelworth's voice that he had no good news. Mr. Kennelworth informed him that no word had been received from Marie by her parents, and that they had called up the school in Sherman, Texas, and not a word had been heard from her there. The school informed them that she had left school on Saturday afternoon and had not been seen since. Of course, Robert knew she had left Sherman to meet him and was now more anxious and worried than ever and freely expressed his great anxiety to Mr. Kennelworth. Mr. Kennelworth was still hopeful and tried to cheer and encourage Robert. Advised him to go on to New York and wait him there.

He had followed Robert's advice and bought Wheat and Cotton on Monday afternoon and Robert told him that he was going to buy the next morning at the Opening. Mr. Kennelworth said that he planned to leave for New York at the end of the week. Robert then decided to stay in St. Louis until he got some definite word, or anyway remain there until Mr. Kennelworth arrived and then go on to New York with him. He was anxious to see Walter as soon as possible but wanted to know something about what happened to Marie before leaving for New York. Mr. Kennelworth was confident that the next day would bring some news from Marie, one way or the other, and advised Robert to keep cheerful; that he would inform him just as soon as news came.

After Robert had time to think over the matter, he decided to place "Personal Notices" in all the newspapers of St. Louis and the towns along the line between Texarkana and St. Louis. If no news was heard of Marie by Tuesday evening, he would place it in the papers the next day. He then wrote out the Notice.

MISS MARIE STANTON—I FOUND YOUR LITTLE NOTE IN MY POCKET ON SUNDAY MORNING. HAVE BEEN WAITING FOR YOU IN ST. LOUIS. MY FAITH IN YOU IS SUPREME. IT WILL NEVER CHANGE. MONTHS AND YEARS CANNOT CHANGE ME, NO MATTER WHAT I HEAR OR DO NOT HEAR OR WHAT MAY HAPPEN, I WILL ALWAYS HAVE FAITH IN YOU AND LOVE YOU. WILL NEVER NEED YOU MORE THAN NOW. NOTHING ELSE THAT I CAN GET, OR MONEY THAT I CAN MAKE MATTERS OR MEANS ANYTHING TO ME WITHOUT YOU. COME TO ME OR COMMUNICATE WITH ME AND EXPLAIN ALL AND I WILL UNDERSTAND AND AGREE TO ANYTHING YOU MAY DESIRE. MARIE, RELIEVE MY ANXIOUS HEART. LET ME HEAR FROM YOU. YOUR FATHER AND MOTHER HAVE

AGREED TO WITHDRAW THEIR OBJECTIONS AND CONSENT TO OUR
BEING MARRIED. I WILL HAVE FAITH AND WAIT IN ST. LOUIS
UNTIL I HEAR SOMETHING FROM YOU.

ROBERT GORDON,
Address—Planters Hotel.

Robert decided to read and study some before he retired that night. He read the poem, "How to Live,"
by William Cullen Bryant:

So live, that when thy summons comes to join
The innumerable caravan that moves
To that mysterious realm where each shall take
His chamber in the silent halls of death,
Thou go not, like the quarry slave at night,
Scourged to his dungeon, but sustained and soothed
By an unfaltering trust, approach thy grave
Like one who wraps the drapery of his couch
About him, and lies down to pleasant dreams.

Robert wished that he might be able that night to lie
down to pleasant dreams but he knew that he would
lay down with an unfaltering trust in Marie, that he
would have the faith in her which would move mountains, that he would never doubt her no matter how
long a time passed and would prove that his love for
her was supreme and his faith unfaltering.

Robert read another poem on "Perserverance" by
Goethe:

PERSEVERANCE

We must not hope to be mowers,
And to gather the ripe gold ears,
Unless we have first been sowers
And watered the furrows with tears.

> It is not just as we take it,
>   This mystical world of ours,
> Life's field will yield as we make it
>   A harvest of thorns or of flowers.

He realized that perhaps all the good things of life do not come to us easily and that we might have to go through sorrows and trouble to try our faith. Robert decided to persevere and try to be philosophic and hope, no matter what happened, and to continue to watch and wait for good news from Marie.

Before he retired that night, Robert read "The Golden Hour" by James W. Foley:

> I'm sending you one golden hour
>   From the full jeweled crown of the day;
> Not sorrow or care shall have power
>   To steal this rare jewel away.
> I'm bidding you join in the dreaming
>   I had in that hour of you,
> When all of the old dreams, in seeming,
>   Were gold like the hour, and came true.
>
> So let's dream like a child in its playing,
>   Let's make us a sky and a sea,
> Let's change the things 'round us by saying
>   They're things that we wish them to be;
> And if there is sadness or sorrow,
>   Let's dream till we charm it away,
> Let's learn from the children, and borrow
>   A saying from childhood: "Let's play!"
>
> Let's play that the world's full of beauty,
>   Let's play there are roses in bloom,
> Let's play there is pleasure in duty,
>   And light where we thought there was gloom.

Let's play that this heart with its sorrow
  Is bidden be joyous and glad,
Let's play that we'll find on tomorrow
  The joys that we never have had.

Let's play that regret with its ruing
  Is banished forever and aye,
Let's play there's delight but in doing,
  Let's play there are flowers by the way.
However the pathway seem dreary,
  Wherever the footsteps may lead,
Let's play there's a song for the weary
  If only the heart will give heed.

Let's play we have done with repining,
  Let's play that our longings are still,
Let's play that the sunlight is shining,
  To gold the green slope of the hill.
Let's play there are birds blithely flinging
  Their songs of delight to the air,
Let's play that the world's full of singing,
  Let's play there is love—everywhere.

Robert knelt and prayed before he went to sleep, always asking for Marie and her protection. He said: "Lord, I ask nothing for myself, but beseech the greatest blessings on Marie and only ask for her happiness. If it be for the best that her happiness be away from me, then I desire to suffer rather than for her to be unhappy. I pray that she may realize my great love and faith in her, my devotion to her and willingness to make any sacrifice for her that might seem right, no matter what my judgment may be."

Robert slept better that night because he was looking

forward to Tuesday, the 7th day of the month. He had learned that the "7th" was a sacred day, and had often talked to Marie about the number 7, and the number of times it is spoken of in the Bible. How God had blessed the 7th day and made it the Sabbath; how many things had come to pass on the 7th day of the 7th month, or the 7th year referred to in the Bible. In some way he felt that on this day news would come from Marie and he hoped that it would be good.

Robert awoke on Tuesday morning feeling much better, had his breakfast early, bought the newspaper and read all about the receptions being planned for Colonel Lindbergh and again the wish stole into his heart and the hope was revived that in some way Marie might be with him when Lindbergh arrived in New York. Later in the day he received telegrams at his hotel from his broker, advising of the purchase of October and December cotton and also the purchase of July wheat.

Robert decided to console himself by reading the Bible. He read Job, and realized that he, too, would have patience to wait until his time should come. Nothing could shake his faith in Marie or shake his faith in the wisdom of Almighty God whom, Robert fully believed, would answer his prayer. He hoped that before the day was over, some news of Marie would surely come.

As he was reading the Bible the bellboy brought him a letter stamped Texarkana, and, of course, Robert hoped it contained some news of Marie. He opened it hastily and read:

Texarkana, Texas.
June 6, 1927.

Mr. Robert Gordon,
Planters Hotel,
St. Louis, Mo.

DEAR ROBERT:

We are deeply grieved over Marie's disappearance but are hopeful that no harm has come to her. From what Mr. Kennelworth tells us of the letter she wrote you, we believe she is returning to school or home, and we are waiting news of her with hope.

While Marie is quite young and we thought too young to marry, and you too, are very young and could well afford to wait a few years, we now realize that if a delay would interfere with your happiness and Marie's, we would gladly consent to an immediate marriage. We regret that we have misjudged you, Robert, and are proud to know more about you from those who have known you intimately. Parents often make mistakes in opposing their children and frequently the interference of parents in the marriage of their children separate two that God has joined together. Man can only put asunder the physical bodies, but what God doeth is forever.

We are very happy to know of your loyalty to Marie, your faith in God and your great ambitions to succeed, according to the rules laid down in the Bible. Shall be very happy to notify you promptly of any news from Marie and will kindly ask you to do the same for us. Believe us

Sincerely your friends,

WILLIAM and MARY STANTON.

When Robert received and read this letter he was deeply touched and felt that a reward must always come to those whose intentions are honest and honorable, so he sat down and answered the letter.

St. Louis, Missouri,
June 7, 1927.

Mr. and Mrs. W. H. Stanton,
Texarkana,
Texas.

DEAR FRIENDS:

I feel like addressing you as friends because sorrow often makes us all friends, and am enclosing a poem—"Trouble Brings Friends," which I think is very appropriate. Materlinck said, "Men help each other by their joy, not by sorrow," but it is my belief that we are often led to extend help in time of sorrow which we would never think of doing in time of joy or happiness. I quote from John 16: 22—"And ye now therefore have sorrow; but I will see you again, and your hearts shall rejoice, and your joy no man taketh from you." I hope and pray that the day is not far distant when our hearts will rejoice together with the return of Marie.

Marie means everything to me and I honor and respect you as her parents. I believe that you acted as you thought best for Marie's future, and can find no fault with your good and honest intentions, regardless of the suffering it has caused me or the sorrow and disappointment it may have brought to Marie. I wish to do only that which is honorable and best for all concerned, and if Marie returns I will agree to submit to your decision and wait until she has finished her course in college before we are married. I wish to take my part of the responsibility for Marie's elopement because I urged her into action. I wanted to go to you and talk the matter over but she felt sure that you would never consent to our marriage and said the only thing to do was to elope.

Marie felt all along when I was a struggling boy without money, that you would never consent to her marrying below her station in life and this, as much as anything else, made me ambitious to achieve success and prove to you that even tho I was born of poor parents and started without anything in life, I could make a great success and accumulate money. To me money means nothing and I would gladly give every dollar I have ever made just to spend one hour with Marie, and I am sure that this is no boyish love affair or trick of the imagination. While it is my first love, it will endure forever. Time will prove that Marie means everything to me.

I thank you for your kindness and consideration and hope and pray that we may soon have good news in regard to Marie.

Sincerely yours,

Robert Gordon.

Poem enclosed with Robert's letter:

It's seldom trouble comes alone,
I've noticed this: when things go wrong
An' trouble comes a-visitin'
It always brings a friend along;
Sometimes it's one you've known before,
And then perhaps it's some one new
Who stretches out a helping hand,
An' stops to see what he can do.

If never trials come to us,
If grief an' sorrow passed us by,
If every day the sun came out,
An' clouds were never in the sky,
We'd still have neighbors, I suppose,
Each one pursuin' selfish ends,
But only neighbors they would be,
We'd never know them as our friends.

Out of the troubles I have had
Have come my richest friendships here,
Kind hands have helped to bear my care,
Kind words have fallen on my ear;
An' so I say when trouble comes
I know before the storm shall end
That I shall find my bit of care
Has also brought to me a friend.

CHAPTER XIII

THAT afternoon, after three o'clock, when the afternoon newspapers were out, he bought a paper and found that cotton and wheat had advanced many points and that he now had a nice profit on the purchases made that morning. Indeed, the gods of good fortune and finance were smiling on Robert, but the Goddess of Love was frowning and he must have patience. As the sun was slowly setting and the day was waning, he watched in sadness because no news had come from Marie. He firmly resolved that he would carry out his intention and place the personal notice in the papers the following day for news of Marie, if something did not come that evening.

Robert called Mr. Kennelworth on the 'phone in Texarkana and again met with disappointment. Not a word had been heard from Marie and her parents were now growing more anxious and feared that there had been some accident or foul play in some way. They were making a search in every direction; City and County officials had been notified and all the schools thruout the country were on the lookout for Marie and making every effort to obtain some information about her. Robert told Mr. Kennelworth about his plan to insert the personal notice and Mr. Kennelworth agreed with him. He thought it would be a good idea and he believed that if she were secretly hiding somewhere, she would surely see the papers because she herself would be anxious to know what happened to Robert and what he was doing.

Robert arose early on Wednesday morning, June 8th, hastened to the newspaper offices and placed the personal notices to appear the following day. When he returned to his hotel, for the first time since Sunday he thought of his birthday, June 9th, when he would be 21 years of age. When he thought of this a great hope came into his mind. He decided that Marie, for some unknown reason, was hiding until his birthday and intended that they should be married on that day and she was going to be his birthday present. Robert's imagination went wild. He was elated over the hope. It seemed like a sudden inspiration to him. It would be just like Marie to wait until his birthday to give him the surprise of his life, and think this delay would only try his faith and patience and she would know just how much she meant to him, but did not think it too long to keep him waiting if he really loved her as he said he did; that he would have patience and wait.

Robert was sure that his advertisements in the papers the following day were going to bring results and that probably Marie, just as soon as she saw it, would come to him. So he really began to plan and hope and get ready for a marriage to take place on his birthday. He was so happy over this sudden thought, so elated that he 'phoned Mr. Kennelworth again that night and told him all about it. Mr. Kennelworth, half-hearted but hopeful, agreed with Robert that there might be something in it, that Marie might have had some plan of this kind in mind, and sincerely hoped that Robert was right and that this birthday would be the happiest of his life.

After Robert talked with Mr. Kennelworth, he immediately called Walter Kennelworth on the 'phone in New York, told him all that had happened, about his placing the personal notices in the papers, about his hopes and theories that Marie would show up on his birthday. Walter said that it would be just like her to do a trick of that kind and that this might be just what it all meant. He thought that Robert had struck on the right idea and was hopeful, too, that the marriage would take place on Robert's birthday. He was to call Robert on the 'phone the next day or Robert should call him just as soon as he got any news. Walter wanted to send congratulations for his birthday and his wedding day. The fact that Walter was so cheerful and shared Robert's views and hopes in the matter, made Robert much happier.

After Robert had talked with Walter, the bellboy came and brought a special-delivery letter and a telegram. Robert opened the telegram hurriedly, hoping that it was something from Marie, but found it was a telegram from his mother in which she congratulated him on his birthday the following day, and encouraged him to hope for the best and not give way to despair in case Marie did not show up. The special-delivery letter was also from Robert's mother, and read:

My dear Son,

Your good friend, Mr. Kennelworth, has been out to see me and told all that has happened. My son, I counsel you to

have patience and faith. Love endures much and is not discouraged. I believe everything happens for the best, my boy,
and it may be that Marie thought that you were both too
young to marry. If this was her view, I would say it would
hurt neither of you to wait a few years longer.

While I cannot understand the mysterious way in which
Marie disappeared, at the same time I hope, pray and believe
that she is alive and will come into your life again when you
most need her and are better prepared for her than you are
now. I know that it will be hard for you to see and realize
that it might be for the best for her to go out of your life
at this time, but even Marie may be wiser than we know. She
may want to test your love and test her love for you. If this
is the case, it will all turn out for the best for both of you.
If your love is strong enough to endure it and wait a few
months or a few years, no harm can come later. If Marie can
bear to be separated from you and remain faithful and loyal
to you for a few months or a few years, then she will mean
more to you when she comes back to you again.

I pray for you each night and pray that everything may
come out all right. I still have great faith and confidence in
you, my boy. Want you to stick to your faith and your
religion. Read the Holy Bible and follow it as you have in
the past and everything that the good God can do will come
to you in due time. Write me of your plans and what you
intend to do. Send me a telegram as soon as you have any
news, one way or the other. I anxiously await news of Marie
and wish that I could be with you to comfort you because I
know you need me when you haven't Marie.

Devotedly,

Your MOTHER.

Robert was happy to get the letter from his mother
because she always encouraged him and he knew that
no matter what happened, her faith in him would always remain the same and her love would endure for-

ever. He retired that night after having a light supper, very happy, looking forward to his birthday with great hopes and expectations. His 21st birthday meant a great deal to him, meant more than any other birthday because he hoped that it would bring Marie. He knew that he had stood the test of her absence and that he had unwavering faith, that the had never doubted her motive, no matter even if he could not understand it, and that he would not censure her actions. When Marie returned and was once sure that she knew all this, he would mean more to her than he had ever before and she would only love him the more. After all, perhaps this little disappointment would mean something good in the future.

That night he read over all the poems that Marie had ever written him or sent him, and read over the poems that he had written her, because he had kept a copy of them. He read the poem where he wrote "If your aim is high and honest, in victory it will tell; Before the pearl is gotten, there must be a broken shell!" Again Robert realized that the shell had been broken worse this time than ever before, or at least it seemed that way to him. Yet at the same time it was not a break because Marie had left him with love, and their last good-night kiss on the train had been one of supreme faith and trusting love which had been built up over a period of years in which there had been many obstacles to overcome, hard struggles and disappointments. Robert prayed his usual night prayer for the protection of Marie and went to sleep, to dream of his birthday.

ROBERT GORDON'S 21ST BIRTHDAY

Robert arose early on June 9th. Hurried down to the desk to ascertain if any telegrams had come over night or any 'phone calls, but found no telegrams and no messages. It was yet too early for the morning mail. Robert secured the morning papers and saw his personal notices which he had instructed the papers to continue to run. He had added the name of his hotel and telephone number so that Marie could reach him promptly. Somehow he had a feeling that just about 11 or 12 o'clock that day Marie would call at the hotel or he would have some good news from her.

After having his breakfast, he waited for the first mail, but there were no letters for him and up to this time no telegrams had been received. He decided to go down to a brokerage office and see how the market opened. Cotton and wheat had advanced the day before and cotton opened higher and was strong this morning, and wheat was also holding up well. Robert found that Major Motors was selling around 203 and he knew that his broker must have sold 500 shares short for him at this price. He figured that Major Motors would not advance above 205½ before it started on a big decline. So he said to himself, "This is going to be a real happy birthday. I am making money fast now in wheat and cotton and will soon be making money in stocks." Right Aeroplane was also strong and his profits were piling up on this. He figured up his profits on Cotton, Wheat and Stocks and on this birthday he was worth $30,000.

The money meant nothing to him. He would gladly give every cent of it to have Marie as a birthday present. His hopes remained high and somehow he felt that he would have Marie as well as the financial success. Just as he was figuring up his profits and thinking about it an old saying came to him: "Lucky at cards, unlucky in love." He wondered if this could be, that he would be lucky in making money in speculation and at the same time unlucky in his love affairs; but hoped and prayed that this was the last disappointment in his love affairs and that this birthday was to be the turning point and that some news would come from Marie.

He decided to forget about the market as everything was moving along his way and returned to the hotel to wait for news of Marie. He still had a hope or an imagination that around 11 or 12 o'clock Marie would either come to the hotel or some news from her would be received. Upon returning to the hotel he found no mail and no telegrams or telephone messages awaiting him. When 11 o'clock came Robert's mind reverted back to Sunday when he was watching the clock in the Union Station, hoping and waiting for Marie to appear. Robert became a little restless and more than anxious as the minutes went by. The clock struck twelve on his birthday and no Marie and no news from her. A few minutes after 12 his bell rang and a messenger boy appeared with a telegram. "Ah," Robert thought, "this is from Marie or some news from her." But it was a telegram of congratulations from his old pal, Walter, who asked that he convey the first news which he received in regard to Marie and stated that he hoped before the day was over he could congratulate Robert on his marriage to Marie. A little later in the day Robert received a long telegram from Mr. Kennelworth, congratulating him on his birthday and offering words of encouragement, also telling Robert that he expected to leave Texarkana on Friday night, June 10th, and arrive in St. Louis some time in the morning and that Robert should be ready to start with him to New York, as he wanted to be there when Lindbergh arrived. Robert received another telegram from his mother congratulating him on his birthday and wishing him every success and happiness.

These messages were very encouraging but it was now 2 o'clock and Robert began to be keenly disappointed—he had raised his hopes so high that Marie would appear or some news would come. He paced the floor in anxiety, his heart beating rapidly and was forced to admit to himself that he had been over hopeful. He started to send a telegram to Mr. Kennelworth asking him to wire or 'phone just as soon as possible if any news had been received of Marie and asked him to call up Marie's parents and find out if they had heard anything. Minutes now began to drag slowly, as they had on Sunday when Robert had watched the clock and saw his hopes slowly waning. They were now waning again and Robert grew heartsick, but cheered himself with the thought that the day was not over yet. There was plenty of time for Marie to show up.

Robert decided to read awhile to quiet his anxiety. He picked up the book of "Poems That Have Helped Me," and read the "Isle of Long Ago."

Oh, a wonderful stream is the River Time,
As it flows thru the realm of years,
With a faultless rhythm and a musical rhyme,
And a broader sweep and a surge sublime,
As it blends with the ocean of years.

How the winters are drifting, like flakes of snow,
And the summers like buds between;
And the years in the sheaf—so they come and they go
On the river's breast, with its ebb and flow,
As they glide in the shadow and sheen.

There's a magical Isle up the River Time,
Where the softest of airs are playing,
There's a cloudless sky and a tropical clime,
And a voice as sweet as a vesper chime,
And the Junes with the roses are staying.

And the name of this Isle is the Long Ago,
And we bury our treasures there;
There are brows of beauty and bosoms of snow—
There are heaps of dust, but we love them so!
There are trinkets and tresses of hair.

There are fragments of songs that nobody sings,
And a part of an infant's prayer,
There's a harp unswept and a lute without strings,
There are broken vows and pieces of rings,
And the garments she used to wear.

There are hands that are waved when the fairy shore
By the mirage is lifted in air;
And we sometimes hear through the turbulent roar
Sweet voices we heard in the days gone before,
When the wind down the river is fair.

Oh, remembered for aye be the blessed Isle
All the day of our life till night,
And when evening comes with its beautiful smile,
And our eyes are closing in slumber awhile,
May that "Greenwood" of soul be in sight.

It made him realize that on the "river of time" there are many trials, tribulations and disappointments. While he was young in years he had experienced many of them, and it seemed to him that the last five days had been five years. When he read the lines of the poem: "Sweet voices we heard in the days gone before, when the wind down the river is fair" and "Our eyes are closing in slumber awhile," he thought of Marie, her beautiful eyes and sweet voice; all the happy things she had ever said; the things that she had written, and like a voice coming across the stillness of the night, he seemed to hear Marie calling as she used to call: "Robert, dear," "Robert dear." He jumped from his chair, startled, because for a moment he thought it was her voice, for he had been hoping and expecting each moment to hear her voice, but alas it was only a ghost of imagination and no Marie was there and no news of her.

Robert turned another page and read: "Crossing the Bar," by Tennyson:

Sunset and evening star,
And one clear call for me,
And may there be no moaning of the bar,
When I put out to sea.

But such a tide as moving seems asleep,
Too full for sound and foam,
When that which drew from out the boundless deep,
Turns again home.

Twilight and evening bell,
And after that the dark;
And may there be no sadness of farewell,
When I embark.

For tho' from out our bourne of time and place,
The flood may bear me far,
I hope to see my Pilot face to face
When I have crossed the bar.

He read the last verse several times.

Robert thought of Marie, his pilot, his star, his hope. When he had driven his ship across the uncertain sea of finance it would be Marie's beautiful face that would keep the lovelight burning upon the altar of his heart, ever to guide her captain safely home. He had looked to her to pilot him into the path of peace, lead him to the fields of contentment and, at last, to the height of eternal peace. He had looked forward to this day, his birthday, when she would return to him and he might claim her for his own. Thought of Marie's words, that hope and anticipation are greater than realization, but felt that nothing in the world could give him greater pleasure than the realization of this moment if he could hold Marie in his arms, kiss her sweet lips and hear the sweet words of love she had spoken to him in the past. Robert's heart for a moment sank within him. It was too much for him. He sobbed and cried like a baby but then he thought of his faith, of God and his power supreme.

Again as he was wondering what to do, he got the crumpled note that Marie wrote and put in his pocket on Sunday and read it again: "According to your faith, be I unto you. Love will always hope, understand and wait. Time proves all things. You will get everything you want. I will come to you when I mean the most and your need for love is the greatest." Only a few short lines, but so much said in them and so much left unsaid, Robert thought. Yet they contained an assurance, they left no doubt about a hope for the future and on that hope and with that faith Robert would cling to the future. Time would prove his love. Marie stated plainly that he would get everything he wanted and he knew that the greatest thing in the world he wanted was Marie. So at the close of another day of disappointment he felt that there was room for hope and that the future was lined with hopes. He resolved never to waver. Then read "A Psalm of Life" by Longfellow:

> Tell me not in mournful numbers
> Life is but an empty dream,
> For the soul is dead that slumbers,
> And things are not what they seem.
>
> Life is real! Life is earnest!
> And the grave is not its goal;
> Dust thou art, to dust returnest,
> Was not spoken of the soul.
>
> Not enjoyment, and not sorrow,
> Is our destined end or way;
> But to act, that each tomorrow
> Find us farther than today.
>
> Art is long and Time is fleeting,
> And our hearts, though stout and brave,
> Still, like muffled drums, are beating
> Funeral marches to the grave.
>
> In the world's broad field of battle,
> In the bivouac of Life,
> Be not like dumb, driven cattle!
> Be a hero in the strife!

Trust no future, howe'er pleasant!
Let the dead Past bury its dead!
Act—act in the living present!
Heart within and God o'erhead.

Lives of great men all remind us
We can make our lives sublime,
And, departing, leave behind us
Footprints on the sands of time.

Footprints, that perhaps another,
Sailing o'er life's solemn main,
A forlorn and shipwrecked brother,
Seeing, shall take heart again.

Let us, then, be up and doing,
With a heart for any fate;
Still achieving, still pursuing,
Learn to labor and to wait.

When he got to the verse

Trust no future, howe'er pleasant!
Let the dead Past bury its dead!
Act—act in the living present!
Heart within and God o'erhead.

Robert now fully realized that he must trust to the future if he intended to live and continue to make a success and complete his discoveries and inventions. He read the last verse slowly and carefully:

Let us, then, be up and doing,
With a heart for any fate;
Still achieving, still pursuing,
Learn to labor and to wait.'

This sounded much better to Robert. He was willing to learn to labor and wait and felt that if he waited there would be a reward, because Marie had promised him and he knew that Marie would keep her promise, and nothing could ever take from him that hope, that knowledge that Marie would keep her promise.

Then he read another little poem: "The Spring of Love."

> A little sun, a little rain,
> A soft wind blowing from the West,
> And woods and fields are sweet again
> And warmth within the mountain's breast.
>
> A little love, a little trust,
> A soft impulse, a sudden dream,
> And life as dry as desert dust,
> Is fresher than a mountain stream.

He knew that he had great love and great trust, and that that love, and the hope of Marie, would give him ambition and courage to continue on. It was now getting late and no news had come of Marie. Robert realized his birthday was passing and his hopes for the present were blasted.

He read the poem, "Lead Kindly Light":

> Lead, kindly Light, amid the encircling gloom,
> Lead thou me on!
> The night is dark and I am far from home,
> Lead thou me on!
> Keep thou my feet; I do not ask to see
> The distant scene—one step enough for me
>
> I was not ever thus, nor prayed that thou
> Shouldst lead me on;
> I loved to see and choose my path, but now
> Lead thou me on!
> I loved the garish day, and, spite of fears,
> Pride ruled my will: remember not past years.

So long thy power hath blessed me, sure it still
Will lead me on;
O'er moor and fen, o'er crag and torrent till
The night is gone;
And with the morn those angel faces smile
Which I have loved long since, and lost awhile.

The last few lines of the final verse impressed him
strongly.   Robert felt that Marie was only lost for
awhile and that on the coming morning he would meet
the future with a smile, face it with hope, courage and
determination and make some new plans; figure some
other new way by which he might locate Marie or obtain
some news of her whereabouts.   Realizing more than
ever that hope deferred maketh the heart grow sick,
Robert read everything in the Bible that he could find
on love.   At last he read the song of Solomon.

Robert knew that he would never leave his first love
and go back on her, that that was the one love of his
life and that it would remain so long as there was life
in his body.   With this resolve in his heart he decided
to face the future with hope.

CHAPTER XIV

ROBERT bought evening newspapers and looked over the Financial Page; noted that cotton, wheat and corn had advanced that day. His birthday had indeed been a success, financially, and his 21st birthday found him on top of the world, but this was not what counted with Robert. The great disappointment was that his hopes for Marie on that day were blasted, but he had not given up. As he looked over the newspapers he saw an advertisement headed, "Madam Cleo," Clairvoyant. The advertisement stated that Madam Cleo could re-unite the separated and bring back lost lovers. While Robert had never been to a clairvoyant and his only faith was in astrology, and science laid down in the Bible, in desperation he decided to grasp at any straw. Early on the morning of June 10th he called to see Madam Cleo. She told him that he had gone thru a great sorrow but that his sweetheart would return to him in a few days, he should be of good cheer because Marie loved him only; that it had been a case of nervous indecision which had caused Marie to disappear, and that she would return just as suddenly as she had disappeared.

Robert felt more hopeful and returned to his hotel, hoping to get some news of Marie. There were no letters or telegrams. He called up the broker's office to find out how cotton and wheat were that morning and found that they were strong and higher. His calculations showed that wheat and cotton should be top for a reaction on June 10th so he wired his broker in New York to sell out his wheat and cotton. Corn was down that morning, so he telegraphed the broker to buy 20,000 bushels of September corn. After sending this telegram, he glanced over the morning paper and saw an advertisement headed, "Professor O. B. Joyful," Astrologer. Robert eagerly read the advertisement because the name attracted him. And he was looking for something to make him joyful. Professor Joyful's advertisement stated that "with the science of Astrology, he could tell when success would start, when trouble would end and reveal when marriage would take place." Robert was a great believer in Astrology because he had found this great science referred to so many times in the Holy Bible. Robert remembered reading in the Psalms 111: 2:

The works of the Lord are great, sought out of all them that have pleasure therein.

He had made notes as he read the Bible at different times where it referred to Astrology or the signs in the heavens and was thoroughly convinced that the influence of the heavenly bodies govern our lives.

Genesis 1: 7, 16 and 18:

And God made the firmament, and divided the waters which were under the firmament from the waters which were above the firmament: and it was so.

And God made two great lights; and the greater light to

rule the day, and the lesser light to rule the night: he made the stars also.

And to rule over the day and over the night, and to divide the light from the darkness: and God saw that it was good.

Genesis 7: 2:

Of every clean beast thou shalt take to thee by sevens, the male and his female; and of beasts that are not clean by two, the male and his female.

Joshua 10:12 and 14:

Then spake Joshua to the Lord in the day when the Lord delivered up the Amorites before the children of Israel, and he said in the sight of Israel, Sun, stand thou still upon Gibeon; and thou, Moon, in the valley of Ajalon.

And there was no day like that before it, or after it, that the Lord hearkened unto the voice of a man: for the Lord fought for Israel.

Samuel 22: 8:

That all of you have conspired against me, and there is none that sheweth me that my son hath made a league with the sons of Jesse, and there is none of you that is sorry for me, or sheweth unto me that my son hath stirred up my servant against me, to lie in wait, as at this day?

Job 22:14:

Thick clouds are a covering to him, that he seeth not; and he walketh in the circuit of heaven,

Job 26:10 and 11:

He hath compassed the waters with bounds, until the day and night come to an end.

The pillars of heaven tremble, and are astonished at his reproof.

Job 37:18:

Hast thou with him spread out the sky, which is strong, and as a molten looking glass?

Psalms 19:1, 4 and 6:

The heavens declare the glory of God: and the firmament sheweth his handywork.

Their line is gone out thru all the earth, and their words to the end of the world. In them hath he set a tabernacle for the sun;

His going forth is from the end of the heaven, and his circuit unto the ends of it: and there is nothing hid from the heat thereof.

Psalms 136: 7 and 9:

To him that made great lights: for his mercy endureth for ever:

The moon and the stars to rule by night: for his mercy endureth for ever.

Proverbs 8: 27 and 28:

When he prepared the heavens, I was there: when he sat a compass upon the face of the depth;

When he established the clouds above; when he strengthened the fountains of the deep;

Ecclesiastes 1: 3 and 5:

What profit hath a man of all his labour which he taketh under the sun?

The sun also ariseth, and the sun goeth down, and hasteth to his place where arose.

Isaiah 40: 22:

It is he that sitteth upon the circle of the earth, and the inhabitants thereof are as grasshoppers; that stretcheth out the heavens as a curtain, and spreadeth them out as a tent to dwell in;

Isaiah 43: 5:

Fear not; for I am with thee: I will bring thy seed from the east, and gather thee from the west;

Ezekiel 1: 22:

And the likeness of the firmament upon the heads of the living creature was as the colour of the terrible crystal, stretched forth over their heads above.

Amos 9: 6:

It is he that buildeth his stories in the heaven, and hath founded his troop in the earth; he that calleth for the waters of the sea, and poureth them out upon the face of the earth; the Lord is his name.

Habakkuk 3: 2:

O Lord, I have heard thy speech, and was afraid; O Lord, revive thy work in the midst of the years, in the midst of the years make known; in wrath remember mercy.

St. Matthew 24: 29 and 30:

Immediately after the tribulation of those days shall the sun be darkened, and the moon shall not give her light, and the stars shall fall from heaven, and the powers of the heavens shall be shaken.

And then shall appear the sign of the Son of man, in heaven: and then shall all the tribes of the earth mourn, and they shall see the Son of man coming in the clouds of heaven, with power and great glory.

Robert knew that the Bible was replete with references that the heavens ruled. He had read where it said:

"Discern the end from the beginning"; where Jesus said: "I will judge you in the place of your nativity." He hastened to the office of Professor O. B. Joyful in the hope that the great science of Astrology would throw some light upon the disappearance of Marie. The secretary told him that the Professor was very busy and as Robert had no appointment, he would have to wait awhile. Glancing around the walls of the office he saw some beautiful cards of poems hanging on the walls. One was entitled, "The power of Love." This attracted Robert's attention:

> Sunbeams after showers are brightest,
> Seeking sorrow is a sin;
> Woman's heart is ever lightest
> When love, the jewel, dwells within.

Robert thought that this was a wonderful poem and he knew that it applied to man as well as woman, because his heart was ever light when love dwelled within; knew that it was Marie's beautiful eyes and the hope of seeing them again, which was guiding him now across the troubled sea of time. He anxiously awaited the time when he could tell his troubles to Professor Joyful, hoping that they would soon be turned into joy. He read another poem on the wall:

> Love is a gift to be used every day,
> Not to be smothered and hidden away,
> Love is not a thing to be stored in the chest
> Where you gather your keepsakes,
> And treasure your best.
> Love is a gift you should use every day.
> —NORAH PERKINS.

Robert knew that he was using love every day and it
seemed that the Professor had prepared his office to receive those in love.   Another poem read:

> We starve each other for love's caress;
> We take, but we do not give;
> We know it is easy some soul to bless,
> But we dole out affection, giving less and less,
> Until the world becomes bitter and hard.

Robert felt that he had not been stingy with his love for
Marie and that he had showered his affection upon her.
The Bible said that love begetteth love and he knew if he
received as he gave, his reward would be the return of
Marie and her love.

By this time, the secretary announced that Professor
Joyful was ready to receive him.   He entered the Professor's office, where he met a middle-aged man whose
kindly face indicated that he had sympathy for those in
trouble.   Robert stated briefly his troubles.   Upon being
asked his date of birth, said he was born June 9th, 1906.
The Professor made out his horoscope hurriedly and
told him that Venus and Mars were in conjunction by
transit in the sign Leo, which ruled the heart; that
Venus applied to a trine of Uranus, and that while he
could give him hopeful news and could assure him from
his horoscope that he would one day find Marie, he
could not offer false hopes and state that he would find
her within a few days.   Said there was a possibility of
his finding her within two years, but it would probably
be three or four years before she would ever come into
his life again.   In view of the fact that Venus was

separating from a conjunction of Mars on the day he
had called to inquire about Marie, the indications were
that his sweetheart, Marie, would be separated farther
from him rather than come closer to him at this time.
He assured Robert that Marie was alive, that no harm
had come to her, and that none would, that she was
carrying out her own secret plans; was faithful to
Robert, and had no other lover. He told Robert that
he was a born genius and in the next few years would
make a great success in speculation and in the field of
aviation. While Robert was disappointed, he felt that
this scientific man was telling the truth and decided
to take his advice, try to be patient, and to face the
future with hope. The Professor told Robert that his
horoscope indicated that he would eventually realize
all his hopes and ambitions. Venus, in the sign Cancer, promised happiness in love affairs eventually, but
Neptune therein indicated a skeleton in the family closet
and some secret mysterious happenings in connection
with the home and domestic relations. Robert told him
of his plans to go to New York and the Professor stated
that New York City was ruled by the sign Cancer, and
in view of the fact that the planet Venus, the Goddess
of Love, was located in that sign, he would eventually
meet or find Marie in New York City. This cheered
Robert greatly because he knew he wanted to go to
New York to make money in speculation and complete
his inventions. Professor Joyful told Robert that Venus
progressed in the sign Leo, which rules the heart, would
cause some great sorrows and heartaches when there
were afflictions to it. He had started the trip with the

Moon in the sign Leo, ruling the heart, but it had separated from good aspects and was applying to evil ones.
His ruling planet applied to an evil aspect of Uranus,
indicating great worries following the starting of this
journey. Said that he had planned his marriage for an
unfortunate day and that it was better that it did not
take place at that time. Assured Robert that there was
no doubt about the realizations of his hopes in the future, but that the delay was inevitable. He told him
that the clairvoyant who promised that he would find
Marie in a few days, was only encouraging his hopes,
and that science, which could be depended upon, did
not confirm these hopes, or at least the immediate
realization of them. There was a possibility of his
finding Marie in a foreign state or country or
that some news would come to him of her from a
great distance. He asked Robert for Marie's date of
birth. Robert told him that he knew she was born
on October 6th, but that he was not sure of the
year, but he thought it was in 1908. The Professor
told him that if this date was correct, it would confirm
all that he had told him and indicated a long delay before he would find her.

Robert returned to his hotel more hopeful and with
the firm decision to face the future and carry out his
plans, living faithful to Marie. On his arrival at the
hotel, he received a telegram from Mr. Kennelworth,
reading:

LEAVING ON THE SUNSHINE SPECIAL TONIGHT ARRIVE ST. LOUIS
SATURDAY MORNING BE READY TO LEAVE IMMEDIATELY WITH ME
FOR NEW YORK.

Robert was more cheerful after reading this message because since Marie's disappearance he had not met a man or woman he had ever known before. Mr. Kennelworth was a dear friend of his and it would be very comforting to meet him and talk over his troubles. He was also anxious to meet his old pal, Walter Kennelworth, so he decided to get ready to go on to New York. The big reception for Colonel Charles A. Lindbergh was planned and would take place in New York on Monday, June 13th, and he wanted to be there, but every time he thought of anything that would give him happiness or pleasure, he thought of Marie and knew that without her it would not mean as much to him. Still he hoped Marie might appear or that some news of her might be received before he left. He wanted to see Captain Lindbergh and his plane, "The Spirit of St. Louis," for Robert was dreaming of the day when he would complete his own great plane according to Ezekiel's plan. Robert went to his room and spent the balance of the day reading the Bible and working out future cycles on wars. Figured that great opportunities would come for making money in the Stock and Commodity markets, and that he was going to make a great financial success and carry out his plans.

On June 11th, Mr. Kennelworth arrived. Robert met him at the Union Station in St. Louis. He had only about an hour to wait before the train departed for New York. No news had been received of Marie. Mr. Kennelworth told Robert that her parents were still hopeful that she was alive, but they were at a loss to understand why she had not communicated with anyone. He told

Robert to keep up his courage for he felt sure that all would end well. On the train to New York they talked of Robert's plans. Mr. Kennelworth said he was anxious for him and Walter to be together again and believed it was for the best. Robert told him that he had been making money in wheat and cotton and that Right Aeroplane was moving his way; that he was Short of Major Motors and expected to make a fortune selling it all the way down. Mr. Kennelworth expressed his continued faith in Robert's ability and told him that he was going to follow him on the market. While he admired him for his great love for Marie and his faith in her, worry would not bring her back, he said, and he should get down to business, study the Bible, work on his inventions and leave the matter of Marie's return to the Lord, trusting and believing in Him who knoweth and doeth all things well. Told Robert that he was a "doer" and not a dreamer; that he had demonstrated the greatest ability of any young man he had ever known. That he had the pep and quoted an epigram, "The pessimist says it can't be done, the optimist says, let George do it: meanwhile the peptomist has done it." He said: "Robert, you and Lindbergh are peptomists. You do it while the other fellow watches and waits, or says it can't be done." He quoted a poem from Tennyson:

> I cannot hide that some have striven
> Achieving calm, to whom was given
> The joy that mixes man with heaven.
> Who rowing hard against the stream,
> Saw distant gates of Eden gleam
> And did not dream it was a dream.

"I am sure you are to make your dreams come true. The Bible says: There is nothing better for a man than that he should make his soul enjoy good in his labor. Work is the only thing to drown your sorrows. If you go to work, complete your inventions and continue to study, the troubles will disapear. Time will fly lightly by and before you know it, Marie will return to you." Then Robert repeated a few lines by Dora Greenwald:

"Joy is a working thing. It builds up while it enlarges the whole nature. It is the wine to strengthen the heart, to brace it to carry noble enterprise."

Mr. Kennelworth said, "That is very fine, Robert, but you must work for the joy that is yet to come and your great love for Marie will strengthen your heart and brace you to attain all your aims. Love is the great power behind the universe and it is the greatest of all powers. Emotions are the motive power behind every great achievement, and without emotion nothing will ever be accomplished. There are three great emotions —Love, Fear and Hate, which actuate every deed, good or bad, and without them, man would accomplish nothing. The great emotion which is going to help you accomplish all your plans and realize your greatest hopes and ambitions, is Love. A man makes money and saves it because he fears the future. Great nations go to war and fight because they are urged by the emotion of Hate. They are also fighting thru the emotion of fear, but if love was the emotion behind all, there would be no war, no sorrows—no troubles and no jealousies."

Robert then showed a poem on "Love" which he had written to Marie and one, "The Garden of Love," which he had written at the time he and Marie had their first break in 1926. Mr. Kennelworth read these poems and was very much impressed with Robert's ability as a writer. He said, "Robert, this proves to me that Love brings out the best in a man and that when he finds a good woman his success is assured."

Robert talked of how he had read the Bible where it said that there eventually would be one God and one united people and that Love would rule the world. How, since a little boy, his Mother had talked against war and prayed for the day when wars would cease and man would follow the command given by Jesus Christ: "Love thy neighbor as thyself." He hoped and felt sure that the day would come but that the Bible made it plain as he understood it, that there would yet be a great war fought in the air, when deadly chemicals would be used and the greater portion of the people on earth would be killed. Then would come peace, when God would rule the world and Love would be the motive behind every act. Then nations would no longer become jealous of each other and go to war. Robert said, "I have made a great study of wars in the past and how conditions changed; how at one time Spain was the mistress of the seas and later Rome was the controlling nation; then England ruled the waves and London was the banking center of the world. Then came the great war in 1914 which changed everything. England lost control of the seas. She lost her power as the great banking nation of the world. The gold supply of the world flowed rapidly to the United States and in the dark days of 1917, when England and France, after being deserted by Russia, were fighting with their backs to the wall, the United States, the land of love and liberty, came to the rescue, helped to defeat the Germans and saved England and France. At that time they were seemingly very grateful, but after the war conditions changed. The United States was no longer in debt to foreign countries but was now the banking nation of the world and the foreign countries owed large sums of money to the United States. This country has continued to prosper since the war, the gold supply of the world now rests here. Our former friends have become jealous of the prosperity we enjoy and the power that we now hold in financial affairs which once belonged to England. Some of the foreign countries do not want to pay their obligations and this jealousy can lead to nothing else but war, as it always has in the past. I hope to be ready when that war comes with my great airplane, and other inventions to help defend my country and later promote a lasting peace based on love and goodwill. The United States began as a land of liberty and has always set an example for the balance of the world and I hope to see the day when our country will take the lead in establishing universal peace and the brotherhood of man. Captain Lindberg's flight confirms my studies and forecasts of the future. Aviation will be developed rapidly and nations will want to try these new discoveries and inventions to conquer other nations, and war is inevitable. The Bible prophets foretold it, and my studies of the cycle theory also indicate that we are in a period where cycles will repeat which have caused war in the past."

On the afternoon of June 12th, Mr. Kennelworth and

Robert arrived in New York City and were met at the train by Walter. Robert was very happy to meet his dearest friend, and it was consoling to be with him. After their arrival, they went to the Hotel Vanderbilt. Mr. Kennelworth went out to see a friend and left Robert and Walter to chat alone. Robert told Walter of the terrible sufferings he had gone thru since Marie's disappearance and of his great disappointment. He talked of the success he had made in the market and of the future when he hoped to complete his great invention with the aid of Walter and his knowledge of chemicals and make discoveries which would end war for all times. But immediately after talking of his future plans his mind would revert back to Marie and he would start talking about her and bemoaning the fact that without her he could not go on in the future. Walter told him to forget about her—that time would bring changes and that he would find another girl who would take the place of Marie. Robert was indignant and told Walter that time would never change him; that he would remain faithful to Marie until death, no matter if he never heard of her again. Walter said that Marie was too young to know her own mind and was probably in love with someone else, or thought she was, which accounted for her sudden change and disappearance from the train. Robert then showed him the letter which he found in his pocket the morning that Marie disappeared. Walter read it.

June 5th, 1927.
3 A.M.

DEAREST ROBERT:

According to your faith, be I unto you. Love will always have faith, understand and wait. Time proves all things.

You will get everything you want; I will come to you when I mean the most and your need for love is the greatest.

Lovingly always,

MARIE.

Walter said: "This is certainly a mysterious letter. I don't understand it and I don't suppose Marie did either. There is nothing in this letter to explain whether she was leaving you or not, or why or where she was going or anything about it. Now, Robert, don't you understand real love could never act like that or write like that? There is some secret behind all this and my opinion is that there is another man in the case." But Robert refused to listen to any such reasoning. His faith in Marie was unshaken. His love for her was great enough to understand, to have patience and wait. Marie could or would do no wrong, and no amount of evidence would ever change him.

Mr. Kennelworth returned to the hotel and after dinner told Robert that he wanted to have a confidential chat with his son, Walter. Robert decided to go out for a walk and see the city. When they were alone, Walter told his father that he had had a long talk with Robert and that his mind was on nothing but Marie. His father said: "The only thing to do is to help Robert get interested in his work so that he will forget about Marie. That is the best thing for him at present. The great love that he has for her will be the incentive to spur him on to success and help him realize his ambitions. Love is the greatest thing in the world and without it men would not get very far. It brings out the noble and better qualities in a man and should always be encouraged."

CHAPTER XV

ON the following day, Monday, June 13th, Mr. Kennelworth, Robert and Walter arose early to be ready for Colonel Lindbergh's triumphant march up Broadway. Robert was very enthusiastic about it and talked about what a great achievement it was and what it meant to the world, especially to the United States. Walter told him that they must get busy and start to lay out the plans to build Robert's great airplane. When they started out on the street, Robert began to talk of Marie and said that he hoped that he would find her that day. Thru all the surging crowds, he stared in the face of every woman, hoping that Marie, if she was alive, might have decided to come to New York for the Lindbergh reception. It was a great day for Colonel Lindbergh, and a great day for Robert, because it encouraged his hope for the day, and believed it would come to pass when airplanes would conquer the world and bring universal peace. He felt that a state of perfection could never be reached until the brotherhood of man, founded on love, was established.

Walter told his father and Robert about a great play that he had been to see: "One for All." He was anxious for them to see it and had secured tickets for that night. Robert was immediately interested. He was attracted to Molly and saw in her great sacrifice for Eric an example of Marie. As the play neared the end, and Molly was in great sorrow, and her secret sacrifice had become known to Eric, Robert could restrain his emotions no longer. He turned to Mr. Kennelworth and said, "I wonder if he'll be man enough to forgive her and appreciate her, as the greatest woman in the world for him. Will his mind be broad enough to realize that she made the supreme sacrifice because of her unselfish love. Now that he has succeeded and has the world at his feet will he turn from her and condemn her as the world usually does?" Mr. Kennelworth said: "You can see that Eric is now weighing the matter in his mind and is hesitating. We can only wait and see." Robert said, "If Eric loves Molly as I love Marie he will now love her more after this." Robert watched Eric with every muscle in his body tense, as Eric read the receipt written by Chattox and also he watched Molly and her expression as she leaned over the staircase and read the receipt over Eric's shoulder. He saw Eric slowly fold the receipt around the little booties for the baby and place them in his pocket and walk slowly away. Robert was wondering what Eric was thinking of and what his decision would be. Then came the final climax—Eric, after knowing all, took Molly in his arms and gave her the kiss which Robert knew meant foregiveness and understanding. He then realized that love, just as Molly said in the beginning, was the greatest thing in the world, and meant more than all the money in the world. Robert jumped to his feet and shouted, "Hurrah for Eric," and said, "that's the kind of love I have for Marie and no matter what may have happened or what she should do in the future, my love is the kind which will understand, forgive and forget." He told them how he was impressed with the story in the Bible where the woman was brought before Jésus accused and how the Jesus said, "Let him who is without sin, cast the first stone," and when they had all disappeared he said: "Woman, doth no man accuse thee," and she answered, "No, Lord." Jesus said, "Neither do I. Go your way and sin no more." Robert said when the world once realized the great power of Love, that jealousy, enmity, all accusations and the desire for personal gain, would pass away. That when Love alone dominated the hearts of men and women, wars would be no more, and that men would see no evil in their fellow-men as Eric saw no evil in Molly's sacrifice but knew and understood that great love for him was the motive that prompted her actions. Robert quoted Daniel 2: 22:

"He revealeth the deep and secret things. He knoweth what is in the darkness and the light dwelleth within him. A kingdom which shall never be destroyed, consume all other kingdoms and stand forever."

He said that when the day came when men were ruled by the law of love and understood each other, a kingdom would be established that would never be destroyed, and that it would consume all other kingdoms. Robert believed that the United States, the land of liberty, was created never to be destroyed, and that it would eventually consume all other nations and rule by the law of love and justice, that it was God's will that it become the most prosperous country and the banking nation of the world. Believed that the nation referred to in Psalms 147: 20 was the United States:

"He hath not dealt so with any nation and as for his judgments they have not known them. Praise ye the Lord."

Walter was not so enthusiastic and sure about the power of Love as Robert. You can never tell what a woman will do, he said and referred to Proverbs 30:18 and 19:

"There be three things which are too wonderful for me. Yea, four which I know not,—the way of an eagle in the air, the way of a serpent upon a rock, the way of a ship in the midst of a sea, and the way of a man with a maid."

Walter said, "The last one is too much for me and I would not attempt to discern the way of a maid without a man. They go where you know not and return when you least expect it. Some wise woman once said, 'When you know one man, you know all.' A wiser man said, 'You never know a woman, for all women are different.' "

Robert said, "It is interesting to go back over history and read the opinions of the smartest men in regard to woman. Confucius said, 'Woman is a masterpiece.' Michelet said, 'Woman is a miracle of divine contradictions.' Lamartine said, 'There is a woman at the beginning of all great things.' I am wholly in accord with him. Go back to the bottom of every great achievement and back of it you will find the influence of a good woman. It may be a mother, sister or sweetheart, but the love of a woman is always the motive behind the great achievements of men. Someone once said: 'Not for herself was woman first created, nor yet to be man's idol, but his mate.' Pythagoras said: 'There are in woman's eyes two sorts of tears, the one of grief; the other of deceit.' I think that is because there are two kinds of men, one who appreciates love and honor and gives sympathy; the other kind who is selfish, expects something for nothing and must meet with deceit. I am a great believer in sowing and reaping. We get out of life just what we put into it. If we give love and faithfulness, the same returns to us. Maeterlinck was right when he said: 'A man's sweetheart is just as pure as his thoughts of her are pure.' I remember reading a poem,

"What thou lovest, Man,
Become thou must,
God, if thou lovest God,
Dust if thou lovest dust.

Napoleon said, 'All the women in the world would not make me lose an hour,' but history shows that Napoleon did lose sleep over his love for Josephine. He wrote to her—'I am sick of men because they keep me away from my love.' Shakespeare expressed it better than all the rest when he said 'Kindness in woman, not their beauteous looks, shall win my love.' A real womanly woman whose heart is filled with love, cannot be other than kind because Kindness is a child of Love. Women may be mysterious and we may fail to understand them. That is one of the reasons why we love them all the more. Fontenelle said, 'There are three things I have always loved and never understood—paintings, music and women.' He might have added that the greatest of the three was, woman."

Then Walter quoted from Southey, " 'There are three things a wise man will not trust, the wind, the sunshine of an April day and a woman's plighted faith.' " Robert replied—"Nevertheless nearly every wise man has loved and trusted some good woman and most of them have not regretted it. Walter, you have never really been in love and you don't know what love is. If you did, you would have faith and trust, regardless of all conditions." "I guess the subject of love and women is too deep for me," said Walter, and the sooner you get down to business and your studies and get love off your mind, the greater success you are going to make." Robert answered, "Without love this world would never have existed. It was God's love for the world that saved it. My love for Marie will make me whatever I am to be in the future. Without that love I know I would be a miserable failure. The time will come when you will go to sleep at night with your last thoughts of beautiful rosy lips, of eyes that shine like Golconda's purest gems, of a voice that is sweeter than a nightingale, of luxurious hair and of a form that to you is more beautiful than Venus, and when you awake in the morning your first thoughts will be of her. You will see her in the beautiful flowers, her face will be reflected from the ripple of the pure waters; everything you think about she will appear in connection with. Your slumbers will be disturbed. When you get a fever like this, you will then know and understand the power of love. Then nothing else will matter, only one thing will count in your life—the woman you love. A great love like this must come to every man. In the Springtime of life it may be, or in those sunny solaces of the afternoon when the waning day brings sadness and man looks back and longs for the time when he might have loved, when he was younger and lived longer. Love is the elixir of life. It is a greater cure than any medicine. It has built up kingdoms and destroyed nations. You have ambitions now and a desire for gold, but after all, Walter, what can it buy? All the gold in the world cannot buy the tender touch of a little child's fingers or the lovelight in angel eyes like Marie's. It gives satisfaction that nothing else can."

Walter said, "Robert, you always drift back to Marie and her eyes. Those beautiful black eyes that you talk about may be wonderful, but you remember the old saying, 'Can you be true to eyes of black or brown, when blue has smiled on you.' You will find that a change will come sooner or later if Marie doesn't show up and you will be the better for it."

But Robert was sure that no eyes could ever take the place of Marie's and Robert handed Walter the following poem to read:

HEAL THYSELF

If any brown-eyed girl has changed her mind
And left you sinking in the consommé,
Calmly smile and let her go, you'll forget about your woe—
(There's a lot of consolation to be found in eyes of gray.)

If any brown-eyed girl has left your heart
In forty-seven pieces at your feet,
Then the proper thing to do is to gaze in eyes of blue—
(And perhaps you'll find the same are twice as sweet.)

If any brown-eyed girl has given you
Your "exit cue," the "go-by" and "the air,"
And your heart in glad amaze'll heed the lure of eyes of hazel—
You can sing that song of Tanguay's, "I Don't Care."

If any brown-eyed girl has—well, she did;
Above, you'll find some good philosophy;
It may do for you, I guess, but I really must confess
It has never been a bit of use to me!

BEN WARREN.

"The last verse expresses my sentiments to a T; no other eyes will ever have any attraction for me except Marie's."

A few days after New York's reception to Colonel Lindbergh, Robert decided to get down to business. He visited his brokers in Wall Street, talked over the market situation and found that they did not agree with his ideas and views. Decided to open an office at 69 Wall Street, and Walter was to work with him when he had time from his studies. They consulted about a stenographer or office assistant. Walter had met Miss Edna Quinton, a very talented girl, whom he thought was the most competent he had ever known, so Robert gave her a position in his office.

Walter was anxious to keep Robert cheerful so went sight-seeing often and to see all the latest plays. Robert was very much interested in the play, "The Student Prince." Was impressed when the old servant told the young King the old saying, "A promise keep, right well you sleep; a promise break, all night you wake." Robert knew that this was what caused the King to return to his former sweetheart, but when he gave her up and married the Princess, he was disgusted and disappointed. Told Walter that he would never break his promise for anyone; and knew that if he did, he would never be able to sleep soundly again.

CHAPTER XVI

ROBERT GORDON'S GREAT CAMPAIGN IN COTTON

AFTER Robert had sold out his October cotton at 17.30 and his December cotton at 17.50 on June 10th, he decided to watch the market very closely for a few days because he thought it would go lower. His forecast indicated last buying level around June 25th. He figured that after this time the market would go higher until September 5th to 6th, when he figured it would be final high.

On June 25th October cotton declined to 16.80 and he bought 500 October at 16.83 and 500 December at 17.15. He figured that it would run up for about thirty days so on July 25th he sold 500 October cotton at 19c and sold 500 December at 19.20 and went short of 500 December at 19.20. The decline followed as he expected. On July 30th he sold 500 more December cotton at 18.60 and on August 6th he bought 1000 December at 17.40 to cover his short contracts. He figured that the Government report on August 8th would be very bullish and that cotton would go up very fast and continue until around September 5th to 6th, or until the Government report in September. On August 6th he bought 1000 December at 17.35. On August 8th he bought 500 December at 17.30. The Government was very bullish as he expected and cotton advanced 200 points on August 8th. On August 9th he sold out his 1500 December at 20.30 and sold 1000 December short at 20.30. A big decline followed and on August 13th he bought 1000 December cotton at 19.10 and also bought 1000 December at 19.10 for long account. He started in to pyramid on the way up. On August 19th he bought 500 more December at 20.10; on August 22nd he bought 500 December at 21.10; on August 27th he bought 500 December at 22.30 and on August 29th bought 300 December at 23.30. On September 8th the Government report was very bullish as he had forecast and the market went up. This was the time when he expected the market to make final top for a big decline. On September 8th he sold 2800 bales of December at 24.40 and on the same day sold 2000 bales of December at 24.50 for short account. On September 9th he sold 500 more December at 23.30; on September 11th sold 300 December at 22.30. On September 13th he bought 2800 December at 21.60 to cover his short contract. On September 14th he sold 1000 December at 22.60. On September 17th sold 500 December at 21.60 and on September 21st sold 300 December at 20.60. September 23rd he figured that the market was bottom for a rally and bought 1800 December at 20.60, and on the same day bought 1000 December at 20.60 for long account. On September 28th he sold 1000 December at 22c and also went short 1000 December at 22.10. On September 29th he bought 1000 December at 21.30 and on September 29th bought 1000 December at 21.30 for long account. On October 3rd he sold 1000 December at 21.50 and also went short of 1000 December at 21.50.   On October 6th he bought 1000 December at 20.75 and went long, because he figured the market would be higher for the Government report on October 8th.

ROBERT GORDON'S GREAT CAMPAIGN IN MAJOR MOTORS

On Sunday, June 19, 1927, Robert Gordon spent the day studying his charts and working out his cycles for stocks, cotton and grain.   He was short of Major Motors and was watching it very closely.   On this day he made a new and great discovery of a time factor from which he figured that Major Motors would decline until about June 30th and then start an advance which would last until about September 16th, 1927, when the Company would be 19 years old and at that time the stock would reach final high and would then go down to February to April, 1929.   He figured that the stock should advance to around 270 by September 16th and made up his mind to watch it closely and cover his shorts if it went down around June 30th, and then start buying the stock.   On June 30th it declined and he bought in his short contracts and bought for long account 500 shares of Major Motors at 192½.   He decided to pyramid it all the way up.   On July 15th he bought 500 shares at 204; on July 21st he bought 300 at 214 and on July 26th bought 300 more at 224.   On August 5th the stock advanced to 230 and he raised his stop on 1600 shares to 225.   On August 8th his stock was sold out at 225.   He still believed that the stock would go up to around 270 by September 16th but he expected a reaction of about 12 to 15 points so he decided to wait for a few days and watch his charts to see how the stock acted. On August 12th Major Motors declined to 218, being down a little over 12 points as he figured, and he bought 1000 shares at 218. He placed a stop at 212, a point which he figured it would not decline to. The advance started, and on August 20th he bought 300 shares at 228; on August 24th bought 300 shares more at 238 and on August 26th bought 300 shares more at 248. When he started pyramiding, his plan was to buy or sell the largest amount first and then gradually decrease buying and selling smaller amounts on the way up or down, and always using a stop loss order. On September 7th the stock advanced to 253 and he raised his stop on his entire amount to 243. This stop was never reached but on September 14th a rapid advance was on and he bought 300 shares more at 258, giving him a line of 2200 shares of stock. He figured that it should advance on September 16th to around 270. When the market advanced to 272 at this time he sold out his 2200 shares at 272.

He cleaned up a profit on this deal of over $80,000.00, and as he figured that the stock would make final top around this time he decided to put out a line of short stock and pyramid all the way down, remaining short for the long pull. On September 17th he sold 500 shares of the new Major Motors stock at 138 and 500 shares at 137 and placed a stop on it at 147.

He had made it a rule that after he had made a large amount of profits that he would never risk more than 10 per cent of his profits on the first new deal, and that if that deal went wrong and he lost 10 per cent of the capital, he would decrease his trading so that the next loss would only be 10 per cent of his remaining profits. In this way he figured that the market would have to beat him ten consecutive times for him to lose all the profits he had made, and his studies of past records showed that this could never happen. He placed orders to sell more Major Motors at 128, 118, 108 and 98 because he expected the first decline to run until the latter part of December, 1927, and after that time he would put out shorts again on a rally to hold and pyramid on the way down into the Spring of 1929. His great discovery of what stocks would do at a certain age enabled him to make enormous profits when stocks reached the age where they would have fast moves up or down in a very short time.

October, 1927, was a beautiful month in New York. The weather was warm and the sun shone brightly every day. It reminded Robert of the Fall of 1926 when he had gone to Sherman, Texas, to visit Marie. He thought of what a great change had taken place in one year, of the fortune that he had made in the market, but money would not buy relief for his aching heart.

Days, weeks and months had drifted slowly by, but no word from Marie Stanton. She seemed to be lost as though the earth had swallowed her up.

The great decline in stocks which he forecast for the Fall and Winter of 1927 took place and he made money rapidly on the short side of stocks. He was selling short Central Steel and Major Motors and other stocks. He had bought Corn and Wheat in October and made big profits later in the year. Money was piling up fast and in the latter part of October, 1927, he had made over $300,000. He had kept Marie's money in a separate account from his own and her original $400.00 was now over $20,000. Robert continued to keep her account separate; he wanted to make all the *money* he could and have it as a surprise for Marie, to prove to her his faithfulness and thoughtfulness when she was away, and also to prove his confidence in her return.

Robert became known as "The Boy Wizard of Wall Street." His fame became known and old men of Wall Street talked about his marvelous success. Robert refused to be interviewed by the newspapers or tell anything about his method of working in the market. Seldom ever visited a broker's office and made very few friends. He worked upon his invention, and Walter was his sole companion. Walter had met an old man by the name of Henry Watson who was a veteran of Wall Street, now over 70 years of age, had made and lost many fortunes and had seen the biggest and best plungers go on the rocks in Wall Street. Walter introduced Mr. Watson to Robert and he became very much interested in the old man's reminiscences. He told Robert the history of Daniel Drew and got him to read the book of Drew's life, which showed how Drew, after making $13,000,000 lost it all and died practically a pauper. Also told the history of Daniel Sully; how he made $10,000,000 to $15,000,000 in the Cotton market, but by violating natural laws lost it all in a few days in the crash of Cotton in March, 1904, and then disappeared from the financial horizon. How Livermore, the boy wonder of 1907 and 1908, had accumulated millions, owned fine yachts, lost everything, had gone thru bankruptcy, but had later recouped his fortunes. How Eugene Scales, another striking example, who at one time had over ten millions dollars paper profit in the Cotton market, had lost all of it. How Allen A. Ryan, at the height of his fame, when he defied the Gods of Chance and the unwritten law of Wall Street with the result that his millions were all lost, had to go thru bankruptcy and paid only about twenty cents on each one hundred dollars.

Mr. Watson also told Robert how Durant had become the giant motor magnate and formed the General Motors Corporation in 1908 and had made a great success, accumulating millions before the war days and afterwards. He was in full control of General Motors and was reputed to be worth over a hundred million dollars when the stock was selling at $410.00 in the Spring of 1920. Durant was very bullish and talked of General Motors going very much higher. Deflation started in the Summer of 1920, and all stocks declined rapidly. He remained bullish, continuing to buy General Motors all the way down. The stock had been split up on a ten for one basis and the new stock which sold at $42.00 in March, 1920, an equivalent of $420.00 per share, declined to $14.00 per share in December, 1920, and finally in the Spring of 1922 sold at $8.25. He had refused to sell; in fact had bought all his brokers would let him have all the way down. When the stock declined to $15.00 per share, Durant was ruined. His fortune of over one hundred millions dollars was wiped out. The Morgans and Duponts took over his holdings at a figure reported to be around $5.00 per share, and he lost control of the gigantic corporation which had made him famous. Later Durant organized a new company and came back fast. He went back into the stock market and in the great Coolidge Bull campaign from 1924 to 1927 was again a dominant factor in General Motors and other stocks and was reputed to have made fifty millions, or more.

The old man said that Durant was one of the very rare exceptions of men who had gone broke in Wall Street and had been able to come back after they were 60 years of age. Told Robert that Wall Street was a place of ups and downs—mostly downs, and that the time to quit was when you were young and had made your money.

Robert explained to Mr. Watson that he was not guessing and gambling on hope but was following science and not trading on human judgment as he followed the law of cycles as laid down in the Holy Bible. Mr. Watson said, "I wish you success, and for your benefit I will give you my opinion as to the cause of most of the failures in Wall Street, for I know the history of the men who have made the greatest amounts of money, and know most of them personally. Selfishness and greed were the cause of the fall of Daniel Drew. He was not loyal to his associates. His idea was to get the money and look out for himself regardless of whom he hurt. Conditions changed and Drew failed to change with them. The result was that he died a pauper. Thomas W. Lawson, the man who wrote, 'Friday the 13th,' was one of the most daring traders that Wall

Street has ever known, worth at one time probably forty to fifty million dollars. He, too, died practically penniless. At one time Lawson had the backing of the Standard Oil crowd and turned against them after they had helped him to make millions. In my opinion, he cut off the hand that fed him and his ruthless attack on men who had been his friends, was the cause of his downfall. Men must be loyal to positions of trust and not reveal secrets of great financial deals by which they profited." Robert said that was his idea. As long as a man remained loyal to his mother, his country, his associates; above all his wife or sweetheart, success was bound to crown his efforts. He believed in the law of compensation; that when a man broke faith with others, he had broken faith with himself, and that failure would follow.

Mr. Watson told Robert that Sully made his money in cotton, and after accumulating millions, quit specializing in cotton and began to trade in stocks and various other commodities, which divided his attention and he was unable to concentrate on cotton alone, the thing that brought him the great success. "I could go over the history of Scales, Livermore, Durant, Ryan and the balance of the great men of Wall Street, and in analyzing their trading, the one weak point would be found in all of them. They diversified too much. Did not specialize in one commodity or a few special stocks, but spread all over the board. The result was they had too many irons in the fire and when one thing started to go wrong and they began to lose money, they would invariably get out of stocks and commodities on which they were making money and keep those that were going against them. Another weak point was that when luck turned against a man in Wall Street, he kept on trying to recoup his losses instead of stopping just as soon as there was an indication that the tide had turned against him. Most men at the heights of prosperity lose their sense of good judgment, become inflated with their success, think they are infallible, refuse to follow science or the advice of anyone, with the result that they continue to buck the tide till all their money is gone."

"Mr. Watson," said Robert, "I believe that if a man starts out to make money for unselfish purposes, he will succeed. That is what I am going to do. Your experience is very valuable to me. Your intimate knowledge of the cause of the failures of other men is a good lesson. I have studied the Bible very carefully because I believe it is the greatest scientific book ever written. The laws are plainly laid down how to make a success. There is a time and a season for everything, and if a man does things according to the time, he will succeed. The Bible makes it plain that not all are born to be prophets, nor to be farmers, doctors or lawyers, but that each can succeed in his own special line, according to time and place. If men would only follow the Bible and know that there is a time to stop trying to make money and to keep what you have, then wait for another season when the time is ripe, they could continue to succeed indefinitely. Has any man ever made a large fortune out of Wall Street and kept it, Mr. Watson?" "Oh, yes," he replied, "if there were not exceptions to the rule, business would not continue to run. I could tell you of dozens of them, but one striking example is that of the late E. H. Harriman who died worth about three hundred million dollars. He had probably made out of the market a hundred million dollars in the last three or four years of his life." Robert asked, "How did he do it?" Mr. Watson answered, "He stuck to one class of stocks—railroads. He studied them day and night, never diverted his attention to other lines. I believe that he possessed some mathematical method which enabled him to forecast stocks many months and years in advance. I have gone over his manipulations and the stocks he traded in, and found that they conform closely to the law of harmonic analysis. He certainly knew something about time and season because he bought at the right time and sold at the right time. He paid a great price for his success, because he neglected his health, sacrificed everything to make his railroads a success and died too young. Such men are the backbone of our country's prosperity. Constructive geniuses of this kind are few and far between and we need more of them. Man's greatest enemy in speculation is 'hope.' He refuses to face facts, and facts are stubborn things. Hope spurs us on. It may be an anchor to the soul, but a very slim anchor in speculation, when facts are against us."

Mr. Watson told Robert that his friend Walter had related to him all about his love affair and the disappearance of Marie. He said, "My boy, the great love you have for her is now furnishing the hope which will carry you to success. When that hope is gone, you will have to find a new one or you cannot go on." Robert told him that Marie had said that anticipation was greater than realization. "Robert," he said, "I want to tell you the story of my love affair. I have made and lost many fortunes in Wall Street, and when things have gone wrong and I have reached the depths of despondency, have seen my last dollar fade away, been deserted by friends of my prosperous days, then when there seemed nothing else to live for, nothing to make me fight on, there would come a hope, the angel of memory would steal over me and I would again hope that some day, somewhere, I would find my Katie." Here the old man's eyes grew dim with tears. He drew an old wallet from his pocket, took out a package, slowly unwrapped it. In there was a picture in a little gold frame. The aged hands trembled, his voice grew weak as he handed the picture to Robert with some faded flowers which he had pressed out and kept and said: "These flowers were picked by her own little hands over forty years ago." He then broke down and wept bitterly. Robert was deeply moved by the old man's great devotion to his long-lost sweetheart and begged him to tell more of the story.

The old man dried his eyes and went on—"Over 50 years ago when I was a young man, I lived near St. Joseph, Missouri. I went to school at a country schoolhouse. Katie Larson was a beautiful young girl. We grew up together. I don't really know when I fell in love with her, but I know that in my school days I loved her and always intended to marry her. The years went by. I had never told Katie of my love. She had grown to be a woman and I kind of took it for granted that she knew and understood that I loved her and intended to marry her. Time went by and we were often together. There was never any trouble or disagreements.

I was anxious to succeed and decided that I should make some money before I proposed to Katie. Time drifted swiftly by, I was not as successful as I hoped to be, and finally one day I received the saddest news of my life—Katie had married. I realized that she had probably waited and hoped for me to make known my intentions but my financial affairs had held me back. I knew it was all my fault. I should have confided my plans to her and asked her to have patience and wait. From that day I was a changed man. My heart was broken and if no hope had been left for me, I would never have gone on, but from that day on, hoped and prayed that I might one day have her, even if for only a few years or weeks, in my declining years. Katie moved away after marrying and probably it was the hope for her love some day that spurred me to action. I worked harder than ever. Success crowned my efforts. I studied medicine, moved to Dallas, Texas, became a very successful doctor. There I met a woman whom I thought I loved. We were married and lived seemingly happy for a few years, but the spark of love for Katie in my heart never died. We had a little girl born and I named her Katie, which proved later a very foolish thing to do. She was the pride of my life, my hope was centered on her. Finally I made the mistake that many men make. I told my wife of my great love for Katie. After that time, she lost faith in me and we slowly drifted apart. Then came separation and divorce. I had accumulated considerable money and now being very unhapy, I decided to leave Dallas and go to New York and try the speculative markets. Success and failure have followed alternately, like the rising and falling of the tides. There has never been a day when I have come to Wall Street that I have not hoped to one day meet Katie again. That hope has kept me alive. I have often tried to find her, but the years have brought changes. She moved away to California and I have never been able to find out whether she is living or dead. I hope that you will never have to go thru the years that I have gone thru without the love and comfort that the woman you love can give. Your faith is supreme and that will carry you safely thru, and even if you never find Marie, it is better to live for that ideal because it will make you a better man, as love always brings out the best."

Robert was very much interested in the old man's story, but very sorry that it had never ended as he had hoped it would with him and Marie. Mr. Watson told Robert that he thought he had wonderful ideas about speculation, and that if he would only stick to them and not be swept off his feet by success, that he would eventually reach the greatest height. He quoted Kipling's "If."

> If you can keep your head when all about you
>   Are losing theirs and blaming it on you;
> If you can trust yourself when all men doubt you,
>   But make allowance for their doubting too:
> If you can wait and not be tired by waiting,
>   Or being lied about, don't deal in lies,
> Or being hated don't give way to hating,
>   And yet don't look too good, nor talk too wise;
>
> If you can dream—and not make dreams your master;
>   If you can think—and not make thoughts your aim,
> If you can meet with Triumph and Disaster
>   And treat those two impostors just the same:

If you can bear to hear the truth you've spoken
   Twisted by knaves to make a trap for fools,
Or watch the things you gave your life to, broken,
   And stoop and build 'em up with worn-out tools;

If you can make one heap of all your winnings
   And risk it on one turn of pitch-and-toss,
And lose, and start again at your beginnings
   And never breathe a word about your loss:
If you can force your heart and nerve and sinew
   To serve your turn long after they are gone,
And so hold on when there is nothing in you
   Except the Will which says to them: "Hold on!"

If you can talk with crowds and keep your virtue,
   Or walk with Kings—nor lose the common touch,
If neither foes nor loving friends can hurt you,
   If all men count with you, but none too much:
If you can fill the unforgiving minute
   With sixty seconds' worth of distance run,
Yours is the Earth and everything that's in it,
   And—which is more—you'll be a Man, my son!

He told Robert the greatest test of a man would come when he reached the stage of great prosperity. That almost any man could stand reverses but very few could stand prosperity. Money could buy so many things which were not necessary to a man's happiness and attracted so many people who would do him harm rather than benefit him that most men started on the down grade as a result of too much money and too great prosperity. Robert agreed that this was right. Said that with him money was only a means to an end and said that he wanted it so he could help others and benefit his country. Mr. Watson told him that as soon as his success was generally known and he was well established in New York many selfish women would be attracted to him and that if he possessed the weak point which had been the undoing of many men, he would be lost. That was being influenced by flattery from beautiful women. He said, "Remember, my boy, they are attracted to the money and not to the man, but few men can keep their heads at a time when women and men crowd around to praise their success. I remember a poem that I used to read when I was a boy, part of which runs something like this:

'They crowd around me, those stately dames and belles,
And pay to me the royal homage that all great success compels;
But where is she, that sweetheart of my former years,
Who stood by me, when others could see nothing in me.'

You will find it so, Robert. Men desert you when money is gone, like pirates fleeing from a sinking ship. I admonish you not to put your trust in money or men. Continue as you have, trust God, have faith in him, stick to your first love, and happiness and success will be your reward."

When the old man had finished talking, Robert noticed that the eyes had become still, his cheeks were pale, his hand dropped limp at his side. Robert rushed to him and soon realized that the old man was very ill. He hurriedly summoned a doctor. Soon after laying the old gentleman on the couch and making him comfortable, the doctor arrived. After hasty examination, he told Robert that the end was near. They decided to send for a minister and when he arrived, the old man was clutching the picture in his hand. The minister bent over him and asked him if he realized that the end was near and if he had made his peace with God, adding, "Will you die in the faith of a Christian?" The old man sprang up from the couch suddenly, as tho new strength had been instilled in his frail old body. He raised his hand and showed the doctor the picture and said, "Will that faith bring me back Katie, the only woman I have every really loved?" The doctor knew that his strength was fast waning and got him to lie down on the couch again. The minister whispered consoling words to him, told him that "God so loved the world that he gave his only begotten son that whomsoever believeth on him should not perish, but have everlasting life." Again he asked, "Do you believe in Jesus Christ? Will you accept the faith?" Again the old man replied, "Will that faith bring back to me my Katie?" His voice was growing weaker, the doctor knew that it was a matter of but a few moments. The minister again bent over him and whispered slowly, "Will you accept Jesus Christ as your saviour and die in the faith of a Christian?" With a faltering weak voice he answered, "Will that faith give me back Katie, the greatest love of my life?" The doctor turned to the minister and said, "He has gone to his reward." "With a love like that, such loyalty and faith to a long-lost love must receive its reward in heaven and a just God will extend mercy to a soul like that," said the minister. Robert was in tears. He felt that he had not only lost a friend, but a very dear friend, and that while the old man's going had taken something from his life, yet the example was one that would be of great comfort and benefit to him. He knew that he would live faithful to Marie, and that he would die, as the old man died, longing for Marie, no matter what happened.

CHAPTER XVII

ROBERT turned to the Bible for consolation. Read every chapter of the Song of Solomon. Was very much impressed with Chapter 2:14:

O my dove, that art in the clefts of the rock, in the secret places of the stairs, let me see thy countenance, let me hear thy voice, for sweet is thy voice and thy countenance is comely.

Robert longed to hear Marie's voice and prayed that she might come forth from her secret hiding place. He read Chapter 8: 6th and 7th verses:

Set me as a seal upon thine heart, as a seal upon thine arm, for love is strong as death; jealousy as cruel as the grave; the coals thereof are coals of fire which have a most vehement flame.

Many waters cannot quench love, neither can the floods drown it; if a man would give all the substance of his house for love, he would utterly be condemned.

Robert realized that nothing could quench his love and that Marie was the only remedy for his aching heart.

Turning to Daniel 9: 21, he read:

Yea while I was speaking in prayer, even the man Gabriel whom I had seen in the vision at the beginning being caused to fly swiftly, touched me about the time of the evening oblation.

Robert knew that this indicated that people did fly in the older days, and that we were now only repeating past cycles. He read Chapter 12: 4th verse:

Let thou, O Daniel, shut up the words, and seal the book

even to the time of the end; many shall run to and fro, and knowledge shall be increased.

Robert thought that we were now nearing the time of the end because man was running to and fro in fast automobiles and traveling swiftly thru the air in airplanes; that new discoveries were being made and that knowledge was increasing. He must hasten his new invention. He read the 12th verse:

Blesseth is he that waiteth, and cometh to the thousand three hundred and five and thirty days.

Robert believed that he understood the cycle and knew the number of years, months and days referred to in Daniel's prophecies. Calculated that from March, 1931, until the end of June, 1932, would be troublesome times for the United States. Depression, war and panic would hang over the destinies of his country. Robert had gone deeply into the Bible study in order to learn more about the great science of Astrology. From the Bible he interpreted that he belonged to the tribe of Issachar, the fifth son of Jacob and that this name indicated price, reward, recompense. He understood from this that he would have to pay the price, but he would receive the reward for his faithfulness and devotion to Marie.

Robert turned to Genesis, Chapter 30, 17th and 18th verses:

And God hearkened unto Leah, and she conceived and bore Jacob, the fifth son, and Leah said God hath given me my hire, because I have given my maiden to my husband; and she called his name Issachar.

He read Genesis 49:14 and 15, where Jacob blessed his 12 sons:

> Issachar is a strong ass, couching down between two burdens and he saw that the rest was good and the land, that it was pleasant; and bowed his shoulders to bear, and became a servant unto tribute.

Robert knew that this was the description of a man born in June under the sign Gemini and that he was born to bear a burden, that he must serve his people and be a comfort and help to carry their burdens. That the sign under which he was born was a double-bodied sign, known as the sign of the twins, that things would repeat in his life, that he would have many ups and downs, but that he would reach his reward thru science. He was anxious to learn of Marie's characteristics from the Bible and thru Astrology and found that she was born under the sign Libra, the sign of the balance, ruled by the Goddess of Love, Venus, which endowed her with her great beauty. Reading Genesis 29 : 32, he found that Marie belonged to the tribe of Reuben, "And Leah conceived and bare a son and she called his name Reuben; for she said 'Surely the Lord hath looked upon my affliction; now therefore my husband will love me.'" The symbol and meaning of this name is "one who sees the sun," the vision of the sun, and indicates great intuition, keen perception and power of foresight. Genesis 49 : 3–4:

> Reuben thou art my first born, my might and the beginning of my strength, the excellency of dignity, and the excellency of power; unstable as water, thou shalt not excel.

Robert understood that this referred to Marie's character and disposition. She was unstable, changeable and moody, but he felt that her love was fixed and that eventually she would return to him. He read all the books he could get on Astrology and began to understand why things had happened as they had. It made him a better philosopher and helped him to bear his sorrows with greater patience.

Robert continued reading Isaiah 45:13:

I have raised him up in righteousness, and I will direct all his ways: he shall build my city and he shall let go my captives, not for price, nor reward, saith the Lord of hosts.

This probably meant that the time would come when the Lord would direct man and that when wars came and prisoners were made captives, they would be set free without price or reward. It was Robert's idea that this was the way it should be when love ruled the world.

Robert read Hebrews 11: 3 and 5:

Through faith we understand that the worlds were framed by the word of God, so that the things which are seen were not made of things which do appear.

By faith Enoch was translated that he should not see death; and was not found, because God had translated him: for before his translation he had this testimony that he had pleased God.

Robert believed that Enoch went away in an airplane and knew that faith was the great sustaining force, and that without faith it was impossible to please God, for he read where it says, "For he that cometh to God must believe that he is, and that he is a rewarder of them that diligently seek him." Robert knew that he had faith and that that faith would sustain him during the time of trials and troubles. In Romans 12: 2:

And be not conformed to this world, but be transformed by

the renewing of your mind, that ye may prove what is that good and acceptable and perfect will of God.

Robert knew and understood how to renew his mind and body because he knew what Jesus meant when he said—"Destroy this temple and in three days I will build it up again." He knew that it referred to the temple of the human body.

Robert read the 9th to 13th verses of the same Chapter:

Let love be without dissimulation. Abhor that which is evil; cleave to that which is good. Be kindly affectioned one to another with brotherly love, in honor preferring one another; not slothful in business; fervent in spirit; serving the Lord, rejoicing in hope, patient in tribulation; continuing instant in prayer.

Robert intended to be patient in tribulations and was going to be kind and show brotherly love; he would have faith, hope and pray for the day when he would again have Marie. Love was the fulfilling of the law and reward was promised for obedience to that law. The more he read the Bible the more he was convinced of its great value and that all of the knowledge and instruction that man needed for any purpose or at any time, was to be found in that good old book. Robert decided that he would not only pray without ceasing, but would spend some of the money that he had made, to try to find Marie, as no word had ever been received of her up to this time. He employed a detective agency to make a search all over the United States.

Mr. Kennelworth left New York and returned to Texarkana in the latter part of June, 1927. He bought cotton heavily on Robert's advice that the Government report would be very bullish and would have a big advance during July according to Robert's forecast earlier in the year. The Government Report on July 9th showed a big decrease in acreage and prices started to advance again. Robert wrote and telegraphed Mr. Kennelworth that October cotton would advance to around 18.50 to 18.75 before there was any important reaction. On July 16th October cotton crossed 18.50 and Mr. Kennelworth wired Robert as follows:

July 16, 1927

Robert Gordon
 69 Wall Street
 New York City

CONGRATULATIONS YOUR FORECASTS ARE WONDERFUL HAVE OVER TWO HUNDRED THOUSAND DOLLARS PROFIT IN COTTON AS SOON AS YOU GET TIME WORK UP YOUR CYCLE ON PRESIDENTIAL ELECTIONS AND WRITE ME WHAT THE OUTLOOK IS FOR 1928

J. H. Kennelworth

To which Robert replied:

July 16, 1927.

MY DEAR MR. KENNELWORTH:

Your telegram just received. Am very happy that you have played the cotton market heavily and are making big profits. I, too, have made over a hundred thousand dollars.

Will get busy in a few days and work out the cycles for 1928 and let you know what the outlook is as to who will be elected President.

Walter and I are getting along nicely. I am making good progress on my plans for the airship. Have employed a detective agency to search all over the United States for Marie. I am patiently awaiting news of her. Believe she is still alive.

Thanks for your good wishes. With kindest regards, I am

Sincerely yours,

ROBERT GORDON.

CHAPTER XVIII

AFTER making his calculations on the Presidential election in 1928, Robert sent the following Forecast to Mr. Kennelworth:

July 20, 1927.

1928 PRESIDENTIAL ELECTION

In order to determine the conditions that will prevail during 1928 and who will be elected, we must look up past cycles. I refer you to Ecclesiastes 3:15—"That which hath been is now and that which is to be hath already been, and God requireth that which is past."

We know that we are repeating past cycles as referred to in Ezekiel's Prophecy—Chapter 20:46—"Son of man set thy face toward the south, and drop thy word toward the south, and prophesy against the forest of the south field, and say to the forest of the south, Hear the word of the Lord, Thus saith the Lord God, Behold, I will kindle a fire in thee and it shall devour every green tree in thee and every dry tree, the flaming flame shall not be quenched, and all faces from the south to the north shall be burned therein."

The troubles in Nicaragua, the destructive floods and storms which have visited Florida, and the destruction by the floods along the Mississippi during the past Spring all show that troubles are starting in the south. We are in a cycle which will repeat and cause wars which will start from the south and southwest, probably Mexico. All of these events will have a great bearing on the Presidential election in 1928, because war will be in the air and the people will be very much upset.

As referred to in Exodus 32:17—"And when Joshua heard the noise of the people as they shouted, he said unto Moses, There is a noise of war in the camp." There will be political wars and revolutionary changes in the United States in 1928. People will want to choose new leaders. Read Judges 5:8— "They chose new gods; then was war within the gates: was there a shield or spear seen among forty thousand in Israel?" The people will need to choose an able leader to prepare for the great war in the air.

I have made a study of President Coolidge's date of birth, name and numbers. ˙ He is the strongest man that the Republicans have, but he has not wanted to accept the nomination and will probably not if he can get out of it. He has the best chance of any Republican for being elected. Along about March or April, 1928, some important event will happen which is likely to cause President Coolidge to refuse to accept the nomination. When the convention meets in June or July there will be long delays, dissatisfaction and fights among the old Republican leaders as to whom they will nominate. From the cycle that we are repeating, there is a strong indication that President Coolidge will not be renominated. He will do something which will cause large financial interests and moneyed men to withdraw their support from him.

Since God requires that which is past, then past cycles and events in the history of the United States must repeat. We look up the names and dates of birth to determine when certain names or initial letters should repeat. The letter "C" is one which repeats in events of the United States as shown by the election of Grover Cleveland the second time in 1892. President Calvin Coolidge, with the "C" strong in both names, succeeded President Harding, August 2, 1923, and was elected in 1924. This was really a repetition of the letter "C" the same as Cleveland's second election, and in view of the fact that President Coolidge has served about 6 years, the letter "C" is not due to repeat its vibration in 1928, but might repeat in 1932 when President Coolidge could possibly be elected again following the war and troublesome times.

The most favorable letters for the Republican Party which could repeat in 1928 are B, J, F, and L. In view of the cycle which indicates war from 1928 to 1932, there is a strong indication that the letter "L" will repeat as it did during the Civil War when Lincoln was President. This might mean the nomination of Borah, Butler, Johnson or Lowden. I haven't the dates of birth of any of these men, therefore, am unable to say before the nominations take place and we know whom their opponents will be, whether any of them would be elected or not.

In regard to the Democratic nomination, the cycle indicates a strong possibility of victory for the Democrats or a new party. Governor Alfred Smith is not likely to be nominated and if nominated would not be elected. The letter "S" has never appeared in the surname of any president of the United States, and as we are only due to repeat past events, he has a very slim chance of being elected.

The letters F, M and R are due to repeat for the Democrats. This might mean Ford, McAdoo or Reed. According to the date of birth, cycle and numbers, McAdoo would have a much better chance of getting the nomination than Smith. Reed looks stronger than either of them. Governor Smith will continue popular and the possibilities of him being nominated will look promising until about May, 1928, when there will be a sudden change of public opinion against him. Support will be withdrawn and some of the strong Democratic leaders will turn to other possible candidates. Smith's name will no doubt come before the convention, but I see no chance of him being nominated.

There is a strong indication that the man who will be nominated will be a "dark horse," a man probably born in May or June. Revolutionary changes are indicated. The question of the 18th Amendment is likely to split both of the old parties. A farm and labor party or some other political party may spring up and defeat both of the old parties. The public will be very much divided and sentiment will be badly mixed in the summer and fall of 1928.

With the present data in hand and the events that are to follow the next Presidential election, my judgment is that a Republican will not be elected.   The President who takes office in March, 1929, will start under very unfavorable conditions similar to those which faced President Wilson at the time he entered his second term and also conditions will repeat similar to those that followed the election of Abraham Lincoln in 1861.   There will be trouble with foreign countries over immigration laws.   Tariff will be a sore spot and cause disagreements with foreign countries.

I will have my calculations made up for the stock and commodity markets for 1928 and 1929 soon and when they are completed will send a copy of them.   There will be some big opportunities for long pull trading in stocks and commodities during 1928.   I want you to be in on the deals with me and hope I can help you make a million dollars.

ROBERT GORDON.

CHAPTER XIX

DECEMBER, 1927, stocks had been declining for several weeks. This month stocks declined rapidly and Robert was heavily short. Wheat and corn advanced. Robert had been on the right side for several months. Just before Christmas he figured that he would cover his short stocks and wait for a rally which he expected would come in January or February. He now had profits which gave him working capital of over five hundred thousand dollars, allowing for all the money that he had spent; so he decided to put more time in working on his invention, as he was now in position to spend money enough to develop his first airplane. He kept in touch every few days with the detective agency, but no word had been received from Marie. Her parents had about given up hope that Marie was alive. Robert wrote them a very encouraging letter because he wanted to cheer them up at Christmas time. Told them that he believed Marie was alive and that he had faith in God and wanted them to have faith and continue to pray for Marie's return. Informed them of his great financial success and told them that he had continued to keep Marie's account separate and had traded very conservatively for her and that she now had over $40,000 which he intended to try to increase and have as a great surprise for her. Robert sent beautiful Christmas gifts to them in memory of Marie.

A few days before Christmas there was a big decline in the stock market. All kinds of unfavorable rumors were afloat. Business conditions were bad. War clouds were gathering thick in Europe. Newspapers talked of the uncertainties in the new year due to the coming presidential election. The public had lost confidence and were selling stocks. Robert decided that this was the time to cash in so he covered a big line of Shorts in Major Motors, Central Steel and others. This was a great Christmas for him, financially. From his beginning with 200 bales of cotton in January, 1927, with a capital of $1,000.00 and $10,000.00 which Mr. Kennelworth gave him later, thru his successful pyramiding he had made over half a million dollars. He was overjoyed with his success because it would help him now to complete his airplane and other inventions. His mind turned back to Christmas, 1926, when he had bought Marie a beautiful ring with the money he had saved. At that time he little realized that so much could happen in one short year. He thought of all he could do for Marie this year if he only knew where she was. Decided that he would buy some beautiful presents for her anyway and keep them until she returned to show her that he was thinking of her on Christmas. He bought a beautiful diamond ring and a bracelet set with sapphires and diamonds. When the jeweler delivered them Robert looked them over and thought of all Marie's beauty and purity. His faith in her was still supreme. He was very sad and wept bitterly because he felt more keenly than ever the need for her. He wanted her to be with him to share his financial success.

His heart turned to his next dearest friend—his mother. He decided to try to make it the happiest Christmas of her life and bought her every kind of a present that he thought would make her happy and comfortable and sent her a check for $5,000.00 to do with just as she pleased and buy anything she wanted. Begged her to come to New York to see him soon after the new year, as he wanted her to see the sights of the city, and thought the trip would be good for her health.

In the early part of 1928 Robert calculated that war was inevitable between England and Russia. He figured that the war would start not later than the summer and that many nations would be involved and that later an attack on the United States would come. His first airplane was now completed,—a small one according to the plan laid down by Ezekiel in the Bible. The plane had four wings and could fly on either one of its four sides. It had a new motor with 12 cylinders and could be operated either with gas, electricity or compressed air. He had constructed a wheel within a wheel so that he could lower his plane and land anywhere he chose and could rise straight up. One motor had a propeller in the center of the plane to lift it up while the other motor started its direct motion. He could drive his plane backwards or forwards. It was a great success and the boy wizard of Wall Street was now hailed as a new Lindbergh of the air. There was an extra motor built with a collapsible propeller so that he could shift it from the center of the airplane to the tail, enabling it to go backward or forward as he willed. The wings were so arranged that they could either remain stationary or be set in motion up or down by motor. This was a new and valuable feature in the construction of airplanes.

Robert's next invention was to build a silent motor, or a muffler, which would prevent any sound. He knew that this would be very useful in war. After he had completed this invention, tested it and proved it a success, he offered it to the United States Government, but after the army officers, who knew very little about this new invention had looked it over, they refused it. Robert then sailed away in his new plane which he had named "The St. Marie." He visited England, France, Germany and in the Spring of 1928 made the longest successful flight to Japan, where he was received with great honor. Japan was very much interested in his new plane and in his muffler. The Japanese Government quickly closed a deal and bought his invention for a large sum of money. Robert felt that probably one day this invention would be used against his own country in time of war, but knew that the United States would have to learn a lesson—that too often in the past American inventions had been sold to foreign countries because his own Government would not buy them.

While in Japan Robert was entertained and introduced to many beautiful titled ladies and prominent men, but he remained loyal to Marie for his great success had not turned his head. He was still searching for Marie, always hoping to find her. He returned to New York in the Summer of 1928 and was now reputed as being worth more than a million dollars, after making more successful deals in stocks, cotton and wheat. He had followed the advice of old Henry Watson and had never scattered over two or three markets at the same time. When he had a deal on in cotton or wheat, he stuck to that until he closed the transaction. When he went into a stock campaign he stayed out of the commodity markets. He was meeting with success in every direction, but his longing for Marie continued and the vision of her beautiful face continued to haunt him.

In May, 1928, Walter received a radiogram from Robert saying that he was leaving Japan the latter part of the month and was going to sail "The St. Marie" back to New York. Walter and Miss Edna Quinton, the secretary, had followed the newspaper reports of the great reception tendered Robert by the officials of the Japanese Government and the report of the large amount of money they had paid for his noiseless patent for air planes. Walter was going to graduate in June so he wrote his father and informed him that Robert was returning to New York soon with great honors and he thought it appropriate to have a big celebration for him when he arrived. As his father was coming to New York anyway for the graduation exercises, he suggested that he be there to greet Robert on his triumphant return.

Mr. Kennelworth, who was a member of the Chamber of Commerce of Texarkana and one of the leading citizens, called a meeting of the Chamber of Commerce, informed them of the phenomenal success of Robert Gordon who had left Texarkana one year previous an unknown boy and who was now the most talked of young man in the world. He had made more than a million dollars following his own discovery of how to use the laws laid down in the Bible for foretelling the future course of cotton, grain and stocks; had built the most marvelous airplane of the age; invented a muffler to make an airplane noiseless; had driven his own plane, "The St. Marie" to Japan where he had been received with great honors and the Japanese Government had bought his invention for making airplanes silent. Mr. Kennelworth proposed that the leading citizens of Texarkana go to New York to honor their favorite son on his return. When he had finished talking there was lasting applause and hurrahs for Robert Gordon. Colonel Stanton was in the audience. He arose and said that he heartily endorsed the proposal and would donate $10,000.00 to the expense fund, that they should go to New York in a special train to greet the greatest young man of the age who was born on a farm near Texarkana. Everyone was in favor of it and the wealthy men all followed Mr. Stanton in offering large sums of money in order to make the reception a success. When the meeting was over, J. H. Kennelworth drove out to the country home of Amelia Gordon, Robert's mother. Told her of her boy's success and the plans to meet him in New York and give him a great reception, inviting her to go on the special train as a guest of honor. She thankfully accepted.

On June 9th Robert Gordon's 22nd birthday, the great reception took place. The special train bearing the leading citizens of Texarkana arrived, Robert had landed at the new airport on Governor's Island without any mishap to his plane. "The St. Marie" had performed perfectly, making the trip from Japan at an average speed of over 300 miles per hour. Robert received the surprise of his life when he saw his mother and rushed to her, and after greeting her affectionately turned to shake hands with Mr. Kennelworth and Walter and seeing Mr. and Mrs. Stanton there was overjoyed and thought sure that Marie had been found. He rushed to greet her parents and his first words were, "Where is Marie?" With tears in their eyes, they informed him that not a word had been received in regard to her. They proceeded immediately to the Commodore Hotel where the reception committee and the entire delegation from Texarkana and arranged for a dinner and celebration. Robert was happy to see all the prominent business men from Texarkana there to greet him. Mr. Kennelworth made the address. Told Robert how proud Texarkana was of him; said that this was the age of the young man and that Robert had demonstrated that he was the greatest young man of his day. Robert was overwhelmed at this great reception. He thanked his friends; thanked Mr. Kennelworth, personally, and above all for bringing his dear old mother to see him; said it was the happiest moment of his life and that his one regret was that Marie was not there, but that he still had hope of finding her. When the reception was over and Robert had a few moments alone with his dear old mother, she said, "My son, do you remember the dream you had when you were a little boy, which you told me about? That you were riding a large bird with white wings across the ocean and how the foreign countries received you with great honor. My boy, when you landed today I thought about that dream and how it had been fulfilled. I hope that all of your other dreams and ambitions will be realized and that you will be rewarded with Marie's love, because you have been faithful and loyal to her."

Robert said, "Mother, I do remember the dream quite well, and when I was in Japan and they gave me such great receptions and honored me, I thought of the dream and I thought of you and how you had taught me how to read the Bible and I thought of Marie and how I loved her and felt that I would gladly give all of the honors just to be with you and Marie alone because your love and Marie's love mean more to me than everything else that the world can give."

Walter Kennelworth was graduated from Columbia College in June and prepared to work with Robert in the office. Edna Quinton had proved to be a faithful employee and a valuable aid to Robert. She had taken care of his business and looked after his financial transactions while he was away. Robert soon went to work on a new invention, and perfected a machine to read the minds of people a short distance away and also a machine which he named the "Tel-talk." This machine was made on the principle of the radio; by raising and lowering it at certain angles it would record all the conferences in the different buildings in Wall Street. Robert also used this machine to get reports on all the conferences of the big manipulators. He knew that manipulators in Wall Street suspected that in some way he understood their plans as he was making money too fast and they were conspiring to find a way to get him

wrong on the market and break him. They changed
their plans often but found that each time Robert was
on the right side of the market. Even his friend Walter knew nothing about Robert's latest invention. He
kept it in a secret room, and no one had ever seen it but
himself. It was a very delicate little machine with
indicators like a compass, delicately balanced and operated by electricity. His success was causing great excitement and schemers wanted to get his secret. They
knew that Edna Quinton had been in his office ever since
he was in New York. She was invited to a dinner at the
Biltmore where she was offered a large sum of money
if she would reveal the secrets of how Robert Gordon
so successfully operated in the market. She told them
frankly that she knew nothing about how he did it,
but if she did know, no amount of money would induce
her to turn traitor to her employer. Edna made up
her mind that when she reached the office the following
morning, she would tell Mr. Gordon just what had happened. Upon reaching the office unusually early she
found Mr. Gordon there. He seemed unusually happy
and she thought that he must have news of Marie. Before she had time to tell him what had happened the
night before, he called her into his secret office, the room
that she had never seen before. There she saw all kinds
of strange instruments which she knew must be some of
his new inventions. He took her to a little machine in
the corner of the room and showed her some peculiar
lines that the machine had recorded on the paper the
night before. He told her that his machine received
the impressions of people's minds and recorded their

thoughts, especially when they were greatly excited or interested in any matter. He read to her from the record on the machine in substance exactly what had been said to her the night before. Then he turned to the Bible and showed her where it said "Everything that is concealed will be revealed, and everything that is covered will be uncovered." Edna was more excited than she had ever been in her life. She knew that the machine had revealed the truth. Then said to Mr. Gordon that she had intended to tell him that morning just what had happened and hoped that he would believe that she was loyal to him and had refused to accept a bribe. He then showed her another record on the machine like a phonograph record which would record people's thoughts and told her that it indicated just what she had been thinking about. The machine had read her mind and recorded her thoughts. He assured her that he did believe her and trust her. Edna was moved to tears at this great confidence. She knew that never before had she been permitted to see this secret room and while she knew of Robert's great love for Marie, she felt that this confidence he had placed in her was more than a matter of business confidence and that he had some love for her. She had always admired him but had never thought of loving him. Now she knew that she did love him.

A few days later Edna had a talk with Walter, because she had known him before Robert came to New York and it was thru his influence she had secured the position. She told him what had happened and confided in him her love for Robert. He was happy to know this and hoped that Robert would fall in love with her as he believed it would be best for him. Walter said, "I am not an expert judge of how emotions work in men and women, but the way for you to find out how Robert feels toward you is to watch his actions, make notes of how often he speaks of Marie, of the letters he writes trying to find her. Continue to be as nice and kind toward him as you have always been. If in a few months his interest in the search for Marie wanes, and he ceases to talk about her, it will be a sure sign that his mind and heart is turning toward you."

Soon after Walter graduated, Robert called Miss Quinton into his secret office one morning and told her he was going to form a new firm under the name of "Gordon, Kennelworth & Quinton" and that Edna was to have an interest in the firm, as reward for her faithful service. She was to help with the work on the secret discoveries. Edna was overjoyed at this and her emotions got the best of her judgment. She flung her arms around Robert's neck, kissed him, told him he was the most wonderful man in the world and that she loved him. He drew himself quickly away from her, sat down in a chair and stared out the window for several minutes before he spoke. Then he turned toward Miss Quinton, faced her with a firm but kind face, told her that she had made a mistake in his actions, that he was rewarding her for faithfulness and that there was no sentiment in the matter, that he did not love her, that he was loyal to his long-lost Marie and would never love anyone else. Edna hardly knew what to say. She begged his forgiveness and tendered her resignation.

He told her that he would refuse to accept it; that they would go right on and work together just the same as in the past, if she felt that she could and wanted to. She assured him that she wanted to remain as long as he wanted her, and that in the future she would always control her emotions.

Walter Kennelworth had completed a special course in chemistry at college and was now prepared for work in the new firm. His father had been following Robert in the market during the past year and had made a large amount of money. He presented Walter with $100,-000.00, part of the profits which he had made out of the market, with the understanding that the money was to be used in helping to further Robert's inventions.

In the Fall of 1928, Robert and Walter completed an invention of Sun-mirrors, whereby they were able to collect the rays from the sun and produce heat powerful enough to melt down skyscrapers in a few minutes. With these mirrors and the aid of electricity, they discovered a powerful light ray. Robert knew that this was going to be of great value in the coming war. They named this machine "The Demon of Death." Miss Quinton had been very much interested in this machine during the course of construction, and she named it "Spit-Fire" because it could send forth such powerful sparks of fire, destroying instantly any metal that it touched. They held a conference and agreed that this new discovery must be kept secret and should never be used except in the defense of the United States in time of war and only then if our country was in dire peril and unable to cope with the enemy. There was one secret connected with the machine that only Robert knew. They intended to start to build a giant airship in a short time equipped with "The Demon of Death." They figured it would send a powerful death ray 3000 to 5000 miles through space, destroying everything within a radius of 700 miles. Work was started on the new machine with all secrecy. It had already been christened "Marie the Angel of Mercy."

Robert and Walter were making money rapidly in the cotton market. The war clouds were gathering and Europe was buying cotton. It had had a big advance and they were playing the fast moves up and down, both on the buying and selling sides. There is an old saying that intimacy breeds contempt, but it did not prove so with Walter Kennelworth and Edna Quinton. One beautiful morning in early September, 1928, Robert Gordon stepped into the laboratory and found Edna in the arms of Walter. He made a hasty exit, but Walter and Edna knew that they had been caught. Robert was very happy at this discovery because he knew that it was just the thing Walter needed to stimulate his ambitions and give him something to work for. He realized what a wonderful woman Miss Quinton was, and that she, too, needed inspiration that love alone could give. That evening he invited Walter to dinner with him and when they were alone said, "Well, Walter, the love bug has got you at last." Walter was bashful at first and didn't want to talk much about it; then he admitted that it had come on very suddenly when he and Edna had realized that they were both in love with each other. Robert told him that it was inevitable and that now was the time it should start and that it would be better for both of them.   They were business partners and it would make them more happy and successful in their work.   Walter asked him if he still had hopes of finding Marie.   Robert told him that he did— that he would never give up the search.

Everything moved along smoothly after this.   Walter and Edna were happy in their work and the Fall of 1928 rewarded them with a new and wonderful discovery. They had been able to perfect a machine which would reflect light in such a way as to make an airplane invisible and this, together with Robert's noiseless invention, solved the problem.   He knew now that in time of war, the plane could be used to sneak upon the enemy and that they would be unable to see or hear it.   After holding a conference, they decided that this invention, as well as "The Demon of Death" should not be patented or offered for sale to any Government, that they would test it out and keep it a secret.   Here Robert's great generosity showed itself again when he decided that this invention should be used in time of greatest need for the benefit of the United States.   Walter said, "Robert, love indeed does make a great man, makes him unselfish, causes him to think of his country, of his mother, his sweetheart and everything else before himself.   No wonder you are making a success and always will, because you are doing right."

The completion of the great machine, "The Demon of Death," which Robert had worked on untiringly day and night, was a great triumph for him, but his wonderful energy had been exhausted.   Walter had noticed before the machine was completed that Robert looked tired and worn. His mind lacked its old-time quickness and he feared for his health. Robert began to reach the office late and ceased to take an interest in his work. He was moody and despondent. Thanksgiving Day, Walter and Edna arranged a big dinner and invited Robert. He appeared very much worn and ate very little dinner. Both Walter and Edna noticed that he was less talkative than ever before. About an hour after dinner was over Robert fell in a faint. A doctor was called immediately and after making a careful examination pronounced it a case of nervous breakdown. Said there must be something preying on his mind or that he had been under a long strain. Walter explained the disappearance of Marie and how Robert had worried over the love affair; his long, strenuous campaigns in the stock and commodity markets and his work upon his inventions; that up to a few months previous Robert had been able to work almost day and night without showing any fatigue, but that in recent weeks he had noticed a great change in him. After the doctor had heard the story of the love affair and Marie's disappearance, he was sure that a long and needed rest was necessary to restore Robert to his normal health. He ordered him to remain absolutely quiet and not attempt to look after any of the details of his business. A few days later Walter persuaded Robert to go to Atlantic City, which he did, and after remaining there and resting a couple of weeks, he returned apparently well and showed his old-time strength and vigor. Was anxious to get back to work and look after his speculative deals in the market.

CHAPTER XX

AS the end of 1928 neared, war was already raging in Europe. England and Russia had already gone to war as Robert had predicted. Complications were developing quick and fast and war clouds were gathering. Robert knew that it was only a question of a short time when the United States with all of its gold supply, would be attacked and there would be a great battle in the air. Great progress had been made in aviation. Airplanes were carrying mail at the rate of 300 miles per hour. Passenger lines were now starting all over the United States. "Marie the Angel of Mercy," Robert's great ship, was rapidly nearing completion. The new 12-cylinder motor had been tested and the engineers had estimated that they would attain a speed of 1000 miles per hour. Robert was elated over the success and knew that he would now be prepared to help his country in time of its greatest need. He had been working early and late and the interest in his work had kept his mind off Marie. Yet not a day passed but what he made some inquiries or had his detectives chase some clew which he hoped would lead to the discovery of Marie, but all efforts were in vain. No news had ever been heard of her.

With the great progress in radio messages thru the air, and radiograms, Robert knew that in time of war, secret communications would be neccessary. Spies could steal codes, and messages sent over the radio could be interpreted; therefore, one of the great needs for the war in the air would be a way to communicate without detection. He finally succeeded in completing what he called "The Pocket Radio." It was no larger than a watch and worked on the same principle of his machine for recording the thoughts of people, only the instrument had to be used by two people who understood how to work it, because the positive radio was carried in one man's pocket and the negative in the other and by pressing the stem, it could be changed from positive into negative. No sound was transmitted thru the air. The machine could be operated by certain motions of the fingers on a little push button which recorded symbols on the other machine that would reveal the message sent. The Pocket Radio made it possible to convey any message without any possibility of detection because only the person sending the message and the one receiving it could understand or know anything about it. This was better than wireless or any other radio discovery up to this time. Robert tested the machine out by leaving one instrument in Walter's pocket, he himself going to Chicago and conveying messages which Walter was able to get without any trouble. He could either speak into this little Pocket Radio and convey the sound without anyone else being able to take it from the air, or use it to convey thoughts or emotions. The test proved perfect and Robert knew that he had another great discovery which would be of great value to his Government in time of war. He decided to keep this a secret and have it ready to aid the United States at a time when they would need it most.

Robert figured that there would be a big bull campaign in cotton during 1929 so he had started buying early in the year, expecting a big advance later. He had also forecast the rapid advance of certain classes of stocks. During 1928 he had closed a successful bear campaign in Major Motors and was still holding his Right Aeroplane stock, which had continued to advance, and he figured that it would have a big rise during 1929. His fortune was piling up rapidly, despite all the money he was spending on his new inventions. The new ship "Marie, the Angel of Mercy," was now about perfected, but Robert intended that this should never be made known to the public until he had it in perfect working order and it was a success beyond doubt.

After preparing his campaign for the market and buying stocks and cotton for the big advance, Walter noticed a great change in Robert. His health began to fail again, and now that he had achieved great success and completed such wonderful inventions, without Marie to comfort him he would probably break down in health and give up. Robert had ceased to talk much about Marie. His interest in the future was waning. Walter and Edna, who were still as much in love as ever, often discussed Robert's physical condition. They decided to encourage him to go away for a long-needed rest. Walter had a talk with Robert in the middle of January, 1929, but Robert didn't show much interest or any desire to travel. A short time after this, Robert appeared at the office one morning looking more haggard and worn than ever. He called Walter and Edna into the office, told them that he had had a very peculiar dream the night before, that he had dreamed that he had gone to Paris and suddenly met Marie. He was so strongly impressed with the dream that he decided to leave at once. Told Walter to give the mechanics instructions to put his old ship "The St. Marie" in shape to sail at once.

It was a matter of only a couple of days until they reported that "The St. Marie" was in perfect shape and could stand a trip around the world. There was to be a great convention of all the nations on aviation in Paris and Robert decided that he wanted to be there for it, but the main incentive for the trip was his dream. Robert had no trouble in securing letters of introduction to prominent people in London and Paris. When he said good-bye to Walter and Edna, they wished him God-speed, told him that they hoped his dream would become a reality and that he would find Marie, but they knew that he was not the same Robert of old. He acted as tho his spirit was broken. On the morning of February 2nd, 1929, Robert started his flight to Paris and arrived there promptly in the evening and went to visit some friends and acquaintances. After talking over the war situation and his forecasts of the great war yet to come, he decided to visit friends in London. England and Russia were waging their battles in the air and doing very little land fighting. Despite the good start that England had made, Russia and her allies were getting the best of the victory. Robert found London very uninteresting. Up to this time he had heard nothing of Marie and decided to return to Paris.

On a beautiful sunhiny morning in the latter part of Feburary, 1929, Robert was walking down a prominent business street in Paris with no special objective in mind. He was feeling sick and gloomy and was walking with his head down, looking at the street. Suddenly he saw a form approaching very closely, and like a flash, a woman quickly passed him. He was sure it was Marie. His heart was in his throat. He turned around quickly to follow her but she had disappeared. Just as she passed him she dropped a letter on the street and he picked it up, put it in his pocket and rushed on down the street, hoping to find her, but after exhausting himself running around, fighting his way thru the crowds, without a glimpse of her, he decided to open the letter. When he opened it it was written in a foreign language which he did not understand. He was not sure whether it was Marie's handwriting or not. His first thought was to go immediately to an interpreter and have the letter read. On second thought, he decided that it might be something confidential and that he would go to an old friend who lived in Paris and ask him to interpret the letter. Robert called on Louis Renan, stated the circumstance of his meeting Marie on the street and told him about the letter she dropped. His friend gladly consented to read the letter. Robert handed it to him and he glanced over it ; handed it back to Robert without a word, told him to get out of his house immediately and never darken the door again. Robert begged for an explanation but in vain. His friend was angry and determined and pushed Robert out of the door. Robert walked slowly back to his hotel, disappointed, mystified, and heart-broken. What could be the meaning of this

letter? Why should his friend offer no explanation as
to what it contained? Had he really met Marie and was
the letter from her? One thing he knew, he must find
out what this mysterious letter contained. He decided
the next best plan was to go to an interpreter, so he
inquired at the hotel the name of an interpreter and was
informed where he could get any language interpreted.
He called at the address, explained his mission to the
manager and turned over the letter. In a few minutes
the manager returned, handed him the letter, told him
there was the door, please get out and ask no questions.
Robert again begged for some explanation but the man
was defiant and refused to make any comment.

Robert returned to his hotel to think matters over.
He bought a paper and looked over the news from New
York and market reports. He saw that cotton and stocks
were advancing as he expected, but money-making now
was of no interest to him when he at last thought that
he had found where Marie was. He decided to place
a personal notice in all the papers in Paris, telling Marie
that he had passed her on the street, had found the letter, was unable to get it interpreted, and beg her to
communicate with him at once. He placed the notice in
the papers that afternoon. Received an invitation from
some acquaintances in Paris to dine with them and go
to a ball. He wanted to refuse the invitation because he
did not feel equal to the occasion, but they insisted that
it would do him good and begged him to come along.
Robert had been so disappointed about the mysterious
letter and the sudden loss of Marie after he had seen
her, that he decided to say nothing about the incident

to his friends. After dinner was over, they chatted with
Robert, and he seemed more cheerful. They told Robert
of the Aviators' Costume Ball to take place in the Hotel
Lafayette that night and asked him to go along. Robert tried to beg off and made the excuse that he had no
costume for this occasion, but they told him that they
had already ordered one for him and there was no getting out of it—he had to go, so finally he consented.

When they arrived at the hotel and entered the ballroom, Robert's friends, who knew of his great fame in
New York and his success in speculative markets, were
anxious to introduce him to the prominent men and
women of Paris. Aviators were there from all over the
world. They had come for the great convention. Each
country was competing for the grand prize for the most
efficient airplane and the best one suited for war purposes. They asked Robert if he did not have a plane to
enter or if he could not demonstrate something with
"The St. Marie." He told them that his health was
not good and that he was not interested in entering a
plane at this time. The ballroom was decorated with
everything connected with airplanes. Miniature planes
were flying around the room, circling up and down from
the ceilings. It was a gorgeous display and while it was
dazzling to others, Robert paid very little attention to
it. His friends, in order to please him and get him
interested, had the radio tuned into New York and were
getting music from the Biltmore. The dance started.
Robert watched but was very little interested. His
friends invited him to dance but he refused. He had
no thoughts of anything but Marie. As he was sitting,

watching the dancers whirl around the floor, suddenly he looked across the hall and again he saw Marie dressed like an eagle, queen of the air. He made a mad rush thru the crowd to the other side of the hall and when he got there, he could see no Marie. The ordeal was too much for him. He fell unconscious on the floor. Friends rushed to his assistance and after reviving him, he explained to them that he had seen Marie again and asked them to find her and bring her to him. After investigation, they told him that there was no one there by that name and that none of the ladies had left the ballroom. They brought them all before him and introduced him, but Marie was not among them. Robert was not only sick at heart but sick physically, and his friends realized it and called a nerve specialist, Dr. Descartes. Robert explained what had happened, about meeting Marie on the street and about seeing her at the ball, altho he said nothing about the mysterious letter to the Doctor. The Doctor, after examining him, told his friends he thought that he was suffering from mental delusions—that he had probably had this woman on his mind so long and after dreaming he had met her on a street in Paris, had hoped so strongly that he would meet her, he had brought himself to believe that she was there and had really thought that he had seen her, both on the street and in the ballroom, but it was probably an optical delusion and after he got better he would realize that he hadn't seen Marie.

Several days passed before Robert fully recovered. In the meantime, he had become quite friendly with Dr. Descartes and told him a great deal about his history. The Doctor was very much interested and had a great desire to help him. Robert finally decided to confide in him about the mysterious letter. The Doctor had a brother in New York and was going to give Robert a letter of introduction to him upon his return. While they were on the subject of the letter of introduction, Robert told him about the mysterious letter and the Doctor agreed to get a friend of his who could interpret it, to read the letter for him. Robert was very happy because he thought that if he could get the meaning of the letter it would throw some light on what the trouble was with Marie. While he had been sick, his mind had wandered and he had imagined all kinds of things, and for a few moments, doubted Marie. He even thought that she might have turned out to be a bad woman and was now in Paris, having a gay time, but as soon as his mind returned to its normal state, his old faith in Marie returned, and he loved her as of old and believed that she could do no wrong.

The next day Dr. Descartes called, took Robert with him in his car to his friend who was an interpreter. Robert handed him the letter and, after looking it over, he handed the letter back to Robert, turned to the Doctor, and said, "Have you no more respect for my friendship than to insult me in a manner like this. Begone, and never let me see you in my house again." The Doctor begged for an explanation and Robert offered his apologies, saying it was all his fault and the Doctor was only trying to aid him, but the man refused to discuss the matter and they hurried away. When they got in the car, Dr. Descartes knew that the shock was too much for Robert so he drove him immediately to the hotel without discussing the mysterious letter. After he had gotten him in his room and made him comfortable, he begged Robert not to worry about the letter, told him that he would think the matter over and call and see him the next day.

Robert was very much worried. His hope was fast giving way to despair. He again realized that hope deferred maketh the heart grow sick. He thought of Henry Watson's story and wondered if he would have to go thru life and die without ever again seeing Marie. Dr. Descartes called the following day and was very solicitous of Robert's welfare. Told him to forget the incident about the letter and advised Robert to try to get it interpreted when he returned to New York. Robert told him more about Marie's disappearance and showed him the note that Marie had placed in his pocket on the train to St. Louis. The Doctor read it and said it certainly left room for hope, and while it was mysterious, he felt that Marie fully intended at some time to come back to him. Robert had received no reply to his personal notices in the Paris newspapers and decided to return to New York in a few days.

In the early part of March a lot of the aviators were returning from Paris to New York after the convention and Robert decided to go home with them. They insisted that he was not physically able to sail "The St. Marie" alone and sent a pilot along with him. The trip was uneventful and on March 5th Robert arrived in New York. On his arrival he went immediately to his office and laboratories where he found Walter and Edna glad to see him. They told him that he looked much improved in health. He related all his experiences in Paris and the mysterious letter. Walter was very much amazed and at a loss to understand it all. He could not understand, if Marie had dropped the letter and had really seen Robert on the street and at the ball, why she would not answer his personal notices in the papers and at least clear up the mystery of her disappearance. Robert decided to go immediately to an interpreter in New York and see if he could get the mysterious letter read. After handing it to the man who spoke about ten different languages, the interpreter handed it back to him and stated in a firm, gentleman-like manner that he would like him to please leave the office immediately and never return. Robert went at once to his office and told Walter and Edna what had happened. They talked it over and advanced all kinds of theories about what the letter might contain, and asked Robert if any of the interpreters had ever given any information or stated whether they could read the letter or not. Robert told them they had not. Edna thought that probably the letter contained a message to the interpreter not to give any information or to reveal what it contained to Robert or anyone else. Walter thought if this were the case, that some of the interpreters who seemed to be insulted by it, would have immediately destroyed the letter instead of handing it back to him. The more theories they advanced, the less plausible the mystery seemed. Robert decided to write to a famous astrologer in Canada whom he had heard of. He sent along his date of birth, telling him the history of the case, to see if he could give him any light on the subject, telling the astrologer that he would pay $50,000.00 or more if necessary, if he could solve the problem and tell him what the letter contained and how to get it interpreted or give him any information leading to the whereabouts of Marie. The astrologer answered as follows after making the calculation from Robert's date of birth:

While it is a very peculiar case, the events were not accidents at all but the result of Natural Law. The young lady still lives and I believe will again come into your life three or four years later. The great trouble was that on the day she disappeared, Mercury, your ruling planet, applied to an evil aspect of Uranus, the great eccentric, revolutionary, mysterious planet, and this indicated disappointment, trouble and delays, over letters or writings and the letters would be mysterious and hard to understand. In view of the fact that Jupiter, Mars, and Mercury, as well as Venus, were all changing signs just around the time she disappeared, it meant that there would be many changes and long delays before the mystery would be solved, that there was great danger of letters being lost or miscarried, and that it was possible that she may have written you letters which never reached you. Neptune has much to do with the sea and its mysteries and as it strongly influences the city of Paris, her appearance there would be shrouded in mystery and there would be much that could not be explained. It is very doubtful if you will get any explanation or interpretation of the mysterious letter. There is something visionary about it, or the appearance of Marie may have been a spiritual apparition.

If you will visit cities near beautiful watering places in the South or Southwest, and could come in contact with an honest spiritualist or clairvoyant, it may be of some benefit and help in some way to solve the mystery. In view of the condition of your health and the planet Saturn is afflicting you, it would be advisable to spend the balance of the Winter and early part of the Spring in a tropical climate. Florida would be especially good for you and might bring favorable results in more ways than one. If you will give me time to figure on your horoscope and have patience I will guarantee to tell you the time that you will find Marie. The progressed Mars is traveling toward a conjunction of Venus, the Goddess of Love, and when this is completed she will probably come back into your life.

CHAPTER XXI

ROBERT was very much encouraged by this letter because he had great confidence in Astrology and in this man's ability. He decided to go immediately to Florida for a rest and visit all the beautiful spots and watering places that he could find, hoping to get some news of Marie. Going directly to Palm Beach, Florida, he met some friends of Conan Doyle's who were very much interested in spiritualism. They told him that a famous spiritualist, Lady Bersford from England, had been there, and that they believed she could help solve the problem. Robert asked where he could find her and was told that she had gone to Ocala, Florida, to visit Silver Springs and investigate the legend of Silver Springs, the story about a beautiful young girl who drowned herself in the Springs.

A LEGEND

(The following story combines the accuracies of fact with the romance of fiction. Aunt Silly lived at Silver Springs until her death, about sixteen years ago, and was seen by many who visited the Springs. It is from the gifted pen of Mrs. Maley Bainbridge Crist):

Near Florida's celebrated Silver Springs lives an old negress, known to the entire surrounding country as "Aunt Silly," whose claim to being 110 years old is borne out by her appearance. Aunt Silly is wrinkled and decrepit, and the wool peeping from her bandanaed head is white as snow, while the blackness and weirdness of her face is intensified by a heavy crop of snow-white beard. As long as the oldest citizen of Ocala can remember Aunt Silly has looked just as ancient as she does now; identified always with Silver Springs, and hobbling about them from morning until night, leaning upon her short, thick staff.

That she was a participant in a tragedy is known only to a very few of Ocala's oldest citizens, and seldom referred to by any of them. In the near vicinity of Ocala, when first it was settled, stood a splendid old mansion owned by Capt. Harding Douglass, a South Carolinian of considerable wealth. His only child was a son, who, with his mother's beauty of countenance, had inherited her tender, shrinking nature, and, like herself, was a slave to the old man's iron will. In the beautiful little City of Ocala lived Bernice Mayo, whose blond beauty won, at first sight, the heart of Claire Douglass. Although of Virginia ancestry, Bernice was a true child of the "Land of Flowers," passionate and impulsive. Her eyes were blue and clear as the waters of Lake Munroe, beside which she had spent her childhood, in the fair little City of Sanford. Her hair was as golden as Florida's own sunshine, and Florida's tropical splendor ran riot in her blood. For six months Bernice Mayo and Claire Douglass were constant companions, and Silver Springs was their favorite resort. For half a day at a time they would drift about on the bosom of the splendid, placid curiosity of nature.

Bernice seemed never to tire of going into the depths of the subterranean world. "If I were a mermaid, Claire," she would say, "and lived in yon crystal cavern, and some fair day I should wander forth among the palmettos and mosses of the springs, and, sitting on yonder ledge of rocks, should 'comb my golden hair with a shell,' and your boat should come drifting by, and you were to see me in the water beneath, would you love me well enough to plunge, plunge to the depths beneath to woo me?" Then would Claire stop her merry chatter with his kisses, and pledge to her his eternal love as they drifted over the transparent mirror of water, pausing now and then to study the rocks and shells, the mosses, palmettos, the fish, which were as visible eighty feet below the transparent water as were the trees and woodland about them. There is nothing fairer than Ocala's "Lover's Lane," and yet no spot held for these young people the attraction of Silver Springs, their constant trysting place. But there came a fatal day, destined to separate them. A day wherein Claire Douglass declared to his father his love for beautiful, penniless Bernice Mayo, and his determination to make her his wife. Stormily, his father vowed it should never be, and secretly planned a separation.

When Claire Douglass had been speedily dispatched abroad on important business for his father, then it was that Bernice learned the truth, and her proud, delicate nature lay crushed and bleeding beneath the cruel blow and still more cruel separation.

Vainly she strove to rally; all life seemed but an empty blank to her. A year dragged wearily by, and the scenes frequented by merry Bernice Mayo knew her no more. Paler and thinner she daily grew. Fragile, she was, as the white blossoms of her well-loved springs. The little chain of gold that Claire had locked on her arm would have slipped across the wasted, transparent hand, but for the ribbon that held its links. One day (her last upon earth) the girl, by dint of desperate energy, crept to Silver Springs. Even Aunt Silly was unprepared for the white, emaciated little creature who tottered into her cabin and fell fainting in her arms. Consciousness soon returned, but it was apparent even to the old black woman that death had set its gray, unmistakable seal upon the young face.

"Aunt Silly," gasped the girl, "I have come to you to die, and you must obey my last request; the grave divulges no secrets. Ere tonight's sun sets I shall be in heaven. This separation from the man I love has been my death, but in that death we shall be united. I have asked God, and He has heard me. But you, Aunt Silly, you must obey my request. You love me; you will do as I ask. Tonight when the moon comes out, row my body to Boiling Springs, and bury me there. You know the spot—make no mistake. Do this, and God will attend to the rest."

"Good Gord A'mighty, chile, you think Aunt Silly am gwine tote dade body off in the lonesomely night?" asked the old woman, her very teeth chattering with the superstitious fear peculiar to her race. The girl realized the risk of her plan being thwarted, and raising herself to a sitting posture she seized the old woman's hands and fixed her dying eyes full on her face.

"Aunt Silly," she gasped, "I am a dying woman; I am very near to God; I have talked with Him, and He has answered me. My will has been crushed in life, I swear it shall not in death. Before twenty-four hours Claire Douglass shall join me in the crystal cavern of Silver Springs. If you do not grant my request every spirit of evil shall surround you. Palsied and blind you shall grow, and deaf—deaf to every sound but the ghosts of the dead, which shall pursue you by day and haunt you by night. Do you swear to obey my dying request, or will you refuse me, and reap the prophecy of a dying woman, which shall rest upon your cowardly head for refusing to obey God's will?"

The old woman was shaking like an aspen. Her eyes protruded with fear, and great beads of perspiration rolled down her cheeks. The strength of the dying girl's will had prevailed, and the old woman answered: "I promises, honey; I promises."

It was a solemn and awful sight that night, witnessed alone by God and nature; the boat, which drifted down Silver Springs in the moonlight, bearing its two strange occupants— the one weird, bent, grotesque; the other, so silent, so white, so pathetic, in its dead loveliness. Not a leaf was stirring, not a sound heard, but the splash, splash of the old woman's oars, as her boat, with its strange, beautiful burden, drifted over the curious, transparent body of water; drifted until it reached Boiling Springs, then veered about and stood still. Gently and easily, as if it had been a babe, the old woman lifted the little body. Something of her fear had departed in the placid smile of the dead face. Tears rolled down her dusky face as she bent forward in obedience to the girl's curious request. For a moment the body rocked to and fro on the bosom of the water, upon which its happiest moments had been spent. The dead face smiled, and the wealth of hair gleamed in the moonlight like a sheen of gold. Every pebble was visible in the depths below. Suddenly, as if by magic, the body began sinking. The boiling of the spring had ceased, showing a peculiar little fissure in the rock from whence all the strange body of water came. The fissure slowly divided, received the dead body and closed again, shutting every vestige of it from view.

"Gord A'mighty, dat chile a angel sho' nuff. She mus' done talked to de Lawd; she knowed how all dat gwine to be," muttered the old woman, as she rowed back to her cabin in the moonlight.

A mocking-bird on the opposite shore sent forth a flood of silvery melody. "Hear dat now," muttered Aunt Silly; "dat bird done sendin' forth de weddin' song o' de bridegroom. Come on, Claire Douglass, yo' little bride am waitin' for you more pacifyin' den she waited many a long day."

The day following the death of Bernice Mayo was one never to be forgotten by the citizens of Ocala. Claire Douglass had just returned after a year's absence. He found his beautiful cousin (whom his father desired to become his wife) a guest at the home of his parents.

"Claire," said his father as they lingered over the breakfast table, "I have a fine, new skiff at Silver Springs, and I wish you to take your cousin for a row this morning; and, by the permission of you young people, I shall make one of your party."

"Delightful, uncle," cried the girl; and Claire, while he turned a trifle pale at the thought of returning to the spot where all that had given color to his life had transpired, could only acquiesce.

Claire Douglass looked unusually handsome as the party drifted down Silver Springs in the April sunshine, but there was a curious pallor on his face, and the uncle and niece were left to carry on all the conversation. What a contrast the blooming girl in April sunshine bore to the one in the solemn moonlight, who had drifted over the same water the evening before! As the skiff neared Boiling Springs the party noted a little boat hovering over it. The boat was rowed by Aunt Silly; and its other occupant was an old woman, whose eyes were swollen with weeping. The skiff paused beside the little rowboat, and the occupants of each gazed into the curious, transparent depths below.

Suddenly the niece cried out, "Oh, see, that looks like a hand; a little human hand!" Plainer and more visible it grew, the little white hand with its gold chain locked above the slender wrist. Ah, little hand, Claire Douglass would have known you among ten thousand hands! His face was white as death and he gasped as though choking. All were intent upon the scene below. Suddenly the boiling of the water ceased, and out upon a rock in its transparent depths, like a broken, beautiful lily, lay Bernice Mayo, her golden hair floating on the sand, her dead face smiling placidly, as if at last a halo of peace had descended upon the tired spirit, and the broken heart had found rest. With a wild cry that pierced even the heart of the mother, who for the last time in life gazed upon the dead face of her child, Claire Douglass dashed overboard, diving deeper, ever deeper, until he caught in his arms the little figure of his dead love.

Then once more the rock divided and closed, shutting from view forever the lovers, who lay locked in each other's embrace. And again the water whirled and boiled in its mad fury, as if to defy the puny will of him who would have separated what God had joined together.

As for the first time the secret bridal chamber of Silver

Springs has been made known to the world, it will be interesting to its future visitors, as they approach that part of it known as "Boiling Springs," to note in the whir of the water beneath (the only part of the water not perfectly placid) the constant shower of tiny, pearl-like shells poured forth from the fissure in the rock, and which Aunt Silly says are the jewels the angels gave Bernice Mayo upon her wedding morning when her lover joined her in their fairy palace in Silver Springs. There is, too, a curious flower growing in the springs—a flower with leaf like a lily, and a blossom shaped like an orange blossom. Its peculiar waxy whiteness and yellow petals are like Bernice Mayo's face and hair, Aunt Silly says, and she calls them "Bernice Bridal Wreath." There is a legend among the young people of Ocala that a woman presented with one of these blossoms will become a bride ere the close of the year.

CHAPTER XXII

ROBERT was greatly impressed with this story and what they told him about the wonderful powers of Lady Bersford. After consulting with his friends, he decided to go immediately to Silver Springs to see her. On Sunday morning about 10 o'clock he boarded a local airplane for Silver Springs and arrived in the afternoon. It was a fitting setting for the scene. The day was beautiful, the sunshine at its best. Robert had watched the plane as it flew swiftly across the country. He had viewed the many beautiful orange groves and thought of the wonderful work of the hand of Nature in painting beauty grander than any hand of man could ever do. Here he thought of something that he would write of Marie in contrast to her beauty.

After thoughts of Marie's beauty had flitted thru Robert's brain and his dream and hope for Marie had revived, he was feeling hopeful and enthusiastic. Lady Bersford upon receiving the letter of introduction from her friends, greeted Robert with unusual courtesy. He told his story. She listened attentively and when he had finished telling her about the mysterious letter, she said that there was an interpreter at the hotel who understood most any foreign language and that she was sure he could interpret the letter. Robert was elated because Lady Bersford showed such a great interest and desire to help him. He related all the obstacles he had met with in trying to get the letter interpreted before, and had almost lost hope of ever getting it interpreted. She assured him that her friendship with the interpreter would at this time bring results.

Robert was anxious to see Silver Springs and Lady Bersford was anxious for him to go and see it immediately and said that after their return she would see the interpreter and get the mysterious letter read. They went to the Springs and slowly rode out on the beautiful waters. Robert had heard the story and when the boat slowly came to a stop over "The Bridal Chamber" and he saw the face of a beautiful woman in the rocks his heart almost failed him. He thought of the sorrows he had gone thru and wondered if such a fate might have been Marie's. The beautiful waters reflected the most radiant colors Robert had ever seen in his life. He secretly prayed the greatest prayer of his life, that he might meet Marie here and with all of her beauty, where they could enjoy the beauty of nature together. When he looked thru the transparent waters into the bridal chamber, it brought him back to Sunday morning, June 5, 1927, when he had expected to marry Marie. Tears streamed down his cheeks and Lady Bersford realizing the situation and knowing that she could say little, remained in silence until Robert's emotions had passed. Then she told of her admiration for his love and devotion to Marie and said that a scene like this, painted by the hand of Nature was calculated to melt the heart of the most cold-blooded man on earth. Robert asked the man who was rowing the boat to row back to the place where the face of the spirit bride showed in the water and as he looked down at the face again, he thought of Marie and this is what he said: "Most beautiful face in all the world, best beloved eyes that inspired the best in me, the days pass by on leaden wings, when only in memory your dear eyes shine for me." Somehow the beautiful waters and the scenery inspired a new hope in Robert, for love must ever inspire hope in man when his faith in a woman keeps the lovelight burning on the altar of his heart.

Robert and Lady Bersford returned to the hotel. After dinner, Lady Bersford met Robert and told him that she had found the interpreter and he had agreed to read the mysterious letter that evening. Robert, having met with so many disappointments, felt that he must make sure this time he would get the letter read. He met the interpreter, went over the whole story with him, told him that no matter what the letter contained, good or bad, he must know the truth and nothing but the truth. Said he would pay any sum that the interpreter might name, and pay it in advance, if he would agree to read the letter regardless of what it contained. His plea was so earnest that the interpreter saw that his heart was breaking and told him that no amount of money would influence him as much to read the letter as the desire to relieve an honest, loyal heart which was breaking for a great love. Such men as he was our country's need in time of peril and such loyalty and devotion to a woman was found in but few men; that it seemed more divine than real, and that he would interpret the letter gladly and willingly. When Robert was fully assured at this time that there would be no disappointment, he was supremely happy. He grabbed the hand of Lady Bersford, thanked her, and fell upon his knees before the interpreter and thanked him in advance for his promise to interpret the letter.

"Now let us delay no longer," said the interpreter, "give me the letter and I will read it." Robert had always carried the letter in a wallet in his pocket, never letting it get out of his possession. Had it carefully folded up in some other papers. He pulled forth the wallet from his pocket, opened it up and looked for the letter. It was not there. He searched the wallet carefully but there was no mistake about it. The letter was gone. The disappointment was another great blow to him. He talked the matter over with the interpreter and Lady Bersford and was at a loss to understand how the letter could have disappeared from his pocket. Was sure that he had it when he was in Palm Beach. He telegraphed the hotel in Palm Beach and after making a search, they reported that they were unable to find the letter. Lady Bersford realized the keen disappointment that the loss of this mysterious letter had brought Robert, so she told him that she would use her spiritual powers every way possible to solve the mystery of the letter and try to help him find Marie, and that if he would leave her alone in silence that night, the following day she would report to him the information she received.

Robert arose early the next morning and decided that he would go to Silver Springs and see this beautiful spot just as the sun was rising. It was a beautiful morning and he rode out upon the waters, listened to the songs of the birds, watched the beautiful fish running to and fro in the clear waters. He again thought of the story of the spirit bride whom the legend said appeared upon the waters on moonlight nights. His mind went back to the fishing trip at Spirit Lake, Arkansas. He thought of the story of Spirit Lake and how he was impressed as a child with that story. Now it seemed more vivid and real. His mind reverted back to the death of Henry Watson and he thought "Is it my fate to visit places and to hear stories of tragedy and disappointment of lovers, and in the end, will my fate be like theirs? Must I sink into the waters of forgetfulness without ever again seeing the best beloved face in all the world, Marie's? After all, is it like Henry Watson said: 'Hope is but an anchor to the soul, but facts are stubborn things and we must face them?'" For a moment, Robert felt that he had been clinging to hope all these years and he was almost ready to bid hope depart and leave him alone to facts, but even then he knew that if hope should depart and not hold aloft a light of Marie's love, he at that moment would follow the course of the lover of the spirit bride and go overboard, to be swallowed up in the beautiful waters, to release his spirit, that it might soar away to find Marie. The man who was rowing the boat, noticed that Robert had fallen into a death-like silence. He asked him if he was ready to return. Robert awakened as if by a shot and said "Yes."

CHAPTER XXIII

HE drove back to the hotel, found Lady Bersford awaiting him. He ate his breakfast hurriedly and retired to a secret corner in the hotel where they would be alone and he could hear what Lady Bersford had gathered from the spirit world the night before. Her first words when he entered the room were, "Mr. Gordon, I have good news for you and I know that you can depend on it. Last night a spirit appeared that I had never seen or heard before. It was an Indian girl, named 'Laughing Waters,' who said she was the daughter of Chief Okeehumkee who once lived near Silver Springs and on account of the loss of her lover had drowned herself in the Springs. At this point Lady Bersford handed Robert Gordon a booklet on Silver Springs containing a legend about the death of Laughing Waters. and he read it hastily.

AN INDIAN LEGEND

A long time ago when Okeehumkee was king over the tribes of Indians who roamed and hunted around the Southwestern lakes, an event occurred which filled many hearts with horror. The king had a daughter whose rare beauty was the pride of the old man's life, and an idol of the braves. She was a coveted prize. Chiefs and warriors vied with each other as to who should present the most valuable gift, when her hand was sought from the king, her father. But the daughter had already seen and loved Chuleotah, the renowed chief of a tribe which dwelt among the wild groves of Silver Springs. But it was a sad truth that between the old chief and the young chief, and their tribes, there had long been a deadly feud. They were enemies. When Okeehumkee learned that Chuleotah had gained the affections of his beloved child, not many weeks passed away before the noble Chuleotah was slain. Slain, too, by the father. Dead! Her lover dead! Poor child. Will she return to the paternal lodge and dwell among her people while her father's hand is stained with the drippings of her lover's scalp? No. She hurries away to the well-known fountain. It was a favorite spot, where herself and Chuleotah met on the glassy bottom of the Springs. The pale ghost of Chuleotah stands beckoning her to come. All was still save the night winds that sighed and moaned thru the lofty pines. Then came the girl to the side of the Springs. For a moment she paused upon the edge of the Springs, then met her palms above her head, and, with a wild leap, she fell into the whelming waves. She had gone to one of those enchanted isles, far out in the Western Seas, where the maiden and her lover are united, and where both have found another Silver Springs.

Lady Bersford said that Laughing Waters' spirit told her that after she drowned herself and her spirit was released, she had been very happy in finding others who met disappointment in love and helping to relieve their sufferings and bring about an understanding and reunite the separated. Laughing Waters said: "Marie is still alive and for mysterious reasons is keeping in hiding from her parents and everyone else, but her love is as strong as the Rock of Gibraltar, and she will keep her promise to return to Robert when he needs her most. It was the spirit of Marie that Robert saw on the streets in Paris. Marie was not there and never had been, but Robert loved her so much and longed for her until Marie's spirit, which had always been closely in touch with Robert, was able to leave her body and appear to comfort him. It was Marie's spirit he saw at the ballroom. She was not there at all. It occurred because Robert needed some hope and encouragement to go on and wait until the proper time when Marie would return to him. The mysterious letter never existed. It was a delusion and a power of the subconscious mind. This power is known and understood by the adepts of India. Some of my tribe knew how to project the subconscious mind, or spirit, as some called it, anywhere they desired. Robert's subconscious mind had received impressions so long and he had hoped and desired so long for a letter from Marie, that when her spirit appeared he expected a message, a letter, or some communication, and he really thought she dropped a letter. This power so strongly impressed the subconscious mind that he was able to make other people feel, believe and see the letter, but of course they could not read or interpret it, because there was no letter or written message and that is why they all acted so strangely about it. When Robert at last met you, a spiritualist and an unselfish woman, and the interpreter, an honest, unselfish man refusing to accept any amount of money to read the mysterious letter, I knew that no letter ever existed and removed the impression from Robert's subconscious mind and when he went to look for the letter, of course it was not there, and never was because it only existed in his subconscious mind."

After this, Robert was much more cheerful and hopeful. His own mind told him that he was at last on the right track. He thought of the laws laid down in the Bible; remembered what Jesus said when they asked him for a sign that the Son of man would remain three days and three nights in the heart of the earth, then rise and ascend to heaven. Robert knew the meaning of this. He knew that sorrows, sufferings and disappointment had to come before joy and happiness; for every day of sunshine comes a night of darkness, for every aching in the heart there is a returning flow. That all the laws of Nature taught the eternal law of action and reaction. He took great comfort in this; knew that the promise was laid down in the Bible of great reward for love and faithfulness and he felt very happy because he believed "Laughing Waters' " story that Marie would come into his life again.

Robert remained a few days longer at Silver Springs. Enjoyed being with Lady Bersford and told her of his understanding of the Bible and natural laws. She said that the pure, clean life he had led was what had brought him in contact with the spirits that had revealed to him the truth. Many seances were held with "Laughing Waters," who was very fond of Robert and anxious to help him all she could. She said that Robert had a love the same as she had, that he had rather die than give up Marie, but that he would attain the greatest honor of any man on earth except Jesus Christ, because he was following the law of love and that law would bring to him his own Marie and he would spend many happy years with her. She told him that the great Chief whose spirit was with her, had confirmed all she had told them.

When Robert prepared to depart from Silver Springs, his heart was filled with gratitude, for Lady Bersford and all she had done for him. He wanted to pay her for her services and if she would name the amount, he would write a check for it. She explained that she was a very wealthy woman, with a large estate in England; that she had gone into this work at the solicitation of Sir Arthur Conan Doyle, for the good that she could do for others and not for any monetary consideration. Her reward for being unselfish and trying to help him was his appreciation, she said. This attitude on the part of Lady Bersford was a great comfort to Robert and gave him more faith in the Bible. He knew that the law that "whatsoever a man soweth, he shall also reap" was a divine law and a natural law, that no man could break it or evade it, and that his reward was just as sure as the law was inevitable. He had read Emerson's "Essay on Compensation," and strongly believed that. He said to Lady Bersford, "Your reward is sure, because you are doing right, giving out the best you can to help others, and only good will return to you."

Lady Bersford said, "Thank you very much, Mr. Gordon, I have enjoyed our visits and hope that we will meet again some time. May I ask where you are going from here?" "I am going direct to New York as I have important business matters to look after there," he replied. "Mr. Gordon, you don't look strong," she said. "It seems to me you need to take more care of your health and have more rest. I am going from here to Sebring, Florida. Have heard so many stories of this wonderful place that I want to go there to recoup my health." "Is it a health resort?" asked Robert. Lady Bersford said, "I understand there is a sunshine sanitarium there. They teach you how to eat and play. The water is the finest in the State of Florida; in fact, one of the few places in Florida where you can get good drinking water. The climate is ideal. Lake Jackson, one of the most beautiful lakes in the State is near there, as well as many others. I am told the fishing and boating is fine. The Kissimmee River is near there. This beautiful river is associated with songs and stories of the Southland and I am anxious to see it. I met some friends in England who spent the past winter at Sebring and they were enthusiastic over the place. They had regained their health and felt that it was the place Ponce de Leon was looking for when he made his search to find the fountain of youth. They said that Sebring had more sunshine than any other place in Florida. I made up my mind that I would never leave Florida before I visited this wonderful spot and see what it would do for my health."

Robert was very much impressed with Lady Bersford's report on Sebring and decided that it must be the ideal place for a tired business man to go and enjoy the sports and recoup his health. It took very little persuading on the part of Lady Bersford to get Robert to go to Sebring with her.

On March 27th, Lady Bersford and Robert Gordon arrived in Sebring, Florida. They found everything just as had been described by her friends. The climate

was ideal, fishing good.   Robert enjoyed the golf links
and his health began to improve a few days after he
arrived.   Time went by rapidly and a month was gone
before Robert knew it.   He had regained health so
rapidly that he felt he had indeed found the Fountain
of Youth.   Having been born on the farm, he loved
nature.   The beautiful scenery around Sebring delighted
him; made him forget his troubles and caused him to
be more hopeful of the future.   He dreamed of the day
when Marie might return to him, and he could take her
to Florida to see beautiful Silver Springs, then to
Sebring to see all the beautiful lakes and the Kissimmee
River.   If her health should ever be bad, that would
be the place to restore her and she would enjoy the
surrounding country as he had.

CHAPTER XXIV

IN the latter part of April, Robert decided that he must return to New York and take up his duties. He said good-bye to Lady Bersford. Was profuse in his thanks; assured her that he owed her a great debt of gratitude for the comforting messages that she had brought to him thru "Laughing Waters" and above all was under lasting obligation for the great kindness she had rendered in bringing him to Sebring where he had fully regained his health. She assured him that it was a real pleasure to her to have been of service and invited him to visit her estate in England on his next trip over.

As Robert started toward New York, his heart was light, his hopes were revived and he had greater faith than ever that Marie was alive and would in the not distant future return to him. When he arrived in New York he went direct to his office and laboratory. Walter and Edna greeted him with enthusiasm. Were happy to see him looking so well. Walter grabbed both of Robert's hands and said, "Old pal, I have never seen you looking so well. You must have found Ponce de Leon's fountain of eternal youth while you were in Florida." Robert replied, "I certainly did. Had some wonderful experience at Silver Springs, the most beau-tiful spot in Florida. It was there that I received information that made me very happy becuse it made me sure that Marie is alive and will return to me. Also while there I heard about the most wonderful health resort in the world at Sebring, Florida, where I went and indeed found the 'fountain of youth,' spending over a month there playing, fishing and boating. It is about the only place in Florida where you can get good water to drink without having it shipped in. The sunshine and climate are ideal. I began to get better the second day after I was there and gained strength every day. You should certainly go to Florida on a vacation next winter and spend your time at Sebring. If you ever get married, be sure to go to Silver Springs on your honeymoon for you will enjoy this beautiful spot and scenery. Take the trip down Silver River to the Ocklawaha, then down the beautiful St. Johns River. If you can make the trip next March or early April, you will find Nature at her best. You will forget all of your troubles, for Nature has so staged the scenery that it reminds you only of pleasant things and inspires hope and happiness in the future."

When Robert had finished telling about the beauties of Florida, Walter acted bashful and Edna looked rather sheepish. Then Walter said, "Robert, we have a big surprise for you. Edna and I are going to be married in June." "Well, this is quite a surprise," said Robert, "but I knew it would come sooner or later. You must have thought I guessed it when I talked about you going on a honeymoon. I congratulate you both and wish you all the happiness in the world. You are entitled to it and I know that you will be happy together."

The news of their coming marriage was not the only

good news they had. Walter and Edna had been working day and night for months on a great chemical discovery and had now succeeded in completing it. This
discovery was a perfectly harmless gas to be used in
war or for medical purposes. It would put people to
sleep and they would remain asleep for 7 days, with no
ill effects. It had always been Robert's desire to have
something to use in war which would not destroy human
lives and he was very much elated over Walter's discovery. Walter told him that he had already tested it
and that Edna had such confidence in him, she had taken
the gas, remained asleep for 7 days, and felt no ill
effects. Walter knew just exactly why it worked, because he was a great chemist and knew the natural law
behind the discovery. He told Robert that this must
be kept a secret until time of war when with the new
ship "Marie the Angel of Mercy," traveling 1000 miles
an hour, they could go from one city to another or from
one battlefield to another, release the gas and put everyone to sleep for 7 days. In the meantime, with "The
Demon of Death"—they could destroy the enemy's
bases and fortifications; would be able to make their
own peace terms with the enemy, and at the same time
obey the divine command of God "Thou shalt not kill."

Cotton had been advancing rapidly and Robert and
Walter were making money fast. Robert told Walter
and Edna that on June 9th, his birthday, he was going
to give them a big dinner and celebration before their
marriage. It was now time to declare a holiday and
have a real jubilee celebration after their great discoveries were completed, that it was but fitting to crown

the event with the marriage of Edna and Walter.   They were now in position to sit calmly by and wait for the great war in the air knowing that, with their secret discoveries, they were prepared to save the United States in time of war and at the same time without sacrificing too many human lives.

The birthday party was a great success.   Robert spared no expense in order to have everything of the best.   Before the dinner which was served in a private dining-room, Robert sprung a great surprise.   He arose and made the following speech: "Comrades and friends, we have traveled the path of life together.   Some of us have run the gauntlet of human emotions.   We have gone down to the depths of despair; have reached the heights of financial glory; have seen our greatest dreams realized.   God has been good to us.   Our great discoveries are now completed.   Fame and fortune have corwned our efforts.   You, Edna and Walter, are now to reach the heights of greatest bliss.   You are to have the satisfaction of being united in marriage, to continue your work together and do the greatest good for the greatest number.   You have been unselfish in your devotion to me and in your loyalty to your country.   The Bible says that where two or three are gathered together, there God will be to own and to bless.   Since God created the world, the Holy Trinity has been the greatest power and it is referred to many times in the Bible as Father, Son and Holy Ghost, and on this mundane sphere we know that happiness comes to husband, wife and child.   The Bible says that one cannot do much alone, that there is need of two together, and that a threefold cord is not easily broken.   Edna, your devotion to Walter has been his inspiration and has led him to the great discovery which will relieve suffering in the world. Your confidence in him in placing your life in his hands to test this great discovery, deserves great credit and no honor or reward is too great for you, but the honor that men can give or the world or your Government, are but empty and mean nothing to the heart of a loyal woman.   You are to have the greatest reward in Walter's love and this means more to you than any honors the world can give.   It will satisfy when the shouts of the hero-worshippers have died away.   When money, with all it can buy, has vanished and nothing else remains but the lovelight in Walter's eyes, you will find happiness."   Robert then presented a beautiful brooch made with the seal of Solomon, constructed with a double triangle, and set with three beautiful diamonds. In the center of the seal was a heart and in the center of the heart was a diamond.   He said, "Edna, I present this to you as your wedding gift.   It will be a symbol to you of how the three of us have worked together in love, loyalty and faith, to accomplish something for others thru unselfish devotion.   With the love of the one must come the love of the many.   One touch of Nature makes the whole world kin, and when once a woman's eyes have looked into a man's with understanding love, he need seek no farther for the philosopher's stone, because after that everything he touches will turn to gold.   This brooch and the diamonds are emblematic of your purity.   The diamonds are the most durable and beautiful of all precious stones.   They reflect all the beautiful colors of the rainbow which reveals God's covenant with man. That is why the diamonds are used as an engagement ring, but few there are who know and understand the real meaning and live in accordance with it. You will ever reflect the beauty of the diamonds. Your love for Walter, which is the love I am sure never changes, will remain fixed as the mountain ranges. Remember that the diamond has gone thru the greatest fire and heat and has emerged with all its strength and beauty. You must learn to go thru trials and tribulations, to help Walter in time of trouble and to emerge unscathed, reflecting love and beauty. Walter, I commend to your care and keeping, a jewel more precious than diamonds or rubies—a good woman. May your loyalty and devotion ever keep her as such."

The dinner was then served and Edna proved that, as an after-dinner speaker, she had some ability. She arose, drank a glass of pure water, pouring part of it on the floor and said, "Mr. Gordon, my vocabulary is now destitute of the poetic rhyme that would be necessary to bring into existence words to express to you my heartfelt thanks for the favor already in hand. I have been so over-generous in loving Walter that I feel that I've neglected to extend to you the friendship due to a man of such noble ideals. As I pour this pure water back to earth, I am following an ancient custom. Before they entered upon any solemn obligation, they washed their hands in pure water, touched their lips with pure water, to purify them and to seal the records of the past. They poured the pure water back to earth, in memory of the absent and dead. I pour this pure water back to earth that in the presence of the living we are not forgetting the absent one, and the greatest wish that I can have for you, Mr. Gordon, is that at a not distant date, Walter and I may have the great pleasure of joining Marie and yourself in an occasion like this. Words are idle now, they mean but little when the heart is touched. I accept your beautiful gift with all gratitude. It is my prayer that the day may come when you may have another brooch made with two hearts entwined, set with a single solitaire, emblematic of your faith and pure love for Marie. I pray for you the gifts of all the Gods, and may your prayers be answered as the prayers of Pygmalion were whose faith and love were so strong that the Grecian Gods turned a piece of cold marble into the living form of a beautiful woman. But, Robert, when Marie returns to you in all her beauty, I am sure that you will not act in the way that Pygmalion did, when he caused Galatea to pray to the Grecian Gods to turn her back to cold marble again. I am sure, yes, I know, that such devotion as yours will keep Marie always when she returns to you."

When Edna had finished, Walter arose and said, "Robert, there is nothing left for me to say, I thank you."

On the 24th of June, Walter and Edna were married. Robert suggested that for their honeymoon they go up thru Canada and see the beautiful scenery there, then go down thru California and in the Fall and Winter, take a second honeymoon trip to Florida and visit Silver Springs and Sebring. Robert's mind always drifted back to the beautiful places where he thought people in love would find harmony and could commune with Nature.

CHAPTER XXV

IN the Fall of 1929, Robert and Walter made a large amount of money in cotton and wheat. Robert was unusually happy. Altho over three years had passed without any direct news of Marie he was sure she was alive; felt that the time was not long to wait before she would reappear. The war clouds had begun to appear as Robert had predicted. Spain and Japan were threatening the United States. Controversies over airplane airports arose. Japan had forbidden the United States commercial ships to land on her soil. Diplomatic relations were not smoothing affairs out and Robert knew that war was inevitable. Spain had made rapid progress with airplanes and was anxious to try her power against the United States. The United States Government was waking up to the fact of their need of a greater air fleet and the Air Department was making some great progress. Robert knew they were working on secret plans and knew that he had something that could be used successfully at the right time. He was spending money lavishly and working to improve on his Ezekiel plane. He was keeping everything secret, sending out plans to different manufacturers and having the parts made, Walter and himself secretly putting the machine together. Robert had made a large amount of money buying oil stocks. A big bull campaign in oil stocks had been brought about by the decreasing oil supply. The Government realizing the increased demand for gasoline on account of the large amount of airplanes used, knew that in time of war their success would depend upon the supply of oil and gas, so a decree was passed conserving the oil resources. There was still a big foreign demand for oil and gasoline as war in Europe was still going on. Affairs in England were in a bad state and revolution was threatened.

APRIL, 1930

Japan declared war on the United States and Spain joined forces with her. They secured the aid of Mexico and established an air base there. The United States was unprepared for war as they had not kept up the programme of building a sufficient air fleet to protect the country against invasion by such a large fleet as commanded by Japan and Spain. There was a hasty call by the Government for volunteers to the Aviation Corps. Robert Gordon and Walter Kennelworth hastened to Washington, tendered their services to the Government and joined the Aviation Corps. They were made Lieutenants and ordered immediately to San Antonio, Texas, where the Southern Aviation Division had its headquarters. Robert offered the benefit of his experience to the officials, but older and wiser heads refused to listen to his advice because they thought he was too young. At that time they knew nothing about his long years of secret work and his great inventions, but they soon learned the value of his discovery and patent which he had sold to Japan,—the muffler which made the airplane silent.

The United States Government fearing that Japan would make the first attack on the Pacific Coast either around Los Angeles or San Francisco, rushed the battle fleet to the Pacific. This proved to be one of the greatest mistakes of the war. As soon as the battleships cruised into the Pacific, Japan attacked from the air with their noiseless airplanes and began dropping deadly bombs from great heights. The anti-aircraft guns from the decks of the battleships were powerless to reach the bombing planes at such great heights. Defeat was swift and severe and only a few of the battleships escaped complete destruction from the first attack. The United States Officers had found that the Japanese planes could rise more than twice the altitude of the United States planes. They knew that Japan had some invention that was superior to ours which enabled them to reach such great heights that their airships were practically immune from attack. This placed the United States at a great disadvantage as they were unable to protect the coast cities from being destroyed by bombs from the Japanese planes.

A council of war was held. The commanding officers were called together. The President hastily summoned the Cabinet. There was no minimizing the danger for everyone knew that the ingenuity of Japan had designed a superior fighting plane; that this was to be a war in the air and that all old methods and weapons of war were obsolete; that the United States must move quick and fast to prevent destruction of the Pacific Coast cities.

They decided to confiscate the large manufacturing plants and start them on making new inventions and the manufacture of airplanes. Central Steel was confiscated; also Major Motors and Major Electric Co. The war council decided that they should scatter their air forces from Brownsville, Texas, up to El Paso to protect the Rio Grande from attack thru Mexico; that the battle line should extend up the Colorado River on across to Portland and Seattle. The land forces were all rushed to the Coast, forming a battle line from Brownsville, Texas, across to the Northwest to Seattle. It was decided that this line should be held with reserve forces to be sent to support a second line of defense running from San Diego up the Coast to Portland, to protect inland invasion by the foe in case they were successful in capturing any of the coast cities. People in Los Angeles and San Francisco were in a state of turmoil. Thousands were leaving every day by train and airplane, going to the Grand Canyon where there were no cities and they hoped they would be safe from attacks. Others went to the central and eastern parts of the United States because they feared attacks any day.

Japan was quick to follow up her victory gained on the water by attacking Los Angeles from the air in the middle of May. Here again the great value of the silent motor was proved and the height to which the Japanese plane could rise. As the enemy stole over the city in the silence of the night, not a sound could be heard from their motors at the great heights which they were sailing. Bombs began to fall in the business section and the skyscrapers crumbled to pieces. Every street light was ordered out, leaving the city in total darkness. The people were aroused at the first noise of exploding bombs and rushed out to find the city in darkness. This caused a panic. Army officers tried to quiet the people and keep them in their homes because they realized the danger if they rushed out into the streets where the bombs were falling. Powerful searchlights were sweeping the sky in an effort to locate the invading planes. Then the giant aircraft guns were trained on the enemy, but the distance was so great and the planes moving so swiftly, that they were unable to do much damage. They only succeeded in bringing down three of the bombing planes. The United States scouting planes were sent out immediately, followed by the fighting planes carrying 6-inch guns. They found that the Japanese planes were dropping bombs from a height of 60,000 to 80,000 feet and the United States planes were unable to rise high enough to attack them.

The battle waged thruout the night and when the sun rose the next morning, the beautiful city of Los Angeles was in ruins. Thousands of people had been killed and the most of the important buildings had been destroyed. The people of Los Angeles were more excited than they had ever been during earthquakes. The destruction and loss of life were so great that everyone forgot all about their property and money and only thought of saving their lives and protecting their loved ones. The commanding officers held a hasty conference, realizing the great damage the enemy had done and the small damage they had been able to inflict upon them and knowing that the enemy would follow this attack by more attacks it was decided that to force the people to remain meant certain death and a destruction of the balance of the valuable property, so the only thing to do was to move the people out as fast as possible and surrender the city. After the commanders had held this council, news of their decision was conveyed to the subordinate officers.

Lieutenant Gordon's heart was broken when he realized that the beautiful city of Los Angeles must be either surrendered or destroyed, yet he knew that unless the Government quickly made some new and wonderful inventions, many more defeats were in store. When Captain George Cooper who was in command of Lieutenant Gordon's company, received orders that no move was to be made and no scouts to be sent out until further instructions, he called Lieutenants Gordon and Kennelworth and conveyed to them the orders. Lieutenant Gordon was desperate. He wanted to do something to help save the situation, but to offer his advice to his superior officers was futile. Finally, he decided to disobey orders and go out on a scouting expedition alone and see what he could find out. He thought he might locate a Japanese base, as he believed they had a mother ship somewhere near from which they were sending out the bombing planes. He was flying very low as he crossed the line below San Diego. All at once a Japanese plane was coming straight toward him. He immediately turned his plane and rushed back across the line followed closely by the enemy who was gaining on him rapidly. Lieutenant Gordon whirled his plane around quickly and charged the Japanese plane. The fight lasted for several minutes.

After Lieutenant Gordon had been gone some time and failed to return Lieutenant Kennelworth knowing that he had disobeyed orders and gone out with his plane decided that some harm might have come to him and that he too must disobey orders and go to his rescue. He jumped into a fast plane and sailed out, going direct toward San Diego. He soon sighted the two planes in combat and just before he reached the scene, they went down together. His heart sank within him. He knew it was his old friend Robert and feared for the worst. Landing along the side of the wreck he found that the Japanese aviator had been killed. Robert's leg had been broken; otherwise he was uninjured. He quickly hauled him aboard his own plane and started back for headquarters and was just in time as other Japanese planes were approaching and followed him close into Los Angeles. Lieutenant Gordon was confined to the hospital three or four weeks before his leg healed and he fully recovered. He was given a severe reprimand for disobeying orders but because he had brought down an enemy plane the Government made him a Captain for this bravery and also promoted Lieutenant Kennelworth, his chum, to the same rank.

In the meantime, the people had been moved away from Los Angeles as fast as possible. There had been several minor attacks by the enemy and more buildings had been destroyed and only a few of the enemy's planes had been brought down. The situation was desperate. People were frantic. The United States was hopelessly outnumbered by the Spanish and Japanese air forces. England was threatening to join forces with Japan and Spain. An attack on San Francisco was expected at any hour. People wanted to get away and move east into the mountains for protection, but the Government had notified everyone to remain. The fact that the foreign planes were noiseless put the United States at a great disadvantage. Robert and Walter were using their secret radio to communicate with each other. They had offered this invention to the Government and it had been accepted. This was a great help as the Japanese were unable to intercept their code messages or take any message from the air because there were none.

The United States Army officers knew that they must fight for time to get some new inventions ready to combat the enemy. On June 14th, Los Angeles was surrendered. White flags were run up all over the city as a signal for the enemy planes to stop attacking. The plan was to send no message to the enemy headquarters in Mexico but to wait and see what action they would take or what terms they would offer to make. General Pearson of the Aviation Corps, General Johnson of the Cavalry, Admiral Dawson of the Navy and General Marshall of the Infantry held a council to decide the next and wisest move to make. A plan was discussed for crossing the Rio Grande into Mexico with land troops and making an attempt to capture the supply base of the enemy. General Pearson said that the days of old tactics and war had changed, that the enemy evidently intended to make this a war in the air and that they would attack troops from the air. To send an army into the mountains of Mexico would not only mean the loss of thousands of lives, which would prove useless, but that part of the air force would have to be sent into Mexico to protect the army and this would weaken the coast patrol and give the enemy a chance to make an air attack on other coast cities. Admiral Dawson said that in the weakened condition of the Navy, since the disaster from the first attack by the Japanese planes, it would be foolhardy to attempt any aggressive campaign by the Navy, that what ships they had were now scattered along the Southern, Eastern and Western shores for protection and to concentrate them at one point would only weaken other joints from which they would have to be withdrawn. General Marshall was of the opinion that the best plan was not to attack, but let the enemy make the first move every time and try to find some way to protect the coast cities, that what we needed was time to get better equipped with sufficient airplanes to cope with the enemy's superior air force. So it was finally decided that the wisest course to pursue was a waiting attitude.

There was a panic in Wall Street when the news came of the surrender of Los Angeles. Edna had been left in charge of the office in New York and thru the secret Pocket Radio, kept in communication with Waltetr and Robert. She was conducting a campaign in the stock market for them and had made a fortune on the short side of the market. Business was bad, and the whole country was in a state of turmoil.

After the white flags were floated over the ruins of Los Angeles, days went by and there were no more attacks by the enemy, nor was any word received from enemy headquarters. The American patrol planes around Los Angeles reported occasionally seeing the enemy planes scouting over the city at great heights, evidently taking observation as to what was going on. This mysterious action on the part of the enemy was a source of worry to the commanding officers of the United States. The people all over the country were in a state of anxiety, wondering where the enemy would strike next. The Infantry and Cavalry were restlessly waiting orders to go into action along the Rio Grande.

On the night of August 1st, the enemy planes crossed the Rio Grande and dropped bombs all along from Brownsville to El Paso, destroying property and killing more than a hundred thousand men among the Infantry and Cavalry. The enemy planes were again flying very high. The anti-craft guns and the attack by our planes did very little damage, only bringing down five of the enemy planes along the entire lines, while more than 200 of the American airplanes were destroyed by bombs dropping on them from above. General Marshall in his report to General Pearson next day said: "Hell turned loose in the sky last night from Brownsville to El Paso. Our loss was terrific and the enemy's loss was very small. There is but one hope and that is to get more and better airplanes. We must get planes that will rise to a height where they can reach the enemy and make the fight in the air."

Captain Robert Gordon was still stationed near Los Angeles and when news came of the terrible loss of life along the Rio Grande, his mind turned to "Marie the

Angel of Mercy,"—his great plane secretly stored away in the Adirondack Mountains for use in just such an emergency as this. He knew what the "Demon of Death" could do and the sleeping gas invented by Captain Kennelworth. He thought of going to General Pearson, telling him of his discoveries and offering them to the United States to put into immediate use, but after meditating over the matter decided that they would only call him a fool and refuse to listen to him as they had before, because he was too young. However, he asked General Pearson for orders to permit him to go on a scouting expedition over Mexico and up and down the Rio Grande to see if he could learn anything of value.

On the morning of August 3rd, Captain Robert Gordon traveled across Arizona and New Mexico and as he neared El Paso saw the largest airship that he had ever seen before slowly drifting over El Paso. It was a giant plane and Robert knew that it was either a mother ship or one of the enemy's great bombing planes which had been so high that he had never been able to see them before. He began circling it at a great distance, watching to see what this monster of the air was going to do. Finally, it slowed down and came to a complete standstill. He saw that it could anchor in the air and knew that the enemy had another discovery that would beat what the Americans had. Waiting for awhile, he saw what seemed to be an observation platform emerge from the side of the plane. An officer appeared on it with some instruments. Captain Gordon thought that they were either taking photographs or making observations over El Paso for some purpose. Fortunately, he had started out on a bombing plane and had plenty of bombs on board. Decided that he had but one life to give for his country and that he would rise as high as he could, sail swiftly over this monster and drop his bombs. When he got as close over it as he could gauge, he released the automatic control and started dropping bombs one after another. The first bomb made a hit and struck the ship near the middle, which was lucky, tearing a terrific hole in it. He knew from the way it acted that it was badly disabled. Now was the time to get in his effective work. Dropping lower, he let go more bombs, this time striking the giant ship both in the front and rear. It started to fall rapidly and he followed it down and got close enough to see that there were still men on board alive so he let go more bombs and in a few minutes there was nothing but a wreck of the greatest dreadnought of death which had ever floated over American soil.

Before venturing to land Captain Gordon ascended to a great height, circled the sky to see if there were any more enemy ships in sight which might endanger his life. Finding the air clear, he immediately radioed the news with his Pocket-Radio to Captain Kennelworth who was then stationed at San Diego. The news was quickly flashed to General Pearson's headquarters. On examination they found that the giant ship was a mother ship more than 600 feet long, bearing the name of "Tokyo J-1" and that it carried 25 bombing planes of the most modern type with collapsible wings and equipped with powerful searchlights carrying bombs and poisonous gases. It was estimated that more than 100 officers and aviators were aboard the airship when it fell. All were killed but two. They were badly wounded with broken limbs and were taken prisoners. There were found to be three of the enemy's planes that were not damaged badly. Captain Gordon and Captain Kennelworth tested these planes after they were put back in working order and found that they were high altitude planes and could rise higher than any of the planes used by the United States. This was a great victory because it would enable the American inventors to find out how these planes were built and they could also be used against the enemy.

News of this great victory was sent to the President of the United States. He ordered General Pearson to decorate Captain Gordon with the Cross of Aviation and convey to him the gratitude of the people of the United States and the President's sincere personal appreciation. The afternoon newspapers in every large city in the United States carried in big headlines "GIANT MOTHER SHIP CAPTURED BY DARING YOUNG AVIATOR, CAPTAIN ROBERT GORDON." The people thruout the United States breathed a sigh of relief; felt that the tide was at last turning and that now some way would be found to destroy more of the enemy's giant ships.

When General Pearson called Captain Gordon before him, he was very modest and meek because he remembered the severe reprimand before when he disobeyed orders and brought down the Japanes plane near San Diego. This time he had acted on instructions from General Pearson and was very happy to have rendered a great service to his country. As the General read the message from the President, tears came into his eyes. He thanked his commanding officer and said that he hoped he might have many more opportunities to render service to his beloved country. At that time his thoughts turned to Marie and he wondered where she might be and if she knew what was happening. He was especially happy because he had brought this enemy ship down in the State in which he was born and that State of which he was very proud. Captain Kennelworth came to congratulate him and said: "Robert, old pal, I am very proud of you and your great achievement. The Lone Star State of Texas which was distinguished by its brave sons at the Battle of the Alamo, has again been distinguished by one of her favorite sons, and Mexico as well as Spain and Japan will be made to realize that the Texans never surrender."

After the night attack and the great destruction along the Rio Grande, the American forces waited anxiously and in peril for another attack. Days went by without any sign from the enemy. Los Angeles had not been molested and the mystery was deepening as to what were the enemy's plans and the next move they would make. General Pearson had ordered one of the planes from the "Tokyo J-1" sent to the Major Electric Company in the East where they could experiment with it and make some planes like it or better ones. He gave one of the planes to Captain Gordon and the other to Captain Kennelworth to be put into service. Captain Gordon asked that they be permitted to go into Mexico, locate the enemy's headquarters and try to destroy more of their ships, but the General refused to grant this request, saying that he would not risk the lives of such valuable men or risk losing the ships which might prove very valuable when the enemy again made an attack.

CHAPTER XXVI

September, 1930

AFTER long days of anxious waiting, with the people nervous and excited, came the attack on San Francisco. The enemy planes attacked from the West, the South and the North, slipping in silently in large numbers. Poisoned gas was turned loose, bombs were dropped all over the city and most of the important business and Government buildings were destroyed. The destruction was the greatest in history, much greater than the earthquake in 1906. Loss of life was terrific. General Pearson ordered Captain Gordon and Kennelworth to lead the defense of the city, using the Japanese planes which had been taken from the wreck of the "Tokyo J-1." As soon as they got in high altitude over San Francisco, they could see that this was a gigantic attack. Thousands of airplanes were circling the air from every direction. It was evident that the enemy intended to destroy San Francisco very quickly. Captain Gordon and Captain Kennelworth were able to keep in communication thru their Pocket Radio. They agreed that one of them should attack the enemy planes approaching from the North and the other, the planes approaching from the South and West, going as high as they could and if possible getting above the enemy planes and dropping bombs on them. When

Captain Gordon got high in the air, he saw another mother ship anchored and with the smaller planes taking off from it. He sailed over and let loose his bombs and destroyed this ship. Other ships were coming from every direction by the thousands. He sailed over them letting loose his bombs cautiously.

Captain Kennelworth also encountered planes by the thousands coming across from the West and succeeded in bringing down numbers of them. Finally, the enemy planes turned on him and when he saw that escape seemed almost impossible, decided to try to race back to headquarters. The enemy planes were firing on him. One wing of his plane was damaged, then a propeller was broken and as his plane was crashing to the earth, he felt that he was sure to lose his life; tried to steer the best he could and finally, seeing that he was going to land on a smooth spot where there were no trees or buildings, he crawled out on top of one of the wings. A few minutes after the crash he regained consciousness, finding himself uninjured with only a few minor scratches. Fortunately he was near one of the army bases and made his way quickly there. He could see to the West that San Francisco was in flames and knew that the destruction was complete. His first thought was what had happened to his old pal, Robert Gordon. Feeling in his pocket and finding his radio safe, he sent the distress signal which they had always used, asking "Are you alive and where are you?" Minutes went by and no reply. He was heartsick and feared that Robert had lost his life. He slowly made his way to headquarters and reported what had happened.

Captain Gordon finally exhausted his bombs, but he estimated that he had brought down several hundred of the enemy planes because he had sailed over them where they were flying by the hundreds in wedge formations, each division being followed by a giant supply ship which could anchor high up in the air and supply more bombs when the bombing planes exhausted their supply and returned for more. Robert thought, "this is just what our Government needs. If there were only a supply ship in the air now where I could go and get more bombs, I could bring down hundreds more of the enemy's planes." He decided to make his way back to the base or headquarters as he was powerless without bombs, but his decision was too late. The enemy planes had located him and were coming straight toward him. He speeded up and tried to make his way to safety, fearing that any minute the enemy would fire on him or drop a bomb on his plane, but the Japanese had discovered that he was flying one of their own planes and they thought he was one of their own aviators and had no intention of harming him. When they got close enough to see that the plane was piloted by an American aviator, they flew close beside him, signaled him to follow them, one plane leading and two others falling in beside him. There was nothing else to do and he was glad of a chance to save his life. They led him up, up, up, thousands of feet in the air, finally reached a giant plane anchored, where they landed, taking Captain Gordon a prisoner.

As soon as they had landed with him, his mind went back to the days of his youth, when he had built his first bicycle to ride on the water, and when he had read the Bible and talked about the wars to come and made his plans for the great airship. He recalled the dream his mother had which greatly disturbed her. She told him she dreamed that she saw San Francisco destroyed by some terrible machine and that one of her sons had nearly lost his life there. He thought of how his mother had told him about his oldest brother losing his life in the San Francisco earthquake and he wondered if now he was to lose his life there, because he felt that the Japs were very treacherous and would probably not keep him a prisoner but would take his life. He prayed for his dear old mother and prayed for Marie that she might be safe and her life be spared, no matter what his fate might be.

Through all this excitement, for the first time he thought of his Pocket-Radio. Before he could get it out of his pocket, he received the S. O. S. signal from Walter and answered, telling him what had happened and where he was.

Ever since the first battle of Los Angeles, the United States officers had felt certain that an attack would come upon San Francisco and had prepared for it the best way possible. They had concentrated a greater portion of their best airplanes there and had thrown them into the fight by the thousands and they had gone down in large numbers, not only being outnumbered by the enemy planes but being unable to follow the enemy planes high enough to destroy them. When reports were made the following morning, more than three thousand of this country's airplanes had been lost.

The loss of life in San Francisco was appalling. Almost half of the population had been wiped out. Most of the valuable buildings had been destroyed. All the ships anchored in the harbor were blown to pieces. A poisonous gas which American chemists had never seen or heard of before had been distributed all over San Francisco and the people who were left were sick and dying by the thousands. The waters in the bay had been poisoned and the fish were dying from this deadly gas. It was indeed a time of trouble such as the world has never known, as spoken of by St. John in the Book of Revelation.

The capture of Captain Gordon and the loss of both of the Japanese airplanes which had been captured at the destruction of the "Tokyo J-1" was a disheartening blow, because Captain Kennelworth had reported how effectively he had worked over the enemy planes and how many he had destroyed. He was sure that Captain Gordon had destroyed many of their planes. When a survey was made of the city it was found that several hundred of the enemy's planes had been brought down. Most of this was attributed to the work done by Captain Gordon and Kennelworth with the high altitude foreign planes. When all reports were in, the commanders of the United States armies got together for a conference. This disaster in such a short time was bewildering and it required quick decision as to the next move. They were at a loss to figure out what the enemy's next move would be, remembering that after Los Angeles had been surrendered and the white flag had floated over it, it had never been molested.

Knowing that another attack would finish the remains of San Francisco, they decided to surrender it, and again the white flag was raised over all the remaining buildings. When General Pearson saw these instructions being carried out, he was overcome with emotion. Tears were flowing down his cheeks and he exclaimed: "My God, my God, is the land of liberty to be destroyed? Is there no way to prevent this deadly destruction?"

As soon as the Japanese had captured Captain Gordon they knew who he was. He was the man who had sold them the great silent muffler. They brought him to headquarters in Mexico where he was questioned as to what other inventions he had. He told them that the only invention he had of value was the secret radio, with which he could send communications without any sound in the air and without anyone intercepting the messages, but made no mention of the other discoveries that he had which he knew could be used in time of emergency and of which he had never told the United States Government officials. The Japanese offered Robert his freedom and a large amount of money if he would sell them this invention. After communicating secretly and silently with Walter, Robert had him tell the commanding General about the proposition the Japanese had offered him and asked for instructions as to what he should do. Their reply was to remain prisoner and not give up any of his secrets to the enemy, because the situation was bad enough at the best. But Robert knew that his services would be of greater value to his Government and that it was bad judgment for him to remain a prisoner. He felt that he could make another invention for communications which would outwit the Japs, so he decided on his own responsibility to give up the secret radio, and after they tested it, they gave him his freedom and conveyed him safely out of the enemy lines. Robert returned to headquarters near San Francisco and reported to Colonel Davis just what he had done. He was immediately sent before General Pearson who was then in command of the United States Air forces. General Pearson after hearing the story and considering Robert's splendid record, decided that clemency should be extended to him but, before doing so, decided to communicate with the President of the United States and await his decision and instructions. A meeting of the Cabinet was called and they voted that Captain Gordon was a traitor to his country, but decided that he should not be court-martialed and shot, but dishonored. Orders were sent that his uniform be torn from him and that he be held a prisoner. This was the greatest blow to Robert that had ever befallen him since the loss of Marie, but he had faith in God. He knew that he had done right and what was for the best, just as the Creator of the universe does all things well and for the best. He read his Bible that night while in prison and was consoled by reading Job, where he said, "Lord, Lord, I'll wait until my change comes." Robert knew that the time would come when he would be able to demonstrate to his Government that his judgment was right and that he was acting for the best. His heart and soul were with his country and he would sacrifice time and money to be prepared to protect his Government. He asked to be allowed to have a conference with

Walter, which was granted. Told Walter to say nothing about his sleeping gas discovery or the "Demon of Death,"—the great light ray destroyer which they could use, and to tell nothing of the great ship "Marie the Angel of Mercy," which they had safely stored away in the Adirondack Mountains. That when the Government came to realize the need of great help and faced defeat, he would then demonstrate the inventions that he had to save the country.

General Pearson was very much interested in Gordon's case. He remembered the great feat of bringing down the "Tokyo J-1" and believed that Robert was a genius and a valuable man to the Government. If the officials had listened to Robert and taken the discovery he had offered them, probably the defeat in San Francisco would never have happened. He did not blame Robert for selling his invention to Japan in peace time, nor did he condemn him for turning over his secret Pocket Radio to the Japanese to secure his freedom. Believed he was loyal to his country and acted as he thought best and had not done it for a selfish motive. The General decided to visit Robert at the prison. After holding a conference with him, ordered him removed and brought to headquarters where he could keep him under his personal supervision. Robert confided to General Pearson that if he could secure his release, and let him return to his laboratory in New York, he could very quickly complete another invention to enable the United States forces to communicate secret orders from place to place, which the enemy could not understand or use. He told him that he had an invention partly completed which when placed a certain distance from an airplane would prevent any communication by his secret radio and that with this it would make the secret radio which he turned over to Japan, absolutely useless. General Pearson believed his story and had faith in him so communicated with the President of the United States and obtained permission to send Robert Gordon to his New York laboratory. The General realized that the situation was much worse than the newspapers were letting the public know. The Government was suppressing their weakened condition. General Pearson knew that with help from England or any other foreign country, it would be easy for the enemy to take New Orleans, Chicago and then sweep down on Washington and New York. The liberty of the United States now hung in a balance and unless something was done, and done quickly, their cause would be lost.

General Pearson wrote to the President that there was no denying the fact that the situation was critical and that the enemy had something up their sleeve and that unless every effort was made to forestall their move, he feared a repetition of the terrible disaster at San Francisco. He sent the record of Robert Gordon. Said that while he was a young man, he was one of the bravest aviators that he had ever known; that he was not only bright but brilliant. He believed he was a genius. That he had had a long talk with him and that Gordon had asked to be released and permitted to return to his laboratory in New York where he believed he could complete a valuable invention which would prove a great help to the country. The General recommended that Gordon be released and permitted to return to New York and given a chance. Said that this was the age of the young men because they were progressive and up to the times.

The President wrote General Pearson to use his own judgment and send Gordon to New York if he thought best. General Pearson gave orders that Robert Gordon be brought to him. He communicated the good news, gave him a passport and told him to proceed immediately to New York and work just as rapidly as possible to perfect any kind of invention that would help defeat the enemy's plans.

CHAPTER XXVII

WHEN Robert arrived in New York, Edna told him about the great fortune which she had made on the short side of the market and how when she received the good news by secret radio of his capture of the "Tokyo J-1" she calculated that as soon as it was generally known, it would restore confidence and stocks would have a big rally. She hastily covered all the short contracts and bought stocks for long account. The following afternoon when the big headlines announced the capture of the Tokyo, traders all rushed to buy and the market advanced rapidly. She said "Mr. Gordon, do you know the market is following the forecast which you mapped out in 1927?" He said, "I have been so worried over the war and my dishonor that I haven't had time to think about making money. If General Pearson hadn't proved to be a good friend, I would still be in prison. Now I must use some of my inventions to help my country and prove to them that I did act for the best and that I am loyal." Edna asked if he thought there was any hope of the terrible war ending soon. "No," he replied, "it will get worse in 1931 when many other nations will join against us. The end will not come until the Summer or Fall of 1932." "That is dreadful," she said, "if it lasts that long, they will destroy every large city in the United States unless something is done to beat them."

In the latter part of October, 1930, Robert returned
to Denver, Colorado, where General Pearson had moved
the aviation headquarters, and was moving heaven and
earth to prevent the advance of the enemy toward the
East. Many people on the coast had become frightened
and moved to Denver for protection. Robert brought
the new invention which he called the "Radio Annulifier." The Spaniards and Japanese were making use
of Robert's secret radio, which was one of the most
valuable discoveries up to that time. The Annulifier
was now placed on scouting airplanes and they were
sent out. They found that it would work a distance of
several hundred miles. This disorganized the enemy
forces because they did not understand what had gone
wrong with the secret mechanism of the Pocket-Radio
with which they were able to transmit orders without
sound or fear of detection. They had to resort to the
old method of using radios and wireless. Robert had
invented a new machine to record either sound or communications by light waves. He soon secured the plans
of the enemy and reported to General Pearson, who was
still in command for the Aviation Corps, that the enemy
was planning to attack from the Gulf of Mexico, follow
up the Mississippi River, take New Orleans and at the
same time make a joint attack across the Great Lakes,
cutting off the Government's forces and the wing which
was holding across from Denver, Colorado to Canada on
the North and the border of Texas on the Southwestern
side. When General Pearson received this disappointing news, he realized that the situation was desperate.
He communicated with the President of the United

States, who immediately called the Cabinet together. All the Army Officers were called in conference to discuss plans as to the best thing to do to forestall the attack. They were forced to admit the painful truth that the fleet of airplanes was not sufficient to withdraw enough forces from the Western line to send to the North and South, to protect Chicago and the Mississippi valley. General Pearson made plain to the War Council the great value of Robert Gordon and suggested that he be restored to his former rank for what he had already done. They agreed with him and Robert Gordon was made Colonel in the early part of November, 1930. Walter Kennelworth, for his great services in working with Robert, was also promoted to Colonel.

When Colonel Gordon informed General Pearson that Mrs. Kennelworth was his sole secret aid in completing the Annulifier which had helped him to get the enemy's plans, this news was conveyed by the General to the President of the United States who ordered Mrs. Kennelworth to report immediately at headquarters in Washington. The President thanked her personally for the great service she had rendered the country and told her that she was the greatest woman since Molly Pitcher, who had taken her husband's place at the cannon. He conferred upon her the title of Captain of Inventions and ordered her to return to her laboratories in New York and continue her scientific work. This brought great rejoicing to Colonel Gordon and Colonel Kennelworth and they redoubled their efforts to do everything to help save the country, but they were not in the War Council and had nothing to say in regard to the plans of protection or attack.

Complications came thick and fast, the enemy was landing more planes in Mexico, bringing up reinforcements. They moved part of their army from San Francisco north, and in December, 1930, after a short engagement, captured Seattle and Portland. The War Council knew that this left the enemy in command of the entire Pacific Coast as most all of the smaller towns had been abandoned because they feared destruction and the next attack would probably be either on the South or the East. They were satisfied that they would probably attack from the Gulf of Mexico and try to get a good hold on the Southeastern part of the United States and, if successful, would then attack from Canada and the Great Lakes. The United States Government was making airplanes as fast as possible, but they were so far behind and lacked trained men to man them, that the situation was very tense and the Government officials freely expressed their anxiety. People in the East were excited and scared. They feared an attack upon the defenseless cities at any time and that the destruction of Los Angelss, San Francisco, Portland and Seattle might be repeated. The crushing blows that the Government had received in the loss of the Pacific Coast had weakened the morale of the people and they had lost confidence in the Government and its officials. The fact that the enemy had made no attempt to set a fixed ransom on any of the cities captured showed that they were looking for something bigger before trying to enforce their demands upon the United States. The

Government officials knew that the Japanese would demand California or the greater part of the Pacific Coast territory. They were hoping that further attacks could be staved off until they were better prepared to meet them. Army officials, as usual, thought they were handling everything for the best and paid no attention to the counsel of men who might be able to help.

Colonel Kennelworth confided to some of the Generals that Colonel Gordon and himself had some great discoveries which, when and if completed would beat the enemy, but they paid little attention to his statements, and after Walter and Robert had a conference, they decided to keep quiet and say nothing further about them until the time when the Government was in desperation and would listen to reason.

1931

After months of waiting and only a few scouting expeditions on the part of the enemy, a sudden attack occurred in March. A large fleet of airplanes sailed up the Mississippi River and attacked New Orleans. Destruction was swift and severe. The United States started to withdraw forces from across the Central part and from Texas, but they soon realized that somewhere out in the Atlantic Ocean or in the Gulf of Mexico, there was a secret base of supplies and they suspected that England had already joined forces with the enemy. The enemy's planes were so superior, their poisonous gas and bombs so effective that New Orleans fell within three days. The alarm spread so fast over the United States that people were panic-stricken.   There was a panic in Wall Street. Stocks crashed rapidly and Captain Edna Kennelworth was again on the short side and had made a large amount of money for the firm of Gordon & Kennelworth.

After the terrible destruction of New Orleans, it was again decided to float the white flag over the city, as had been done in Los Angeles, San Francisco, Portland and Seattle. People were badly frightened; were leaving their homes and property and going in every direction, not knowing which was the best way to go to save their lives. Many of the old darkies went to the swamps, hid out until they were starving to death, feeling that they were safer away from any of the cities or buildings. The most mystifying thing to the Government officials was that up to this time when the enemy had succeeded in destroying a city, they had never returned or attempted to do any more damage after the white flag floated over it. They knew that the enemy had several bases in Mexico and were at a loss to understand why more attacks had not been made on the towns along the border of Texas; but now that they had started up the Mississippi River, it was plain that they were bent on destroying only the largest cities in the country and that, eventually, they would make demands for large amounts of indemnity and territory. Why no demands had been made up to this time and why the enemy had not tried to land troops and take charge was hard to understand. The wiser heads among the Government officials felt that the enemy wanted to sufficiently frighten the people all over the United States and destroy enough life and property that when they did make a demand, that no matter how unreasonable, the United States would be forced to accept. It was thought that there was some secret treaty between Spain, Japan, Mexico and other foreign countries, and that they had started their campaign in the South and would later attack the Eastern Coast because they knew that they would get help from other countries if it was required.

After the fall of New Orleans, the enemy continued their march up the Mississippi valley. One by one important cities were bombed. Natchez, Vicksburg, then Memphis fell under the fire of the enemy. The devastation was the greatest ever known. Not only were the buildings destroyed by bombs, but fire and poisoned gases were used. Hundreds of thousands of people lost their lives. People were so terrified that they wanted to flee to the mountains and forests and get away from all the towns. The march up the Mississippi thus far had cost the Government the loss of thousands of their best airplanes. The enemy's loss was very small. On account of flying at such great heights, it was hard to reach them with the anti-aircraft guns or the army planes.

The United States army officers knew that the next objective would be St. Louis, and that if St. Louis were captured, they would probably attack Chicago, close the lines, prepare to attack the Eastern Coast and try to take Washington and New York. Colonel Gordon and Colonel Kennelworth were doing great work, but were fighting against terrific odds. They had to take orders from their superior officers, and were not able to act on their own initiative. Colonel Gordon was permitted to sit in at a conference of the War Council in April, 1931, but after listening to his plans, they refused to accept them; at the same time they knew the country needed help because further attacks were imminent, and the enemy was pushing on to victory and gaining more help all the time. Some of Colonel Gordon's plans were to ask France to come to our aid in view of the fact they had helped us in the Revolution of 1812 and that we had gone to their rescue in the Great War in 1917 showing our appreciation for the services rendered by Lafayette. He also wanted to ask Canada to join us and protect the Northern border of the United States.

After the first battle of New Orleans, the United States transferred all the planes they could spare for patrol of the Eastern and Southern coasts along the Atlantic and Gulf of Mexico. Commercial and passenger airplanes were crossing daily to and from Europe. One foggy night in the month of April, scouting planes flying as high as they could, sighted a large fleet of airships flying toward Savannah, Georgia. They decided that they were enemy planes making for Savannah, to attack it. Commander Rooker in charge ordered his company to sail over the fleet and start dropping bombs. They were quickly destroyed, all falling into the ocean. When our planes descended to see how many had been destroyed and what country they were from, they found that they were not enemy planes at all, but were commercial planes from England, Germany, Austria and Italy. This complicated matters more and diplomatic communications failed to smooth out the difficulties. England refused to accept an explanation or apology and all the other countries took sides with her. Our Cabinet officers held a conference. They decided that England and the other countries, knowing our weakened condition, had intended to join the enemy all along and were only waiting for an excuse, but they now knew that with all these countries against them, without some aid or new discovery, the cause was lost. General Pearson said "Colonel Gordon was right. We should have asked the help of France and Canada long before this. We must now seek aid from any country that is friendly to us. We went to the rescue of the Allies in the darkest days of the World War and surely some of them will stand by us in this, our greatest hour of need."

In May, 1931, England, Germany, Italy and Austria joined forces against the United States. The wealth of the United States had caused so much jealousy that it now began to look as tho Uncle Sam were a lone eagle against the world. England began to land her forces and establish a base in Canada, and the War Council, knowing that England would attack the Eastern Coast, made all preparations to try to protect the Northern border and the Eastern Coast, withdrawing forces from other strategic points to try to protect the North and the Eastern part of the United States.

In the latter part of the month, England and the other allied enemy forces sailed across the Atlantic, bringing their entire fleets on the water escorted by thousands of modern airplanes. They had been preparing for war for years; had built fast hydroplanes which could travel on the water at more than 150 miles an hour. When this fleet arrived off the Atlantic Coast, the United States air patrol attacked them, but were so far outnumbered that it was futile. The patrol was quickly destroyed. All of the United States commercial planes were stopped from carrying mail, passengers or express across the Atlantic. The enemies were now in position to blockade the United States on every side. The Japanese, Spanish and Mexican planes were patrolling the Gulf of Mexico and the Pacific Coast. We were now in a worse position than the Allies were in 1917 when they were fighting with their backs to the wall and the United States went to their rescue. The War Council knew that England would now close the Northern border, shut us off from Canada and would probably attack all along the border sooner or later.

The United States had concentrated all the available forces which could possibly be spared to try and forestall attacks upon Chicago and the Central part of the country. While an attack was hourly expected in St. Louis, part of the English, German and Italian battleships, under the protection of their air fleet, moved to the mouth of the Mississippi River. The airplanes, numbering thousands, led the advance up the river, followed by the hydroplanes and battleships. The planes destroyed cities and drove the people away in terror. When this march started, the United States War Council decided to move the Infantry and Artillery as fast as possible to try and protect the territory along the Mississippi and prevent the advance up thru the

Central and Northern parts of the United States.   The enemies took charge of New Orleans and placed their officers in control of the city.   Fierce fighting continued all the way up the river.   The United States was hopelessly outnumbered and the loss of men and planes was enormous.   It began to look as if resistance was folly. It was plain that this was a move to take charge of our territory and showed that Japan, Spain, and Mexico had only been waiting for the time when England and other countries would join them to start taking over captured cities.

The move up the Mississippi was swift.   Every town was taken over and placed under the control of English officers.   Finally, when Cairo, Illinois, was reached the United States had perfected a new invention for dropping chemicals from airplanes into the water and then using an electric current from an airplane to discharge the chemical hundreds of miles away.

When the enemy advanced and the airplane attack was on at Cairo, the inhabitants had been moved to Louisville and Cincinnati and there was no attempt to try to save the city.   The plan was to let the enemy hydroplanes and battleships move up the river and destroy them by the powerful electric charge in the water.   When they had completed great destruction in Cairo, the hydroplanes and light battle cruisers which followed up the advance, taking charge of cities, moved up to the mouth of the Ohio to land and take charge of Cairo.

Colonel Walter Kennelworth had been sent to Cairo with a new plane which had been completed by the

Major Electric Co. This plane was equipped with an electric machine which could take the electric current from the air, charge into the water, and destroy battleships for miles in every direction. He was circling the sky at a high altitude and watching for an opportunity. Finally, seeing the airplanes receding from Cairo when they thought they had completed the destruction, he pressed a button and turned loose the powerful electric ray. In less than a minute every cruiser and hydroplane was blown to pieces or burnt up by the electric current. The enemy lost every man on board their ships. While Cairo had been almost completely destroyed, this was the first real victory for the United States since Colonel Gordon destroyed the "Tokyo J-1." The news was flashed all over the United States and people on the Eastern Coast, from Boston to Miami, who feared destruction at any minute, breathed a sigh of relief and hoped that this would turn the tide. The old-timers talked about the Yankee ingenuity and said that the brains of the United States were the greatest in the world and would find a way to overcome any obstacle and defeat the enemies no matter how powerful they were.

After this disaster to the hydroplanes which had been marching up the Mississippi, the enemy air fleet ceased its attacks for awhile, but about the end of June, an air fleet swarmed over Cairo, landed without much resistance, and officers were put in charge of the town. The United States had already asked France to come to their rescue and implored Canada to forbid England or any other foreign countries to cross their borders to attack the Northern and Eastern borders of the United States. France had quickly responded and informed the United States Government that they stood ready to order their air fleet to the United States or to attack England and Germany at home. This was another piece of good news which cheered the country and put courage into the hearts of the soldiers who had been fighting for more than a year against such great odds and had been meeting with such disastrous defeats. The newspapers were optimistic, but the Government official knew that the odds were still greatly against us and that we were out-classed and outnumbered in the air, where the decisive battles would be fought.

CHAPTER XXVIII

ON July 4th, 1931, the people all over the United States were celebrating the victory at Cairo where the English and German battleships and hydroplanes had been destroyed. Everything had been quiet and there had been no more air attacks on the cities. A large fleet of the enemies' planes were seen constantly scouting up and down the Mississippi. Colonel Gordon had sent out a scouting expedition with some of the planes equipped with powerful searchlights and they had discovered several mother supply ships, like the "Tokyo," anchored at great heights above Cairo. He knew that this meant that preparations were being made to attack St. Louis and continue the advance up the Mississippi, that the enemy was making for Chicago and the Great Lakes to form a line across the United States so that their airplanes could control this territory, shut off any attacks from the West while they advanced on the Eastern and Northern borders of the United States.

The Nation's birthday brought more good news. Canada informed the United States that she would join hands with her, order England's forces to leave Canadian territory and forbid them to cross Canada to attack the United States. This news was received in Washington just before the President delivered his an-

nual Independence address. While his speech was
short, he called attention to the fact that this was the
155th anniversary of the independence of the United
States and that the liberty of this country was threatened greater than at any time since the days of the
Declaration of Independence, but stated that cheering
news had just come from Canada which would be a
great help; that France, our old friend, who had stood
by us before, had also come to our rescue and that there
was room for hope. The recent victory of Cairo was of
great importance. The new inventions which were rapidly being completed would surely save the United
States in her hour of greatest need. He urged the
people to be courageous, not leave their cities or desert
their homes unless absolutely necessary. While no one
could be sure of the end, he hoped that a decisive victory
would be gained within a few months.

Colonel Gordon reported what the scouting planes had
discovered and said that this could mean but one thing,
that the enemy is concentrating at Cairo and that
the next attacks would be on St. Louis, then probably
Louisville, Cincinnati, and Chicago. At a conference
of the War Council, he suggested that there was no use
risking the lives of the women and children in these
cities; that arrangements should be made to move them
to places of safety at once, that camps should be established in the Catskills and Adirondack Mountains where
they could remain until the danger had passed. The
Council, after discussing the matter, decided that this
would prove to be a bad move on the part of the Government because it would disclose their weakened condi-

tion to the enemy who might be scouting around St. Louis at high altitudes and would see the people being moved away and know that the country was frightened and make an attack immediately. The Council decided to prepare for an attack, believing that with the help of Canada and France, this country would emerge a victor.

In the early part of August, 1931, the attack upon St. Louis started. The United States had concentrated every available force there. Canada had sent her airplanes to patrol the Northern border, enabling the United States to withdraw more forces to protect the Central part of the country. The battle raged on and off, day and night. There were attacks and counter-attacks. The United States factories were turning out airplanes now at the rate of more than 1000 per day. The Henry Motor Company of Detroit had made great improvements on bombing and scouting planes and were turning them out rapidly. A new long-range gun had been completed which would reach the enemy's planes at greater heights and this proved to be of great value in the battle of St. Louis. On the third day of the battle, General Pearson ordered Colonel Gordon and Colonel Kennelworth to lead their men against the Southern and Eastern wings of the enemy. They succeeded in bringing down over 500 of the enemy's planes, and the United States in the encounter only lost about 200 planes. This was very encouraging and General Pearson ordered more of the reserves thrown into the fight on the following day and this seemed just what the enemy was waiting for. One mistake after another was made by the subordinate officers of the United States in carrying out instructions for attacking. The bombing planes ran short of ammunition and were destroyed by the enemies in trying to return to their bases for supplies. The enemy had concentrated more than 30,000 planes for this giant attack on St. Louis. Buildings were being destroyed daily and the loss of life was great. Frightened women and children were rushing in every direction only to get into the path of the exploding bombs. The enemy's planes proved superior, larger and better-manned. Their large supply ships anchored at high altitudes enabled them to get in their effective work of destruction when the United States planes ran out of ammunition.

After the battle had waged for 14 days, with the United States losing thousands of planes, the cause seemed to be hopeless and St. Louis was surrendered. The situation was getting more desperate all the time and the people again were losing hope. The large loss of airships at the battle of St. Louis had weakened the U. S. Army regardless of the rapidity with which new planes were being turned out. The enemy took charge of St. Louis and moved part of their supply bases there. The food situation was acute thruout the country. Farmers had been afraid to go to the field to plant anything. Canada was not able to supply all of our needs and we were blockaded on the South, East and West. The Cabinet now awoke to the fact that many mistakes had been made and that the situation instead of improving was growing rapidly worse.

Before the fall of St. Louis or the news of it had had

time to be fully understood by the people all over the United States, the English and the Germans attacked the Northern border, making for Chicago. The lines were tightly drawn, the enemy was still holding the Western Coast and it now meant only a matter of capturing Chicago, close up the lines between Chicago and St. Louis, and complete the enemy's lines across the Central part of the United States. Council after council was held while the fighting was going on around the Great Lakes. The Government rushed reinforcements and the new long-range gun on our large cruising airships was able to do effective work for a long time in protecting Chicago. England lost heavily in the battle around the Great Lakes because Canada was helping us there, but the blow was heavy to the United States. Our losses in men and planes were tremendous.

In the early part of September, 1931, it was plain from the skirmishes which had been taking place around the Great Lakes that the enemy was trying to attack Chicago and it was only a question of time when they would break thru and make the attack. The United States officers were well aware of the fact that if Chicago fell into the hands of the enemy, it would place the United States at a greater disadvantage than ever to defend the Eastern Coast. The United States War Council decided to urge France to attack England and Germany and make them withdraw forces from the United States to protect their home cities. France was well equipped with airplanes and could rapidly destroy the large cities in England and Germany and she was the only country on the other side that we could look to to help us. When America's appeal was received in France, the President of France sent the following message to our Government:

"France is mindful of the perilous position in which the Land of Liberty is now placed. She has not forgotten the days when she came to your rescue during the struggles of the young republic, and you proved that you did not forget when your loyal sons crossed the Atlantic to help save France when she was fighting with her back to the wall in 1917. We placed the Statue of Liberty in the harbor of New York as a signal light to the world to welcome the oppressed from every land to the Land of Liberty. It has ever stood as a beacon light of truth, liberty and justice to all. We now stand ready to defend that statue and its principles. We appreciate the generosity of the American people toward us in the past and now extend them every aid within our power. Our supplies and forces are at your disposal."

About this time England and Germany knew that France was getting ready to aid the United States and they had been preparing to enlist the aid of other countries in order to complete the victories already won and gain control of the United States and divide up the territory. On September 6th, France made the first attack upon London and the same night attacked Berlin from the air, destroying many buildings, with the result that there was a large loss of life. Quickly following this, England, Germany, Austria, Spain, Italy and Japan called upon the other countries with whom they had treaties to join them in the final battles against the United States, promising a division of the spoils. All the world had become so jealous of the prosperity and success of the United States previous to this War of the Air that they were eager to join in the conquest and share in the great gold supply that had been gathered from all parts of the world by the United States. Turkey and Russia were the first to join the enemy; then quickly followed Rumania, Denmark, Greece, Hungary, Morocco and Portugal. These new supporters to the enemy's cause rushed their airplane fleets to the Eastern shores of the United States; sent aid to England and Germany to help hold off France and keep the enemy from having to withdraw any forces from the United States to protect their own countries.

The enemy, knowing that they now had practically all of Europe against the United States, were confident that it would only be a matter of a few weeks to take Chicago, Boston, New York and Washington, then make their own terms and the United States would be forced to accept. The United States knew that the most desperate battle of the war was now impending and another council was held. They were expecting the first blow to be struck in Chicago. The enemy's reinforcements had arrived and were scattered in every direction. The night of October 1st proved to be one of the worst so far of the war. The enemy attacked Omaha, Kansas City, Denver, Cincinnati, Louisville, Milwaukee and St. Paul. The forces from Mexico attacked El Paso, San Antonio, Galveston and Houston. The greater part of the United States forces being concentrated around Chicago and the East, this scattered attack all over the South, West and North was disorganizing to our forces. There was great loss of life and property in all of these cities because they were not properly prepared for the attack which came suddenly and unexpectedly.

On the morning of October 2nd a Council was held and it was decided to immediately send as many airplanes as possible to help protect these cities because an attack was expected again that night. This was just exactly what the enemy wanted,—to get the United States to scatter forces, withdrawing part of their armies which were protecting Chicago.

On the night of October 2nd the enemy concentrated an attack of more than 50,000 planes against Chicago and broke thru the United States lines on every side. England, Germany and Russia turned loose their giant dreadnought battle planes, the largest that had ever yet been used in the War in the Air. Many of these planes carried 12- to 36-inch guns. They were equipped with the latest improved 12-cylinder motors; were operated by electricity as well as gasoline. These giant planes could be supplied with power thru the air by radio current. The attack was well-timed and they had every advantage of the United States forces. The first attack destroyed Chicago's great skyscrapers. The Board of Trade Building, Post Office and other Government buildings were completely destroyed. Loss of life was appalling. Over a million people lost their lives. More defenseless women and children were killed than in any other battle during the war.

When the sun rose over the greaty City of Chicago on the morning of October 3rd, buildings were smouldering in ruins in every direction. It was the greatest destruction that had ever been in the history of the world. No mortal tongue could describe the terrifying sights. There was a brief respite. As the sun rose the enemy's planes which had wreaked their vengeance, withdrew. The United States had lost more than 25,000 planes and their best aviators had gone down in this terrible disaster.

Colonel Gordon and Colonel Kennelworth had done wonderful work and fortunately their lives had been preserved for future use to their country. As Colonel Gordon made his way to headquarters to report to General Pearson, he thought of what he had read in the Acts 2:17: "And it shall come to pass in the last days, saith God, I will pour out of my Spirit upon all flesh: and your sons and your daughters shall prophesy, and your young men shall see visions, and your old men shall dream dreams: and I will shew wonders in heaven above, and signs in the earth beneath; blood, and fire, and vapour of smoke." He thought of how he had dreamed and prophesied and how he had believed the Bible knowing that these terrible things would come in the latter days. As he saw the blood, the fire, the smoke and the ruined city, for a moment he wondered why God should permit such destruction as this in order that the Scriptures might be fulfilled, but then he thought of what he had read in Isaiah 2:2: "And he shall judge among the nations, and shall rebuke many people; and they shall beat their swords into plowshares, and their spears into pruninghooks; nation shall not lift up sword against nation, neither shall they learn war any more." He prayed to God to hasten the day when men shall not make war any more.

The United States officers knew now that if they held out, Chicago would be completely annihilated because England's giant bombing planes were able to destroy every building and kill every living soul. General Pearson called all the commanding officers together and they quickly agreed that with the enemy outnumbering them 50 to 1, another attack would be soon over with and that it was a useless sacrifice of human life and their remaining planes to offer resistance. But before surrendering, they decided to ask the consent of the President and his Cabinet. The President hastily called the Cabinet together and when they assembled, their faces were grave. They all knew what had happened the night before in Chicago. The President with sadness in his voice read the decision of the commanding Generals and said: "This is the gravest crisis this country has ever faced. To surrender may mean the loss of our country and our liberty; to go on and fight may mean even worse. To surrender Chicago and wait for time to determine the next move may be the wisest plan. We can only trust to God and hope. What is your decision, gentlemen?" Not a man rose to discuss the matter. One by one they answered: "It seems best to permit our commanding officers to surrender Chicago."

News was quickly flashed to headquarters at Chicago and about 10 A.M. the white flag was hoisted from the few remaining tall buildings and a large plane was sent out to circle the sky with white flags floating from its wings. As soon as Chicago was surrendered, the enemy planes and land forces were brought up and they closed the gap between Chicago and St. Louis, leaving the Central lines intact and the Western lines holding the Pacific Coast.

The New York Stock Exchange closed to prevent complete panic because the people were panic-stricken and selling stocks regardless of price. They soon discovered that the enemy had bases for supplies and ships all up and down the Atlantic and in the Gulf of Mexico. They were in control of the Northern border and in position to attack the Eastern Coast from the North, South, East and West. There was no minimizing the seriousness of the situation. The fall of Chicago had broken the heart of the American people. They were panic-stricken and it looked as tho for the first time in history, Old Glory would trail the dust. There was a great War Council held. To make a plea for peace at this time meant surrender to the enemy and accepting any terms that they might want to dictate. The leaders of the War Council were puzzled. They didn't know what move to make next since they were overwhelmed by great odds. The United States was practically alone in the fight. France and Canada were the only countries which had not joined forces against the United States. When the news of the fall of Chicago reached France, they realized that America was doomed.

The United States Government officials knowing the seriousness of the situation made no attempt to conceal it, but decided to play for time. They replied to the note from the enemy and asked for an armistice to last thirty days, in which neither side would make any attack until they discussed plans to see if it were possible to arrive at any acceptable terms. The enemy taking this as an admission of defeat and weakness on the part of the United States granted 15 days' time for a discussion of terms, and sent the following note:

The Allied Powers demand the complete surrender of the United States and a division of territory; Japan to have the Western coast, England to have the Eastern coast and Northern territory bordering on Canada; Mexico to have Texas, and Spain to have the territory along the Mississippi and Gulf of Mexico. The United States is to turn over to the Allied Powers its entire gold supply and the people to submit to the various Governments to which the territory is allotted and there is to be no longer any United States of America. If the Government of the United States refuses to accept these terms, we will destroy Boston, New York, Philadelphia and Washington, and take charge of the Eastern coast of the United States. Your answer must be received within the allotted time.

CHAPTER XXIX

WHEN these terms were received, everyone was gloomy at headquarters. The President called his Cabinet for a conference. A United War Council was also called, and after a long discussion, they were forced to admit that it was not only a probability but a possibility that the enemy would take New York City, capture the Eastern ports, and Washington, and then dictate any terms they might desire. To submit to the terms already offered would mean ruin and disgrace but the question was what to do. Men high up and Government officials who had relied upon their judgment before, now realized that one mistake after the other had placed the country in this terrible position. Colonel Charles Manson, a descendant of the family of General Lee, arose and asked the War Council if he might have permission to speak. It was promptly granted because he was a man highly respected for his good judgment, and one who had had advocated the building of greater air fleets and preparedness years before the war started. His speech was as follows:

GENERAL PEARSON AND SONS OF LIBERTY: This country now faces the gravest situation since the days of Washington and the winter at Valley Forge. We are not only menaced by England, our old enemy, but practically by the whole world. France now is our only friend. The enemy is in control and can attack from every side. It is a time to think, and think seriously; a time for action rather than words.

We need the man of the hour, and in times past, the United States has always produced that man. I am a great believer in the Bible. I have read the predictions made by Colonel Robert Gordon ever since he was a very young man. Just what is happening now he predicted years ago. He has made some remarkable inventions. Was born under the sign which astrologers call the Ascendant Sign of the United States, the sign Gemini, ruled by Mercury, the Messenger of the Gods. This sign is symbolized by the ancients as the double-bodied sign. It is a sign of genius and intellect. Ancient mythology tells us that one of the twins was a great warrior, and his brother a great inventor and that he invented all of the war instruments which helped his brother to win his victories. He was said to be so swift and shrewd that he had wings on his heels and wings on his shoulders. Could sip the wine from the cups of the Gods while they were drinking, without getting caught.

This sign has always symbolized the United States and Yankee ingenuity. The greatest inventions that have ever been were made by United States inventors. The airplane was invented here, the submarine, the great guns which have been used in war, the steamboats, electricity, radio, and other valuable inventions too numerous to mention. From what I know and have read, I still hope and believe that the United States has the brains to outwit the entire world. I believe this because it is the land of liberty, because there never has been a nation to conquer it. The United States has never been an aggressor, never entered a war on its own accord. I believe that God is with us and that this is the country established for God's kingdom.

I have read the Bible and followed Colonel Gordon's writings and believe with St. Luke, Chap. 7: 22, "Then Jesus answered and said unto them 'Go your way and tell John what things ye have seen and heard, how that the blind see, the lame walk, the lepers are cleansed, the deaf hear, the dead are raised, to the poor the gospel is preached, but what went ye out for to see—a prophet—yea, I say unto you, and much more than a prophet, for I say unto you, Among those that are born of woman, there is not a greater prophet than John the Baptist, but he that is least in the kingdom of God is greater than he.' "

I say to you, gentlemen, that I believe there is not a greater prophet than Colonel Gordon. Further, I believe that he is the greatest inventor that the United States has ever produced, and believe that he can save the situation or find some solution of the problem. The Army Officers made a mistake not to listen to Colonel Gordon when he offered them advice and told them he could complete an invention to save the country.

I believe the prophecy of Daniel which has often been referred to by Colonel Gordon, Chap. 7:27, "And kingdom and dominion, and the greatness of kingdom under the whole heaven, shall be given to the people of the saints of the Most High, whose kingdom is an everlasting kingdom, and all dominions shall serve and obey him." I believe that refers to the United States. If we can win this war, then as we are one against the world, it shall be a kingdom of the United World. In my judgment it would be wise to place Colonel Robert Gordon in supreme command and follow his instructions to the letter.

After Colonel Manson had ceased talking and sat down, complete silence reigned for several minutes. The War Council knew that there were only three more days left until the time of the armistice was up when the enemy would attack. General Pearson was the first to rise. He said, "Gentlemen of the Council, I have known Colonel Gordon ever since he entered the service. I interceded for him and obtained his release from prison. He has proved to be one of the most valuable men that we have had in the Aviation Corps. His bravery and genius have surpassed all others. I am willing to surrender my office to him and if agreeable to the rest of you I make a motion that he be made Supreme Commander of the United States Army and we will abide by his decision."

General Pearson was held in great respect by the Army officers, and his judgment was not questioned. A vote was taken and it was unanimous.

General Pearson arose and said, "Colonel Gordon, by the authority and power vested in me, I now confer upon you the title of the Supreme Commander of the Armies of the United States and place upon your shoulders the greatest burden ever placed on any man. Our country's life hangs in the balance. The situation is desperate. Something must be done and done quickly. We must give an answer to the enemy, and when that answer is given, it either settles our doom forever or if we can win, means that the Stars and Stripes will ever stand supreme to the world. Sir, what have you to say?"

Supreme Commander Gordon arose. His face showed new responsibility which rested upon his shoulders. He said simply, "I thank you for the honor and confidence, but before completely accepting I want to ask if I may have the unanimous consent of the entire War Council to carry out my plans no matter how absurd they may seem to the War Council." The entire Council arose in a body and voted their unanimous consent. General Pearson then said "Supreme Commander Robert Gordon, we await your orders." He saluted and sat down. Supreme Commander Gordon arose and said, "Dispatch immediately the following answer to the enemy's Headquarters.

" 'The Government of the United States of America, the land of Liberty, refuses your terms and will never surrender or accede to any of your demands. You may strike as soon as you are ready. We have not yet begun to fight.' "

When he had finished speaking, there was not a whisper. He sat down and Colonel Walter Kennelworth arose and said: "Gentlemen of the War Council, you have heard Supreme Commander Gordon's answer to the enemy. You must know and realize that in hurling defiance like this at the enemy, there is something which gives him supreme confidence. He knows exactly what he has and what he is going to do, and you can rely upon him in this emergency." Colonel Kennelworth saluted his Supreme Commander Gordon and said, "I await your orders, Sir."

Supreme Commander Gordon said, "I appoint Colonel Walter Kennelworth as aide-de-camp in carrying out my plans. I appoint Captain Edna Kennelworth second aide and confer upon her the title of Colonel." He turned to the Council and there was not a dissenting voice.

When Supreme Commander Gordon had finished his appointments and gave his instructions to his officers, General Pearson arose and said, "Supreme Commander Gordon, I do not wish to in any way inquire into your plans or interfere with any course which you may pursue, you have my heartiest support, but if you don't mind, I should like to have you explain to me what the trouble has been in the past, why we have been outclassed and have lost the war thus far and what is now the remedy or what you propose to do."

Supreme Commander Gordon replied: "The trouble in the past has been that the enemy used noiseless airplanes. Our next great handicap was the fact that they could rise to heights to which we are unable to attain, giving them the advantage in the fighting. Of course, we have been hopelessly outnumbered from the start, by that I mean, in the amount of equipment. Another thing that we need and must have, which the enemy already has, is an airship that can be anchored and remain anchored in the air for an indefinite length of time. We need a ship that can take its power from the air, giving it an unlimited cruising radius. We need other ships for cruising purposes and scouters that can take their power from the air, not having to return to the base at any time for fuel or ammunition, working from a base in the air at all times. The next and most important thing we need is an invisible plane. An invisible, noiseless plane will be one of the things to beat the enemy. When our planes can travel high or low, no longer be seen or heard, we will be able to obtain information about the enemy's position and plans and thereby know their weak points, when and where to attack.

"The great mistake that the army officers have made from time to time was in not listening to the counsel of younger men. By this, I do not mean myself alone. My authority for this is taken from the Bible,—Prov. 20:18: 'Every purpose is established by counsel, and with good advice make war.' Prov. 24: 6: 'For the wise counsel thou shalt make thy war, and in a multitude of counsellors there is safety.' There have not been enough counsellors and enough changes in plans at the proper time when the enemy was winning.

"My strength and power is in the Lord and I shall follow the rules laid down in the Bible in my future campaign. 2 Samuel 22:33: 'God is my strength and power: and he maketh my way perfect.' 1 Chronicles 5:22: 'For there fell down many slain, because the war was of God and they dwelt in their steads until the captivity.' This great War in the Air is according to the will of God and to fulfill the Scriptures and to work out God's plan for an eternal united kingdom of the world. You may wonder at my confidence and my defiance of the enemy at this time when it looks as if our chance for victory is absolutely impossible. I refer you to St. Luke 1:37: 'For with God nothing shall be impossible.' Again Luke 1:52: 'He hath put down the mighty from their seats, and exalted them of low degree.' I believe that if it is the will of God for us to win he will give us the power to bring down the mighty who have tried to oppress and destroy this nation, the land of liberty.

"Read Acts 17:26: 'And hath made of one blood all nations of men, for to dwell on all the face of the earth; and hath determined the times before appointed, and the bounds of their habitation.' All men are brothers and it is God's will that they should dwell together on the earth in peace. This great war, the last of all, is brought about to teach men that they can not defy the laws of God.

"Romans 8:25 and 31: 'For we are saved by hope: but hope that is seen, is not hope: for what a man seeth, why doth he yet hope for? But if we hope for that we see not, then do we with patience wait for it. What shall we then say to these things? If God be for us, who can be against us?' I am confident that God is for us, that he established this land of America never to be destroyed. Then no matter how dark the situation is now, even if all the nations of the world join against us, if God is for us they shall not prevail.

"Getting back to what we need to defeat the enemy, man has always found a way to do things. The genius of America has never been defeated. We only have to go back over the histories of wars in which America has engaged to find evidence that in emergency they have always found a way out, because they were led by the divine power of Almighty God. In time of war, man has dug tunnels under the earth in order that he could pass safely, concealing and protecting himself. During the great World War, Germany was the first to succeed with the submarine, passing secretly under the water, doing great damage and at the same time, suffering very little damage to her submarines. While the submarine was what caused her to lose the war, it came very near enabling her to win it. Man has dug tunnels thru mountains and under rivers when it was impossible almost to go over them or get thru any other way. In New York City, in 1927, one of the greatest engineering feats up to that time was completed, when a tunnel for vehicular traffic was opened from New York City under the Hudson River to the State of New Jersey.

"What we now need and need more than anything else is a Tunnel thru the Air. With such a tunnel and noiseless, invisible planes so that we can pass thru the air without being interfered with or harmed and without being seen or heard, our victory is assured. To make a Tunnel thru the Air is not at all impossible. It is just as easy as to put a tunnel under the earth or drive a submarine under the water. While the air is invisible, it is one of the strongest forces that we have. If the water can be separated or a submarine can push it each way and travel under it, if dirt can be removed and a man put a tunnel under a river or a mountain, we can find a way to put a Tunnel thru the Air so others can not see us, hear or enter unless we so desire.

"One of my first plans will be to put a Tunnel thru the Air. With a Tunnel thru the Air from New York City to London and Germany, our airplanes may safely pass thru without being seen or heard and the enemy will be unable to attack them, placing us in position to leave the tunnel at any time and return to it for safety.

"We need a Tunnel thru the Air from the Great Lakes to New Orleans and the Gulf of Mexico so that our planes may pass safely thru this tunnel, take observations of the enemy's position without being seen or heard, and when necessary leave this tunnel, attack the enemy, return to the tunnel again for protection. We can also have a Tunnel thru the Air so that when the enemy's planes enter this tunnel and do not understand it, they will be unable to get out of it and we may keep them there in prison as long as we wish, capture or destroy them.

"I have the plan already worked out for this Tunnel

thru the Air. I expect to accomplish it by the use of certain light rays and light waves, sending a strong current thru the air on one side and another current on the other side anywhere from 100 yards to miles wide and then thru another process that I have in mind, remove the air from between these lines or currents, making a vacuum or space between the air which will really be a tunnel. We can drive our planes thru this tunnel by radio rays, directing them from a great central station which I expect to build. All the aviators know that often they run into what they call air-pockets in the air, which means nothing more than a vacuum made by Nature in some way and that when these air-pockets are encountered an airship will drop right down until denser layers of air are reached. If Nature can construct a tunnel thru the air, then certainly man with the guidance of God's divine power can do it. It may be hard for you to understand and believe my theories, but they are founded on faith and the knowledge that with God nothing is impossible.

"I have demonstrated in the past that every law laid down in the Bible is provable, every prophecy has been fulfilled or will be fulfilled. I again refer to Roman 1:17: 'For therein is the righteousness of God revealed from faith to faith: as it is written, The just shall live by faith.' At this moment there is nothing for this nation to hang their hope on but faith in a divine Creator, and if I am right in my interpretations that the United States was God's kingdom which he created never to be destroyed and if it is to be the united kingdom of the world, then we must live by faith. If every other man, woman, and child in the United States, yea, and the world, turns against me, I will believe and follow that faith, knowing that no power can harm me and that no matter how many may be against me, I can win so long as I believe in the divine Creator.

"Romans 5: 3–4: 'And not only so, but we glory in tribulations also: knowing that tribulation worketh patience; and patience, experience; and experience, hope.' These trials and tribulations which we have gone thru have brought knowledge. We have learned patience and thru patience, experience. I propose to put that experience and knowledge that I have gained in the past into execution to preserve and protect my country which means more than life to me."

When Supreme Commander Gordon had finished talking, there was new life and new hope in the face of every man in the room. It was plain to see that they had caught the divine inspiration; that their faith had been strengthened and that they now believed that God would lead them safely to victory and preserve the nation which He had created to be a land of love and liberty.

General Pearson arose and said: "Supreme Commander Gordon, I offer you my heartfelt thanks and sincere gratitude. You have placed in my heart a new hope; made me understand our Lord and Saviour Jesus Christ better than ever before. I believe I bespeak the sentiments of the entire Council and that they, too, have supreme confidence in you and now understand what the great faith that you have had in your Creator has done for you. Had the world and all of us understood

the Bible and God's plan as you do, this war would
never have taken place. I plainly see now that it is
God's intention to teach man thru trials, sorrow and
bitter experiences to reverence and respect the law
which he has laid down for man to follow. Man must
learn to love his neighbor as himself and to do unto
others as he would have them do unto him. When that
law is understood and obeyed, then men will no longer
want to make war because war is not based on brotherly
love, but on greed, jealousy and hatred. When we decided to surrender Chicago, I felt that that meant the
end of our glorious country. I could see no hope, no
way out, but you have shown us the way and our combined faith in you, together with the inspiration from
our holy Father, will guide us to victory thru your lead-
ership. We are with you, in all confidence, to victory."

Supreme Commander Gordon then ordered each officer and commander to return to his respective post of
duty and to await further orders. He said, "If my
plans develop as I think, you will not need to take further action." He asked for the use of the largest building in New York, "The Mammouth" and wanted the entire top floor of this 110-story building at 42nd street and
Broadway. His wishes were immediately granted. Was
told that the Government already had taken over control of all the large buildings in the United States and
that he might use the building as he chose. Supreme
Commander Gordon departed from Washington that
night in the old "St. Marie" which he had ordered
brought to Washington to convey him back, taking with
him Colonel Walter Kennelworth. He had instructed

Colonel Edna Kennelworth to meet him at the Mammouth Building in New York. On arrival he proceeded at once to put the top floor in order for the "Demon of Death" to be moved in. Colonel Kennelworth and another assistant were sent at once to the Adirondacks to the secret hiding of "Marie the Angel of Mercy," to test out this giant Ezekiel airplane, and bring it to New York City. The machine for distributing the sleeping gas which would reach a radius of 700 miles, was made in readiness on the top floor of the building. "Marie the Angel of Mercy" was in perfect working order, and arrived in New York ship-shape.

The whole United States was waiting in anxiety because it was known that within a few days the armistice would end and the United States must either fight or surrender. The people in Washington, Boston, Philadelphia, and New York had not slept for more than a week. They knew that an air attack had been threatened and feared the consequences. Supreme Commander Gordon dispatched the sleeping gas by "Marie the Angel of Mercy," and it was distributed to the planes all across the country. Colonel Kennelworth returned at the end of the second day in "Marie the Angel of Mercy," after distributing the sleeping gas and giving instructions how to use it. The "Demon of Death" was tested out and found to be in good working order. For many months previous to this, all of the large cities had been kept in darkness because they feared night attacks.

CHAPTER XXX

WHEN the commanders of the Allied Enemy in Chicago and St. Louis received the defiance hurled at them on October 15, 1931, this reply was signed by Supreme Commander Robert Gordon. The English, German, Austrian, and Russians had never heard of this United States officer before and were at a loss to undertand whom the United States had placed in supreme command. The reply was conveyed to Japanese and Spanish headquarters in Mexico and the Japanese quickly understood just who Supreme Commander Robert Gordon was and feared that he had made some wonderful invention which had made him confident of winning the war. The Japanese Generals, knowing what this might mean and fearing the great genius, Robert Gordon, asked for an allied war council to convene before making another attack. On October 21st it was decided that the War Council should be held in the City of Mexico. The allied enemy were confident that the United States would not make any attack in the near future, but would wait for them to make the next move. They felt that the great losses which had been suffered by the United States Army at the battle of Chicago placed them in no position to make an immediate attack and that they would try to strengthen their position for the next attack by the allied enemy. It was decided that the commanding generals of all the allied enemy nations should proceed at once to the City of Mexico to hold a council and decide what the wisest and next move should be. They left in the dead hours of the night in the fastest planes and those which could rise to the highest altitudes, enabling them to travel noiselessly and at a height at which they could not be detected or captured. The scouting and cruising planes were left to patrol the lines between Chicago, St. Louis and New Orleans and watch for any move that might be made on the part of the United States forces.

When the Council had convened in the City of Mexico, General Nagato, the commander of the Japanese army, arose and said: "Supreme Commander Robert Gordon now in charge of the United States forces is well known to us. He is the man who made the first flight from New York City to Japan in 1927, traveling at a speed of more than 300 miles per hour. He is the man who invented the muffler which made our airplanes noiseless. We bought it from him and it helped us to successfully wage this war. When we attacked the Rio Grande and were preparing to bombard El Paso, Gordon, we believe, was the man who successfully brought down our greatest ship, the 'Tokyo J-1.' Later we captured Gordon at the battle of San Francisco. He was flying one of our planes which was on board the Tokyo. We found that he had a wonderful Pocket-Radio by which we could communicate without any sound passing thru the air, thus avoiding our orders being intercepted. After negotiating with him, we gave him his freedom, conducted him safely back to the American lines in consideration of his turning over to us his secret Pocket-Radio, which we worked successfully for many months. Finally it failed to work and we have always believed that he invented something by which he could prevent our communications.

"He is one of the ablest inventors that the United States has. The fact that he has been placed in command means that he must have made some great discovery or new invention which has inspired the United States with confidence of winning the war. While we have all the advantage in numbers, both in men, ships and ammunition, and to all appearance the United States is hopelessly crippled and will not be able to hold out much longer, one new invention by this man Gordon may mean our defeat. It is my opinion that the factories in Detroit, Michigan, have been working on some of his new discoveries. Our next attack should be directed at Detroit. We should capture that city and destroy the factories of the big automobile concerns and other manufacturing concerns there. All of these manufacturing concerns have long since been commandeered by the United States Government and are working on war weapons and ammunition."

When Colonel Nagato had finished speaking, the Spanish, English, German, Austrian and Russian Generals discussed war plans for many days and there were numerous disagreements before it was finally agreed as to just what the next move should be. Finally they united on the plan to make the next attack upon Detroit and if successful there, proceed to attack Boston,

New York, Washington and the Eastern Coast of the United States.

The delay by the Allied Enemy was just what Supreme Commander Gordon wanted. It gave him time to prepare. He had ordered the Henry Motor Company of Detroit to proceed at once to manufacture according to his plans which he sent them, two large machines, one positive and one negative, by which he could send currents of electricity thru the air and produce a vacuum, or as he called it, a "Tunnel thru the Air." These plans had been worked out years before and there was no question but what the machines would work successfully. The Henry Motor Company had been commandeered by the United States Government and as soon as they received the order and plans from the Supreme Commander, they started running day and night working to build the two giant machines.

The fifteen days' armistice expired on October 18th, 1931. Supreme Commander Gordon was in readiness and waited the first attack of the enemy. Less than thirty days from the time that he ordered work started on the machines, they reported that the machines were completed and ready to test out. He called Colonel Kennelworth to his office in New York and explained to him that the great Vacuum Producer, as the machine had been named, had been completed; ordered him to proceed at once to Detroit and test out the machines both for short and long distance work.

Colonel Kennelworth arrived in Detroit on November 17th. The following day tested out the Tunnel machines; reported to Supreme Commander Gordon that they were working in fine shape and producing results according to the plans. The Supreme Commander then decided to go immediately to Detroit and establish one of the machines at a base there and have Colonel Kennelworth take the other machine to Cincinnati and set it up. The machine was transported secretly and successfully to Cincinnati and set up in one of the largest buildings in the city.

On November 20th, Supreme Commander Gordon and Colonel Kennelworth tested the Tunnel machines over this long distance. The machines were set to produe a tunnel 100 yards wide at first and were set in motion. The American scouting airplanes were sent off over a described area and on entering between these lines found that they were in a complete tunnel. They could travel quickly back and forth thru the Tunnel in the Air. This was a great triumph. Commander Gordon instructed all those connected with the test to keep it a complete secret. He knew that this was going to be a great surprise to the enemy when they started their next attack.

Supreme Commander Gordon had now completed another new invention on the same plan of the radio that he had to use in his office in New York several years before to record conversations when the manipulators were trying to catch him in the stock market. He had enlarged this machine so that it would record voices 3000 miles away and named it the "Tel-Talk."

On the night of November 19th, 1931, the Supreme War Council which had convened in Mexico City broke up and the commanding generals returned to their various posts around St. Louis and Chicago. Supreme Commander Gordon had his powerful Tel-Talk directed so that he would get all the conversation along the lines between Chicago, St. Louis and New Orleans. When he went to his headquarters in Detroit on the morning of November 20th, he went into look at his Tel-Talk, saw that there had been a conference of the enemy held the night before. He pushed the needle of the machine back and turned it on; put his ear to the receiver and listened. He found that the commanding generals had talked over the conference in Mexico and had now decided that their next attack would be on Detroit in order to destroy the factories there and prevent the United States continuing making airplanes and inventions which might help them to win the war. He was very happy to get the plans of the enemy. It was just what he wanted. He was anxious to test the Tunnel thru the Air, capture the enemy's planes and keep them there because he knew when once he got them in the Tunnel, thy would be unable to get out of it and he could keep them suspended in the air indefinitely, moving up and down in the Tunnel, or could capture them and destroy them. He was impatient and anxious for and attack upon Detroit and decided to defy the enemy and urge them on.

With the plans of the enemy in his possession, Supreme Commander Gordon decided to change the location of the Tunnel machines so as to protect the factories and large buildings in Detroit. He arranged the machines so that when the attacking planes came over Detroit at a high altitude, he could drop them into the

Tunnel thru the Air and thus prevent any harm to the factories or buildings in Detroit. He waited patiently for an attack upon the city, but no move of any kind was made by the enemy. When it was near Thanksgiving, he had a great desire that the battle should start around that time so that the United States might have the greatest Thanksgiving in history because he was confident that if the attack came, Detroit would be successfully defended and the enemy for the first time would find that we had outwitted them. He decided to urge the enemy to make an attack on Detroit as soon as possible, so ordered a large electric sign built with letters twenty feet high, "DETROIT IS READY— WON'T YOU COME AND TAKE US WE WANT TO BE YOUR THANKSGIVING TURKEY." The sign was placed on an airplane and lighted. This plane passed in full view of the enemy's lines at St. Louis and Chicago. What the enemy thought of this, perhaps no one will ever know. Colonel Manson later wrote that this electric sign put the fear of God in the heart of the enemy; that the Germans recalled the days when the Yankees arrived at the time of the great World War. The Japanese, the Spanish and the English realized that this was not meant for a bluff and thought they had made a mistake in allowing 15 days' armistice, now that the United States had decided to fight again. How they could hope to win, the enemy could not see. They decided to teach this young, boastful commander a lesson that he would never forget.

On Thanksgiving night, November 24th, the attack was ordered. Supreme Commander Gordon was at dinner and a messenger interrupted him to tell him that "Tel-Talk" had picked up an important message. He rushed to the secret room and noticed that a conference had been held and orders given by the enemy to attack Detroit that night. He immediately communicated this information secretly with the new Pocket-Radio to Colonel Kennelworth in Cincinnati. Told him to be in readiness to adjust the Tunnel machine and change the location and altitude any moment that he instructed. He ordered all the lights in the streets of Detroit to be kept on that night. It has been the custom for many months, since long before the attack at Chicago, to keep all the cities in darkness at night.

He had just completed another new invention which he called the Radium Ray. With this Ray he could locate anything in the sky 75 to 100 miles away. He had the Radium Ray machine in readiness to search the sky for the first attack that night. Just before 10 o'clock he was sweeping the sky with the Radium Ray when he discovered the enemy planes approaching from the direction of Chicago. There was a large flock of them flying at very high altitudes, followed by three large supply ships. He knew that these supply ships would anchor in the air somewhere over Detroit and the bombing planes would make the attack. He decided to send Captain Morrison, the famous aviator who had distinguished himself at the battle of Chicago, to lead a fleet of decoy airplanes to meet the invading planes and to lead them into the Tunnel thru the Air. Captain Morrison led his swift cruisers into the air to the greatest heights they could rise, and as they neared the approaching enemy they began to turn loose the rapid-firing anti-aircraft guns. As soon as the enemy discovered the firing, they turned their searchlights on our planes, located and started after them. Captain Morrison obeyed orders and retreated rapidly with the other planes following. He made straight for Detroit to the vicinity of main buildings and factory districts with the enemy planes in hot pursuit. Suddenly he received a radio message from Supreme Commander Gordon to descend very low and fly Northwest. At this time the Supreme Commander was in communication with Colonel Kennelworth and they had adjusted the Tunnel machines and established the Tunnel thru the Air.

Supreme Commander Gordon was atop one of Detroit's giant skyscrapers over 80 stories high watching the action of the enemy planes. Suddenly he saw the first battalion of more than 250 planes, which were flying in a wedge formation, dive into the Tunnel. He followed them with the Radium Ray and saw immediately that the Tunnel was doing its work and that the giant battle planes were now powerless. Next came the three giant supply ships. Following the same course as the bombing planes, they dived into the Tunnel thru the Air and were powerless to proceed further. Once the planes were in the Tunnel, they were unable to communicate with headquarters or make any move because the Tunnel was a complete vacuum and no plane could move in it except the American planes which understood the combination how to navigate thru the Tunnel. As soon as Supreme Commander Gordon saw that the great Tunnel machines were doing their miraculous work, he sent another defiant message to the enemy headquarters in Chicago and St. Louis:

We have given your first battalion a wonderful Thanksgiving reception. Won't you send some more of your famous aviators to have Thanksgiving supper with us.

Immediately after this message was received, the commanding generals ordered a message sent to the supply ships which were supposed to be anchored over Detroit, asking information as to what was happening. No reply was received. This caused consternation in the enemy camp. They knew that the first battalion had either been captured or destroyed. The news was quickly flashed to headquarters in the City of Mexico and General Nagato replied: "This is some devilish trick of that genius, Gordon. Be careful what move you make. Send out scouting planes around Detroit and ascertain what is going on." Their fast cruising scouters were immediately dispatched to Detroit to see what had happened to the bombing planes and the mother ships. These planes soon came in view of the Radium Ray. After circling high over Detroit, finally came lower and lower until suddenly they plunged into the Tunnel thru the Air and like the others, were powerless to move or to communicate with their headquarters.

Supreme Commander Gordon decided to take no chances with the captured planes which were in the Tunnel thru the Air and ordered the sleeping gas turned on to put all the aviators to sleep for seven days. After waiting till after 12 o'clock for further attacks and finding the air clear with no signs of the enemy in sight, he decided to retire and get some sleep. This was the greatest day since the beginning of the war. He was very happy and knelt to offer his thanks to Almighty God. He said: "Lord, thou workest in mysterious ways thy wonders to perform. I know that by faith and thru faith were all things made. I have put my trust and my confidence in thee. Thou hast guided me safely and helped me protect my country in time of greatest need. God, not my will, but thine be done, but if it be thy will, I pray thee that when these trials and troubles pass away and once the United Kingdom of the World is established and all men live as brothers according to the law of love, it be a part of thy divine plan to return to me in safety my beloved Marie. Guide me in this great task to protect and save my country from the enemies who would destroy it. Amen."

November 25th, 1931, was a great day for the United States. They had more to be thankful for than any day since November, 1918, when the great World War had come to a close. After conferring with his commanding officers and Government officials, Supreme Commander Gordon gave orders that no newspapers were to be permitted to publish anything about the attack upon Detroit, that it was to be kept strictly a secret.

There was not much to be thankful for in the camp of the enemy. Failure of any of the planes sent out the night before to return and no message being received from them, made it plain that the United States was not bluffing and that Supreme Commander Gordon knew what he had up his sleeve when he hurled defiance at the enemy and refused to accept any terms. They were not aware of the fact that when he defied them to come and take Detroit, he must have been anxiously awaiting the attack and had something new that he wanted to try out on the enemy planes, and that it had been successful. It was now a time to move cautiously. The next and future moves must be made in a way to conserve their resources and assure final success.

Everything was quiet and no move or attack was made until December 7th, when the enemy held a council and decided that a gigantic attack on Detroit should be made; that they should concentrate a large part of their forces there; destroy the factories and take Detroit; then proceed to attack New York and the Eastern Coast. The plan was to make a daylight attack and, if possible, to surprise Supreme Commander Gordon. About 3 o'clock in the afternoon the enemy planes were seen approaching from the East and West. He saw that this was to be a gigantic attack because there was a larger number of planes than they had used at any time since the attack of Chicago. Before he could get the Tunnel machines in working order and establish a wider range in the Tunnel thru the Air, the enemy planes had begun dropping bombs on the outskirts of the city and had destroyed many of the smaller buildings. The United States planes were attacked and being unable to rise to the heights at which the enemy planes were flying, a great many of our planes went down, but in a few minutes the Tunnel thru the Air was in working order and the enemy planes began to be drawn into it. Within less than an hour more than 2500 planes had been captured. The loss of life around the city had been small because the bombs which had been dropped had not reached the thickly populated sections of the city and no plane had been able to reach the factories or business sections where the large buildings were. The Tunnel thru the Air was protecting and keeping them away from these sections. Canadian planes had come to the assistance of the United States on the Northern border and were patrolling the other side of the river and preventing the enemy from attacking from the North.

About 5 o'clock, the gigantic concentrated attack took place. It was estimated that there were more than 25,000 planes of the enemy in this attack. They were supported by about 10 supply ships which sailed at a great distance and were attempting to anchor. Supreme Commander Gordon knew that it was necessary to sacrifice some of the American planes in order to draw this attacking force into the Tunnel thru the Air. He sent more than 1000 of our best planes to meet the attack and lead the enemy in the right direction. The enemy turned loose their large 12-inch guns and they destroyed our ships rapidly. Planes were falling all over Detroit. The people were very much frightened and thought that this was going to be another disaster such as had occurred in Chicago. Finally Captain Morrison changed plans and led the enemy toward the Tunnel thru the Air. Soon more than 10,000 of their planes had gone into the Tunnel never to return again. When this large fleet of planes went down and evidently were no longer able to communicate with the giant supply ships which were not yet anchored, the enemy quickly changed plans and the supply ships sailed back toward Chicago, followed by the balance of the invading fleet which had not been captured.

When all reports were in, Supreme Commander Gordon found that the United States had lost about 400 of their best planes, but had captured more than 12,000 of the enemy planes. He was very greatly elated over this victory because he knew that when the enemy planes retreated, it was the first time they had ever returned to their base without a report of victory. He felt that this would break the morale of the enemy; make them more cautious in the future; give him more time now to complete his invisible airplane and the one which would rise to any altitude. When this was completed together with other machines for establishing Tunnels thru the Air, the balance would be easy and a mere question of time until the enemy could all be destroyed or put to sleep. People thruout the United States were still in a panicky, restless state. Ever since the attacks at Los Angeles, San Francisco, Chicago, Kansas City, New Orleans and the Southern part of Texas, every large and small town all over the country had remained in a state of fear, expecting an attack at any moment. Hundreds of thousands of people had moved from the Pacific Coast and from the Central and Eastern parts of the United States into the mountains of the West and the Grand Canyon. They felt that there were no large cities and nothing to attack around the Grand Canyon and that it was the safest place to go. Thousands of people were living in tents and there was a great scarcity of food and much suffering.

Supreme Commander Gordon decided that the people

should be given some encouragement and that the news of the failure of the second attack upon Detroit should be given to the newspapers; thought it would encourage and cheer the people. On the morning of December 8th, all the newspapers thruout the United States, carried big headlines: "DETROIT ATTACKED THE SECOND TIME BY THE ENEMY FORCES BUT DEFEATED. THOUSANDS OF THEIR PLANES HAVE BEEN CAPTURED. THERE HAS BEEN PRACTICALLY NO LOSS OF LIFE AND NO IMPORTANT BUILDINGS DESTROYED." The papers emphasized the fact that this meant the turn of the war and that the placing of Supreme Commander Gordon at the head of our forces had saved the country and that there was no longer need for any great alarm. It was a question of only a few months till the war would be over and the enemy would be driven from our soil.

The defeat at the second attack of Detroit had indeed put the fear of God in the hearts of the Enemy, but they had not by any means lost hope. They were getting recruits rapidly from Europe. Every nation was building airplanes as fast as the factories could turn them out and sending them to the United States to aid their allies. Practically every nation on the face of the earth, outside of France, Canada and a few countries in South America and Australia, had joined against the United States. This encouraged the Enemy and they felt that no matter what the United States had, in the end they would not be able to win. The great problem now was to find out what the Americans were using in order to capture the enemy planes and what discovery they had to prevent their communications. The Enemy were unable to find out anything about the American plans. They demanded to know what had happened to the captured aviators, whether they were living or dead. Supreme Commander Gordon refused to give any information whatsoever about prisoners; replied that reports of anything in regard to prisoners or planes would be made after the war was over and after the Enemy had surrendered and were ready to leave our soil. This greatly aroused the Japanese, Spanish and Germans who decided to redouble their efforts to take Detroit and then attack the Eastern Coast of the United States.

Days went by and everything was quiet in Detroit. No attacks were made anywhere in the United States. December 25th, 1931, arrived and the United States had much to be thankful for. There was a great rejoicing and merry-making on Christmas. Supreme Commander Gordon had a great Christmas. The Major Electric Co. had been working on the process for making planes invisible and reported to him that they had completed the process according to his plans and that it was a success. They had also completed a new motor which he had designed with 24 cylinders. This motor was to be used in lifting our planes to great heights. It was estimated that it would carry a ship 50 miles in the air if necessary. A stabilizer and anchor had been completed in accordance with his plans. The Major Electric Co. informed him that these machines were all ready for him to test out. He ordered these new inventions to be sent to New York headquarters. A large 24-cylinder motor was placed in "Marie the Angel of Mercy" and she was made an invisible airship. This motor was able to take its power from the air.

Supreme Commander Gordon went to New York on January 1st, 1932, leaving Colonel Morrison in charge in Detroit and ordering General Pearson to Detroit to hold the fort until he completed the test in New York. Supreme Commander Gordon accompanied only by Colonel Edna Kennelworth made the first flight in "Marie the Angel of Mercy," ascended to a height of more than 20 miles and anchored the "Marie" in the air. The new inventions were a perfect success and the machine could rise to any height and anchor and remain as long as it was desired and was absolutely invisible.

He was now in position to construct a Tunnel thru the Air from New York to Europe and sail the "Marie" in safety thru it, then rise to a height of 20 to 50 miles over any of the cities, anchor and start destruction. "Marie the Angel of Mercy" could carry enough sleeping gas to destroy or put to sleep people over thousands of miles of territory. After remaining anchored in the air for two days to test "Marie the Angel of Mercy," Supreme Commander Gordon descended to New York, anchored at the Mammouth Building to get a report of what had been happening and prepare for any attack. The Enemy were keeping quiet and making no move, evidently trying to find out what America's new inventions were before making the next great attack.

"Marie the Angel of Mercy" was now equipped with the Tunnel machine which would automatically put a

Tunnel thru the Air anywhere in any direction. The Supreme Commander had enlarged and improved upon the Tunnel machine or vacuum until it could be made 25 to 50 miles wide in any direction from a large city. He had also discovered how to send ships thru the air without an aviator, directing them by radio rays, which would enable them to distribute sleeping gas among the enemy's lines and prevent loss of any of his valuable aviators. He now had confidence that every city would be safe from an attack and no destruction could take place. The Henry Motor Co. and the Major Electric Co. were ordered to manufacture more of the Tunnel machines just as fast as possible so that one might be placed in each city in Boston, New York, Philadelphia, Pittsburgh, Washington and Savannah, Ga., to protect the Eastern Coast of the United States. It was the opinion of Supreme Commander Gordon that the Enemy would eventually concentrate their final attacks on the Eastern shores of the United States and if unsuccessful in attacking New York and Washington, the war would be over. He intended to be fully prepared so that the United States would emerge victorious without much loss of life and was especially trying to protect the women and children in the large cities.

February 15, 1932—Supreme Commander Gordon was informed by the Henry Motor Co. and Major Electric Co. that the Tunnel machines were completed, that gas-distributing machines and equipment for sending airplanes by radio ray without an aviator to distribute the sleeping gas were ready for delivery. Two more "Demon of Death" machines were ready and ordered sent to Washington and Boston. The Supreme Commander was hourly expecting that the enemy would attack the Eastern Coast, concentrating on Boston, New York and Washington. The "Tel-Talk" had recorded conferences which had been held and plans which were under way to concentrate the Enemy's combined forces on the Eastern Coast. He figured that they were trying to make improvements to overcome the defeat at Detroit because the enemy had been mystified by the new invention which had been used to capture so many of their planes. He was now ready and waiting for the attack on the Eastern shore, feeling confident that he was prepared for victory.

CHAPTER XXXI

APRIL 1st, 1932, arrived and no attack had been made.   The enemy was evidently making gigantic preparations for an attack and Supreme Commander Gordon decided to make the first move.   He then sent instructions to France to begin attacking England and Germany again.   France was well prepared with a large number of airplanes.   The attack started and they were successful.   When this news reached the enemy headquarters in the United States there was great consternation.   They thought that this was the secret behind the United States refusing to accept peace terms, but felt that France could not hold out long alone.   Spain and Japan ordered their reserve planes from home to England and Germany to help fight France.   The "Tel-Talk" recorded that a large fleet of planes had been sent across the Atlantic to attack France.   Supreme Commander Gordon ordered the French to go out and meet the attack.   A great battle raged over the Atlantic for hours with the French winning.   Thousands of the enemy planes went down into the ocean.   The Spanish and Japanese withdrew.   This stopped Germany and England from striking back at France.   The news reached the enemy headquarters in the United States and they figured that in some way the United States had a large number of planes out guarding the Atlantic and realized that the time had come to strike at the Eastern Coast of the United States before France and the United States could do more damage on the other side.

In June, 1932, the enemy decided to make the attack on the Eastern part of the United States. Supreme Commander Gordon had time to make ample preparations to meet it. He had established Colonel Kennelworth in Boston with one of the sleeping-gas machines and he remained in New York in the Mammouth Building, with a "Demon of Death," awaiting the attack upon New York.

BATTLE OF BOSTON

On June 6th, the enemy attacked Boston. The planes came in large numbers from every side, some from across the water, some from the North and West. Colonel Kennelworth let them approach within a reasonable distance and then turned loose the sleeping gas among all the enemy planes. The aviators immediately went to sleep and the planes all dropped slowly to the earth and some landed on the water and were not damaged. Hundreds after hundreds of planes followed up, each one sharing the same fate. Of all the planes sent out by the enemy, not one returned. Colonel Kennelworth reported to Supreme Commander Gordon that Boston was safe,—that there had not been the loss of one life and not a bomb had been dropped upon the city.

The Commanders of the Allied Enemy armies were unable to get any report of what had happened to the planes that went to attack Boston. They waited until the next day; and when not a plane returned and there was no report of any kind, decided that the same fate had befallen them as at the attack on Detroit; that the Americans certainly had something by which they were destroying every ship and plane which attacked them. This was unusual and unheard of. The fact that thousands and thousands of planes had attacked Boston and not one had escaped capture or destruction, made it plain that Yankee ingenuity had discovered something that was turning the tide of war in their favor. They now knew that they had made the greatest mistake by not pressing us hard after the fall of Chicago. They should have refused to grant the 15 days' armistice without demanding the surrender of the Eastern Coast. Another great mistake was the long delay between the attack on Detroit and the attack on Boston. This had enabled the Americans to get better prepared. There was no denying the painful truth. Something must be done and done quickly. They decided to order every plane that could possibly be spared from the Pacific Coast and from the lines extending from New Orleans to St. Louis and Chicago; to concentrate a supreme attack upon New York and Washington, making Washington the final goal. Planes were concentrated and mother ships anchored out in the Atlantic Ocean to prepare for the attack upon New York City. This was to be the greatest battle in all history.

On the night of June 7th, Supreme Commander Gordon had grown tired from his long vigil waiting for an attack upon New York. He placed Colonel Edna Kennelworth in charge of the "Demon of Death" while he went to get a few hours' sleep. While he was sleeping, the "Tel-Talk" machine and the secret radio communicator began to work. Colonel Edna Kennelworth listened in and soon had the plans of the enemy. She knew that Supreme Commander Gordon needed rest and she did not awaken him until early next morning. When he entered the headquarters on top of the Mammouth Building, she saluted him and said, "Supreme Commander Gordon, this is going to be a great birthday for you. The enemy is going to attack New York City with probably 100,000 airplanes and you and I are alone to defend it. It will be the day of all days for you." He replied: "I had forgotten all about my birthday. We have been so busy preparing for the final attacks of the enemy that I have had no time to think of myself." She reminded him that five years ago he arrived in New York just after his birthday, then of the birthday parties that they had had since and that always something unusual happened around his birthday. "You remember the birthday party we had the year Walter and I were married. Last year we had too much trouble to think of your birthday. The enemy was sweeping up the Mississippi, making complete destruction and taking every city; but there was something eventful around your birthday. About that time you discovered how to take electricity from the air and completed the machine for sending an electric discharge into the water which destroyed the battleships and hydroplanes of the enemy at Cairo. This was our greatest victory up to that time, and while the disaster at Chicago and St. Louis followed, it gave us the first ray of hope. Now, one year later, complete victory is in sight. I know that you have supreme faith in our new machines and that our recent successes will be followed by greater successes. This attack upon New York is going to be the greatest in history because the gain will be the greatest should the enemy win. Should they fail their cause is lost, and they will fail." She saw that Supreme Commander Gordon was very happy and that there was a note of confidence in his tone. While she shuddered to think of what might happen if they should fail, she knew that Supreme Commander Gordon had great confidence in the "Demon of Death" and the sleeping gas machine and knew what they would do, because he alone knew all the secrets of working these machines.

At 8 o'clock on the evening of June 8th, Supreme Commander Gordon stood near the "Demon of Death" watching his different instruments and soon noticed on the other side of the room the radio interceptor start to work. He stepped up to it and listened, caught the orders going from the different enemy headquarters, giving instructions for the combined attack on New York City at 10 o'clock that night. He immediately gave instructions for all the electric lights to be kept on all night and all buildings to be well lighted to show his confidence and let the enemy know that he expected the attack. Colonel Edna Kennelworth was ordered to instruct all army headquarters to send radio messages to the enemy that Supreme Commander Gordon had ordered the City of New York and all buildings lighted up for the night so that they would not miss the city and that he awaited their coming with pleasure. Asked them not to overlook the Mammouth Building which was 110 stories high; that he would be there alone, waiting for them to destroy the building.

GIGANTIC ATTACK ON NEW YORK CITY

When the news reached the enemy, they knew that in some way their plans had leaked out, but it was too late now to make any change and to delay attack might mean defeat later, so the orders were carried out. About 10 minutes after 10 o'clock, Supreme Commander Gordon sighted the first airplane of the fleet approaching 40 or 50 miles up the Hudson River. He watched them until they got within about 20 miles of New York City, near Yonkers, then he slowly swung the "Demon of Death" around on the revolving base and turned on the rays, at the same time starting the sleeping gas machine working. He swept the territory for 50 or 60 miles in every direction, and as the rays from the "Demon of Death" struck the enemy planes, their motors leaped into a liquid flame. Supreme Commander Gordon saw that the "Demon of Death" was doing its work so he pressed a button and Colonel Edna Kennelworth appeared. He told her to put on powerful glasses and to look at the planes going down. One by one she saw the motors dissolved by the flame from the rays of the "Demon of Death" and the planes falling, one by one, to the ground.

A few minutes after the Northern army was wiped out, the signal came that a great fleet of airplanes was making its way across Long Island Sound. Supreme

Commander Gordon swung the "Demon of Death" around and watched the approach of the enemy planes as they came out from the Atlantic Ocean and crossed Fire Island. He let them get within 30 to 40 miles as they came up across the Great South Bay, then he again turned loose the "Demon of Death." Swiftly the planes went down in flames, ending the attack from the ocean.

He watched a little while longer and saw across Staten Island another flock of planes which he knew was coming from Southern headquarters. He called Colonel Edna Kennelworth and said: "This time you may operate 'Spitfire' and destroy the Southern wing." She was a little nervous at first but knowing what this great machine could do, she turned it on, slowly lowered and raised it, moving to the right and left, until she gauged the distance of the approaching planes. One by one she saw their motors turn to liquid fire and sink to the earth. Turning to Supreme Commander Gordon she said, "Look." He focused his powerful glasses toward the South and saw that the air was clear. Turning around he said: "Edna, you are a wonderful woman and I am happy to have you take this part in saving your country. This is the day of women and their influence must help to win war forever." "It seems a shame," she replied, "that the lives of all these brave men from so many nations should be sacrificed. Among the planes that went down by the thousands, I could see some were English, German, Spanish, Austrian, Russian, Japanese, Turkish, and Arabian planes. Certainly almost the entire world is against us and we are winning. This must mean the end of the war. While I know that it is God's plan to teach man a lesson so that he will cease to go to war any more, it does seem a shame that we should take the lives of any more of these innocent men who are forced by selfish rulers of their countries to attack us."

"You are quite right," the Supreme Commander said. "Your noble husband invented the sleeping gas because it was my desire to protect my country and win the war with as little loss of life as possible. From this time on, no more lives will be sacrificed. We will use the sleeping gas, put all the attacking aviators to sleep for seven days and the war will soon be over. I know that there will be another final attack upon New York in a few minutes and I am going to allow you the honor of using the sleeping gas machine and ending the final attack upon the great City of New York without loss of any life."

About the time that Colonel Kennelworth was transferred from Cincinnati to Boston, General Pearson had been sent to Cincinnati to operate the Tunnel machine from there. Immediately before the final attack on New York City, Supreme Commander Gordon ordered General Pearson to swing the Tunnel machine to the East and establish a Tunnel thru the Air between New York and Cincinnati, informing him that the expected the final attack upon New York would come over the mountains of Pennsylvania and that this final attack would be from the West; that he wanted a Tunnel thru the Air at least 30 miles wide so that he could protect the Jersey shores and prevent the attack upon New

York City. In a few minutes a test was made and the Tunnel was ready to receive the invading army of planes and airships. He knew that New York was now safe and awaited the final combined attack of the Enemy planes that would come across from St. Louis and Chicago to meet on the Western side of the Hudson River.

About 12 o'clock he sighted the enemy planes across the Western coast of Jersey moving in triangle form, and knew that it was the combined forces with probably more than 50,000 planes ready for the final attack. Swiftly they approached, closer and closer. He played his powerful searchlight upon their glistening wings, until they were within 15 to 20 miles of New York. Fearing that they might start dropping bombs on Newark, Jersey City and the towns on the other side before attacking New York, he adjusted the Tunnel thru the Air until it was high enough to reach the enemy planes flying at the highest altitude; then turned to Colonel Edna Kennelworth and said: "Turn on the sleeping gas machine. The Tunnel is ready and as the aviators go to sleep, the machines will plunge into the Tunnel thru the Air and remain suspended without the planes being destroyed or the loss of any lives. This will be a silent, painless victory, but it will demonstrate our power to the enemy and the world."

Slowly and carefully, with a trembling hand, she swung the powerful gas distributing machine into action and as she saw the planes coming by the thousands begin slowly to plunge into the Tunnel thru the Air, she thought of how she had risked her life taking the sleeping gas for seven days to prove its success for the love of her husband, who invented it, and for the love of her country. She thought of Supreme Commander Gordon naming his great ship "Marie the Angel of Mercy" and then realized what was in his mind at the time; that the sleeping gas should be named the "God of Mercy" because it was winning the war in a humane way without taking human lives. Her mind went back to the great destruction of Los Angeles and San Francisco and above all, she remembered the loss of more than a million lives at the battle of Chicago; how merciless the enemy had been, sparing not the lives of women or children. We were now indeed merciful unto our foes and heaping coals of fire upon their heads and she believed this would be a great example to the world. She knew that the enemy had used poisoned gas of all kinds, poisoning the water and foods in the various cities and resorted to every means to destroy both life and property.

As these thoughts were flitting thru her mind, battalion after battalion of planes followed and she was pouring the sleeping gas into the noses of the aviators and the planes were diving into the Tunnel. This was indeed a great victory and she was glad to help accomplish it without the loss of life. The great Tunnel machines had worked successfully and perfectly. The sleeping gas had done its silent, painless work and the army of more than 50,000 planes—the giant attack from the West—rested safely in the Tunnel thru the Air, not a single one having escaped.

At 12:30 the sky in the West was clear and there was not an enemy plane in sight in any direction. During the minutes of the final battle Supreme Commander Gordon had remained as motionless as a statue, standing with his hand upon the levers of the Tunnel machine, with the powerful searchlights playing upon the enemy planes, and watching thru his field glasses the planes as they dived swiftly into the Tunnel thru the Air after the aviators inhaled the sleeping gas. When the last plane had landed safely in the Tunnel, his features relaxed and his face showed a smile of victory. His first thought was of Marie, his next thought was of his old friend Walter Kennelworth. He sent the first message of the victory over his secret radio to him. "The enemy has attacked New York from four sides, more than 100,000 strong. The 'Demon of Death' has done its work. The Tunnel machines have performed a miracle. More than 50,000 aviators are sleeping in our nets. Your great discovery has made this a painless victory. Edna, your noble wife, performed the painless herculean task and played her part in the final stage of the great victory."

On receiving this message Colonel Kennelworth was overjoyed, knowing that it meant that the end of the war was near. His reply was brief—"Congratulations, Robert Gordon. Love to Edna. I hope that you may yet have Marie to share with you in the great victory."

Supreme Commander Gordon's next thought was of General Pearson who had been his friend and had saved his life after his capture by the Japanese at the battle of San Francisco. The next informed him of the great victory. This was the greatest news that General Pearson had ever received in his life. He felt doubly happy because he had had faith in Robert Gordon from the first and had been the one to offer to turn over his command and authority to Gordon and make him Supreme Commander. He answered: "Supreme Commander Gordon, our country made no mistake when they placed their fate in your hands. My faith in you has been supreme and I had confidence in you from the first time I met you. Accept my sincerest gratitude for the great service that you have rendered our country. You deserve all the honor and reward that we can give you."

When reports came to headquarters in Washington that the enemy had attacked New York with more than 100,000 airplanes; that they had all been destroyed or captured; that New York was safe, and prepared for further attacks, there was great rejoicing. The President of the United States hurried to the War Office, ordered the swiftest plane to convey him to New York City to congratulate Supreme Commander Gordon. He was given a fast plane which could travel more than 300 miles per hour.

After the last attack and Supreme Commander Gordon had relaxed from the terrific strain, he walked to his desk and picked up the Bible. Turning to Ezekiel 5:2, he read: "Thou shalt burn with fire a third part in the midst of the city, when the days of the siege are fulfilled; and thou shalt take a third part, and smite about it with a knife; and a third part thou shalt scatter in the wind; and I will draw out a sword after them." He knew that Ezekiel was talking about the Tunnel thru the Air and the scattering of a third part of the army in wind and that they were caught while traveling in the Tunnel thru the Air. Then he read Chapter 17:3: "Thus saith the Lord God, A great eagle with great wings, long-winged, full of feathers, which had divers colours, came unto Lebanon, and took the highest branch of the cedar." This referred to Uncle Sam, the great eagle that was winning the war. The cedar referred to the tall building of 110 stories where Supreme Commander Gordon now had his headquarters.

He next read Ezekiel 31:4: "The waters made him great, the deep set him up on high with her rivers running round about his plants, and sent out her little rivers unto all the trees of the field." He knew that this referred to England when she had been the mistress of the seas, but that Uncle Sam had proved to be the eagle of the air and would conquer all nations on the face of the earth.

He read Ezekiel 33:21: "And it came to pass in the twelfth year of our captivity, in the tenth month, in the fifth day of the month, that one had escaped out of Jerusalem came unto me, saying, The city is smitten." He interpreted this to mean the City of Chicago where the enemy gained their last great victory.

Then read Ezekiel 37:22: "And I will make them one nation in the land upon the mountains of Israel; and one king shall be king to them all; and they shall be no more two nations, neither shall they be divided into two kingdoms, any more at all." He was sure that this meant that North and South America were to unite all nations of the world and that there was to be one ruler, one king, and he was God.

He continued with Ezekiel 39:11: "And it shall come to pass in that day, that I will give unto Gog a place there of graves in Israel, the valley of the passengers on the east of the sea; and it shall stop the noses of the passengers; and there shall they bury Gog, and all his multitude; and they shall call it, The Valley of Hamon-gog." He thought that this referred to the battle of New York. Where it said "it shall stop the noses of the passengers," this referred to the sleeping gas, which had caused the aviators to fall into the Tunnel thru the Air, and indeed the multitude had been buried above the valley and meadows of New Jersey. Again in the 39th Chapter: 9th verse: "Shall go forth and shall set on fire and burn the weapons, both the shields and the bucklers, the bows and the arrows, and the handstaves and the spears, and they shall burn them with fire seven years." This meant the "Demon of Death" which had burned up the motors of the attacking airplanes.

He then wondered when the war would end. He knew that Daniel's 70 weeks indicated the end in 1932, or about 3½ years from the time that war first broke out in Europe in 1928. He read Daniel 7:12: "As concerning the rest of the beasts, they had their dominion taken away: yet their lives were prolonged for a season and time." And again the 25th verse: "And he shall speak great words against the Most High, and shall wear out the saints of the Most High, and think to change times and laws; and they shall be given into his hand, until a time and times and the dividing of time." He had proved by study and comparing past cycles that a time or a season referred to in the Bible meant 360 days, 360 years, or 360 degrees,—a measure known and used by the astrologers in olden times and still understood and used by modern astrologers for measuring time. He knew that half a time meant 180 degrees, 180 days or years, because Ezekiel had said that the Lord had appointed a day for a year. He figured that America began with the discovery by Columbus in 1492 and that in October, 1932, would be 440 years since the discovery. The measurement used thruout the Bible was by scores and man's span of life was three score years and ten, and that four hundred and forty years equalled twenty-two scores, leaving two scores, or forty years, more for the completion of the jubilee years. He read Matthew 18:21 and 22: "Then came Peter to him, and said, Lord, how oft shall my brother sin against me, and I forgive him? till seven times? Jesus saith unto him, I say not unto thee, Until seven times; but, Until seventy times seven." Robert figured that seventy times seven meant four hundred and ninety years from the discovery of America until we would cease fighting, forgive our brothers and live in peace. He knew that the seventh period was always a jubilee period, that there was a jubilee period of seven years at the end of each forty-ninth year period and that there was a great period of forty-nine jubilee years at the end of seven times seventy; that the sixth period would end in 1933 and that from 1933 to 1982 would be the forty-nine years of the great jubilee following the end of wars and the United Kingdom of the World.

He read Daniel 7: 25: "And he shall speak great words against the Most High, and shall wear out the saints of the Most High, and think to change times and laws: and they shall be given into his hand, until a time and times and the dividing of time." Then read Daniel 12: 7: "And I heard the man clothed in linen, which was upon the waters of the river, when he held up his right hand and his left hand unto heaven, and sware by him that liveth for ever, that it shall be for a time, times, and an half; and when he shall have accomplished to scatter the power of the holy people, all these things shall be finished." He figured that a time equalled twenty years or a score, and that a time, times, equalled four hundred years, and half a time equalled ten years.

Again, Daniel 12:11 and 12: "And from the time that the daily sacrifice shall be taken away, and the abomination that maketh desolate set up, there shall be a thousand two hundred and ninety days. Blessed is he that waiteth, and cometh to the thousand three hundred and five and thirty days." Twelve hundred and ninety days are to be added to the time the war broke out in Europe in 1928 and the thirteen hundred and thirty-five days being forty-five days more, the blessed jubilee days will follow from the time the war ended in 1932 until the great celebration and signing of peace and establishing the brotherhood of man. He read Daniel 9: 24: "Seventy weeks are determined upon thy people, and upon thy holy city, to finish the transgression, and to make an end of sins, and to make reconciliation for iniquity, and to bring in everlasting righteousness, and to seal up the vision and prophecy, and to anoint the Most Holy."

This again proved that four hundred and ninety years from the discovery of America, that there should be an end of sins, an end of war and of troublesome times.

Ezekiel 4: 5 and 6: "For I have laid upon thee the years of their iniquity, according to the number of the days, three hundred and ninety days; so shalt thou bear the iniquity of the house of Israel. And when thou hast accomplished them, lie again on thy right side, and thou shalt bear the iniquity of the house of Judah forty days: I have appointed thee each day for a year." This made it plain that a day was to be used in measuring years and that there were to be forty days or forty years after peace for a jubilee period in which the sins of the past were to be atoned for.

Ten years after the armistice in November, 1918, would bring us to November, 1928, or half a score, and from November, 1928 to 1932 are indicated the troublesome times for the United States. May, 1928 to July, 1928, are very important and troublesome periods when the nominations for President of the United States will arouse the people and start a time of trouble. Using the time of three score years and ten, and doubling this period, making one hundred and forty years and adding it to 1776, the Declaration of Independence, brought us to the election of Wilson in 1916 and the war followed in 1917. The next score from this period ends in 1936.

New York City was evacuated by the British on November 25, 1783. If we add three periods of forty-nine years to this, it will bring us to 1930, the starting of the war against the United States which ended with the final attack on New York City in 1932.

New York City was founded in 1614. Adding a period of six times forty-nine brings us to 1908 and adding 24½ years or one-half the time of forty-nine years, brings us to 1932, when the name of the city was again changed. The last half of the seventh period of forty-nine years, or from the dividing of time, is another jubilee period for New York City

The first English settlement in the United States was established by Raleigh at Roanoke, Virginia, in 1585. Adding the seventh forty-nine year period, or 343 years, brings us to 1928, indicating more troublesome times to start.

The smaller cycles and seven-year periods mentioned so often in the Bible, also indicated that twice seven, or fourteen years from 1914 would bring war again in 1928, and adding half a period of a cycle of seven, or forty-two months, would indicate the duration of the war, as spoken of by Daniel in the dividing of times and seasons.

Robert figured that after October, 1932, there would be only three years left to prepare for the great feast of the jubilee of the maximum period which was to follow the establishment of universal peace. He was very happy because he felt that we were now near the end of the war and these troublesome times.

CHAPTER XXXII

ABOUT 4 A.M. the President of the United States landed on the Mammouth Building in New York and was taken down in the elevator to the 110th floor to Supreme Commander Gordon's office. He found Colonel Edna Kennelworth sentinel at the door. She had met the President before and after saluting him asked if he wished to see Supreme Commander Gordon. He replied that he did and she immediately conducted him to his private office.

The President rushed in and found Supreme Commander Gordon sitting peacefully reading a newspaper. The President could hardly believe it and asked him for the facts of the attack upon New York City and if all enemy planes had been destroyed. Supreme Commander Gordon told the President that it was a fact. The President asked Supreme Commander Gordon if there had been any losses to our airplane fleet in destroying the enemy and where our fleet was now located. The Supreme Commander pointed to the "Demon of Death" and the sleeping gas machines and said: "There is the fleet which has destroyed and captured probably 100,000 of the enemy's planes. Mr. President, would you like to go on a little sight-seeing expedition?" The President said that he would. A button was pressed and in a few minutes "Marie the Angel of Mercy," Robert's big ship, appeared in front of the window. The President told Supreme Commander Gordon that he had neither seen nor heard of such a ship before and asked him where it came from. Robert said, "Mr. President, this ship was built according to the plan laid down by Ezekiel in the Bible. I worked on it for years and completed it just before the war broke out. Its most useful work is yet to be done." Supreme Commander Gordon then explained fully the working of the "Demon of Death" to the President.

They stepped upon board "Marie the Angel of Mercy," sailed out across Long Island, slowed the plane down, drifted very low and passed over the thousands of airplanes which had been destroyed.

They sailed over Staten Island and saw the wrecks of the planes which had been destroyed there. Then swung up the Hudson River above Yonkers, descended close to the water and anchored in the air. The President had never been on an airship that was anchored in the air and was amazed at Supreme Commander Gordon's marvelous invention. He handed the President a pair of powerful field glasses and told him to take a look. The river was almost choked with the wrecks of the airplanes which had gone down defying the "Demon of Death." Bodies of aviators wearing the uniforms of the various nations were floating upon the waters. When the Supreme Commander explained to the President that he believed that not one of the enemy's planes had escaped, he marveled at the wonderful invention and the fact that two men and a lone woman could accomplish such a feat. Supreme Commander Gordon then said: "Mr. President, your greatest sight is yet to come."

He then started "Marie the Angel of Mercy," sailed out across the New Jersey hills, slowed down the big ship and entered the Tunnel thru the Air. There the greatest sight that human eyes had ever witnessed greeted the President. They passed slowly thru the Tunnel where there were thousands and thousands of planes unharmed suspended in the air with the aviators all sound asleep. The Supreme Commander then said: "This work was done by the sleeping gas. As this giant horde of probably 50,000 planes moving in sections of hundreds and thousands, one following after another, tried to attack New York, General Pearson and myself worked the Tunnel machines and Colonel Edna Kennelworth operated the sleeping gas machine. You can see the effective work and our mission of mercy. We have not taken human life and have gained the greatest victory in the world. These aviators will sleep for seven days and then awake unharmed. There will be no ill effects of the sleeping gas. We will of course remove the airships and aviators to the Wilson, Coolidge, Roosevelt, Lowden, Harding and Washington airfields and when they awake they will be our prisoners and the enemy's airships will be in our possession."

The President was astounded. He had never dreamed that man could make such marvelous inventions. Turning to Supreme Commander Gordon and grasping his hand, he said: "You have been inspired by Almighty God. You are an instrument in his hands to save this country according to God's plan." The Supreme Commander replied that he had always felt that way and had never taken any credit to himself; that since he was about eight years old he had been reading the Bible and knew from it that this war was inevitable; that he had spent his time and money to complete these inventions for the day his country would need them.

On the way back, Supreme Commander Gordon told the President that the Marie the Angel of Mercy could make a speed of 1000 miles an hour and that he could easily go round the world in 24 hours. On their return all was quiet in New York City. No one knew what had happened that night. The President could not find words to express his appreciation for this wonderful work. He asked the Supreme Commander what his future plans were. Supreme Commander Gordon told the President to read the Bible, especially Daniel's prophecy and the book of Ezekiel, and he would know what was yet to take place. It was agreed that the news of the success with the "Demon of Death" and the sleeping gas machine was to be kept secret and that the President was the only one to know of Robert's great invention.

The President returned to Washington on the forenoon of June 9th, feeling much elated over the wonderful victory, proud of his native land and thankful that the Divine Power had given them the man of the hour at the right time.

It had been a great birthday for Robert, because his country had been saved. His years of labor had been rewarded but yet no news had come of Marie. He wondered if she were alive and if she had been watching this terrible war, the greatest of all with its great destruction. When the war was over and the world was once more at peace, what would happen to him or what would he do? It seemed to him that when the war was over, his life work would be finished. Without Marie, there would be nothing left, nothing more to work for. Supreme Commander Gordon knew that there would be no more attacks that day, so he ordered Colonel Edna Kennelworth to get some sleep. He communicated with Colonel Kennelworth in Boston and found that there had been no further attacks there. The Colonel reported that he was ready and waiting to put to sleep more of the enemy as soon as they arrived.

The Allied Enemy headquarters at the different points in the United States were absolutely without any news as to what had happened to all the planes and airships that had been sent out to attack New York, but in this case, they felt that no news was good news. They were trying in every way with the wireless and radio to reach the commanders of the different fleets but not a word was received.

On the afternoon of June 9th, when not a word had been heard from any of the ships or planes sent out the night before to destroy New York City, the Allied Enemy headquarters were in gloom. Hope was giving way to despair. They feared that the disaster at Detroit and Boston had been repeated. General Nagato was communicated with and his reply was: "This is a great disappointment. We had all hoped that New York could be destroyed or captured and this would mean the end of the war. It now seems our hopes are blasted. Some devilish invention by the Americans is being used to destroy or capture our ships. Their success seems to be so complete that it is almost unbelievable. Not one report from any man or ship has been heard since we attacked Boston. Now, if the flower of our army has been lost in this attack against New York, our cause seems hopeless. The facts are desperate but we must face them. Let no further move be made until we know more about what the Yankees have."

Supreme Commander Gordon had made up his mind that he would keep everything secret and not let the enemy know anything, but he dispatched a message by radio to enemy headquarters reading:

Very much disappointed. Lost a good night's sleep last night waiting for your army to take New York City. When may we expect the pleasure of a visit from your planes?

This mysterious message was as much a mystery to the enemy as the letter that Robert found on the street in Paris was to him. The fleet sent out to attack Boston had never returned and no word had ever been heard of them. France had been instructed by Supreme Commander Gordon to cease attacking and await further instructions. Everything was quiet on the other side and Germany and England were awaiting reports of the success of the campaign of the United States before making further attacks on France.

On the morning of June 13th the aviators who had been put to sleep by the sleeping gas around Boston, awoke. They were feeling good. They knew that something had put them to sleep suddenly but did not know that they had slept seven days and nights instead of one night. Instructions by Supreme Commander Gordon had been given that no harm should be done any of the aviators when they awoke. Scouting planes were sent out by the United States Army to capture the aviators when they awoke or started to drive their planes away, but a few of the planes were permitted to escape and return to the headquarters of the enemy. When they reported that while they were attacking Boston the night before, they suddenly went to sleep and the planes dropped to the earth and water, they were informed by the Commanders that they had been away one week.

This was a great blow to the enemy and they knew now that the Americans had some kind of a sleeping gas which was harmless and would put men to sleep and keep them asleep for 7 days. The enemy had all kinds of poisonous gases and bombs, but they had never discovered a gas to put people asleep for a week, then awake without any ill effects. They now realized what Supreme Commander Gordon's answer meant,—that it was some new discoveries which the United States had made that caused them to fight on and not accede to any peace terms. After days of waiting, scouting and trying to secure information as to what had happened, the attack on New York was left a mystery. They waited until the 16th day of June, thinking that if their aviators had been put to sleep there some of them would return. When none of them returned by the 21st of the month and no word was received, they knew that the fleet had been destroyed or captured and that their army had been greatly weakened, but still they held the Pacific Coast and controlled New Orleans, St. Louis, and Chicago and their Western lines were unbroken. After holding a conference, they decided to adopt a waiting attitude for a time and see what the next move of the United States would be.

CHAPTER XXXIII

TIME drifted along until the early part of July without any further attack by the enemy, but Supreme Commander Gordon believed that they would make another attack soon before giving up. He was simply watching and waiting, biding his time. The United States Army scouting planes reported that the enemy scouts were going out more frequently each night and some of them had been seen 50,000 or 60,000 feet in the air. They thought that they were getting ready to make another attack and were trying to get a line on what the United States forces were planning to do. The Supreme Commander went to Washington to test out the "Demon of Death" which had been installed in the Capitol Building and found it in good working order. A sleeping gas distributing machine and the Tunnel machine had been set up there and he also tested them out.

In view of the splendid work done by Colonel Edna Kennelworth at the time of the attack on New York City, Supreme Commander Gordon decided to send her to Washington and put her in charge of the sleeping gas distributing machine, the "Demon of Death," and the Tunnel machine. He instructed her that if an attack came upon Washington, she was not to use the "Demon of Death" unless the sleeping gas failed or they failed to get the enemy aviators into the Tunnel thru the Air. He believed that if attack came upon Washington, it would be the last and end the war. Because his country had ever stood for love and liberty, if its Capitol was attacked he wanted it to be saved by a bloodless victory. It would mean much to the United States in future years if the seat of government could be protected without taking the life of one of the enemy. With the Tunnel machine in New York, another one in Cincinnati and a third machine in Washington, D. C., he would be able from New York City to place a Tunnel thru the Air in every direction around Washington to capture the invading army of planes. Colonel Edna Kennelworth said that she thought he was placing on her shoulders a great responsibility, but that if he had confidence in her, she would go and do her best. He told her that she could not fail and that there was nothing to fear; that it would be much easier now to protect Washington than it was New York from attack. So Colonel Edna Kennelworth went to Washington. She arrived there on July 2nd, and did not have long to wait before seeing action.

Battle of Washington

The enemy was losing confidence and decided to risk 50,000 planes, the best that they had, on a concerted attack upon Washington. They figured that if they could take the Capitol, it would be a telling blow and help them on to further victory. This was to be a supreme test and they decided to make the attack in broad daylight because they thought it would be a surprise and there would be more people on the street, and the attack would have a greater demoralizing effect on the people thruout the country.   July 4th, Independence Day, was the time selected for the attack.   The plan was to send one fleet up the Potomac, have another fleet come down the Potomac from the North and Northwest and the third wing come across by Baltimore. Colonel Edna Kennelworth was on duty when the Tel-Talk buzzed and a scouting plane reported to her that the enemy were approaching in large numbers up the Potomac.   She had never operated the sleeping gas machine in daylight before, but knew that it would work just as effectively.   Having seen the attack upon New York and knowing how swiftly one attack followed the other, she realized that she must work fast. She adjusted the gas machine toward the enemy approaching down the Potomac and set it for a certain range, about 75 miles.   She looked thru her telescope and saw the enemy when they were about 50 miles away and decided to let go the sleeping gas.   She swept it quickly right and left and in the glistening sunshine saw hundreds of planes going down.   In fifteen minutes the entire fleet was safely asleep in the Tunnel thru the Air.   By this time report came that another fleet was making from Baltimore in a direct line for Washington. She set the machine again, looked thru her powerful glass and saw the enemy approachingg.   She started discharging the gas, and in twelve minutes the entire fleet had been plunged into the Tunnel.

She had a few minutes to wait and immediately

picked up the radiophone and told Supreme Commander Gordon in New York that the sleeping gas machine had worked wonderfully and that the Tunnel thru the Air held in captivity thousands of the enemy's airships and planes. Almost before she had finished making her report, the Tel-Talk buzzed. She ran to it and was informed by the scouting planes that the largest fleet of planes ever seen was approaching from the West and Northwest. Knowing that this was a combined fleet from the enemy's Western lines, from the same direction as the final one that attacked New York City. This was to be the supreme test. The first formation approached with about 1000 planes. Swiftly and silently, the gas machine did its work and they went down into the Tunnel. Then came the second, third, and fourth formation and so on. More than 50,000 planes had gone down and not more than one hour's time had elapsed. When it was over with, Edna realized that she had not been a human being during this ordeal, that she had worked just like the machine, forgotten everything but the responsibility for the protection of her country. When she knew that the Capitol of her beloved country was safe and that more than 50,000 of the enemy's airships were safely suspended in the Tunnel thru the Air and that the aviators had entered upon their seven days' sleep, she was supremely happy because not one life was required to save the Capitol. It was the greatest victory of all history thus far and she knew what it meant to Supreme Commander Gordon and how this victory would be hailed with rejoicing all over the United States. It would relieve the tension which had existed for two years when every hamlet, town and city had feared every night that they might be attacked and destroyed by bombs from the enemy's planes.

The news had been flashed to all the Departments and Army Headquarters. When the scouting planes reported that more than 50,000 planes had been captured in this attack and not one of them escaped, the President and Army officers breathed a great sigh of relief and knew that this meant certain victory for the United States because the enemy had concentrated their attack on New York and Washington with their best planes, and had very few large bombing planes left, and if this was not the end of the war, it was the beginning of the end.

The President and his Cabinet rushed to the Capitol Building to congratulate Colonel Edna Kennelworth. They found her carefully powdering her nose. By this time she was calm and collected and prepared for the unexpected reception, but was overwhelmed with the suddenness of the arrival of high officials. She had met the President before when he had come to New York after the great battle. He was the first to grasp her hand and, after kissing it, told her of the great debt of gratitude her country owed her. The President said, "Your great service demonstrates that woman is the equal of man and I hope to live to see the day when a woman will be President of the United States. This country owes to you and Supreme Commander Gordon and your good husband, Colonel Kennelworth, its liberty and freedom. There is nothing too good for you.

You have performed the greatest act of any woman in history. I speak for the American people and extend their heartfelt gratitude. We can never repay you."

Colonel Edna Kennelworth thanked the President, told him that she had only done her duty and that she felt any other good woman in the United States would be glad to do the same under the same conditions. The President and members of his Cabinet were greatly impressed with her modesty and expressed their pride that one so young in years possessed such kill and daring. She told them that this was imperative and that there was no one else who know how to handle the sleeping gas machine except Supreme Commander Gordon and Colonel Kennelworth and that she had been placed there for that purpose and had only done her duty. Supreme Commander Gordon in New York sent a simple message congratulating Colonel Edna Kennelworth: "You're a real woman—a thorobred. I knew you could do it."

The President and the War Council met and voted that a message of congratulation and appreciation be sent to Supreme Commander Gordon telling him that everything would be left in his hands and to proceed as he had in the past. The President and other Government officials asked him if he would not give his consent to permit all of the newspapers in the United States to publish the details of the attack upon New York and how it had been successfully defended and to give details of the great victory at Washington. They felt that the people had so long been in a state of fear and anxiety, this would bring great relief and give them a chance to get some peaceful sleep because it would remove from their minds the fear of their cities and towns being destroyed; give them confidence that the United States had proved equal to the occasion; help the general business situation and bring comfort to thousands of people who were suffering. Supreme Commander Gordon replied that there was no question but that the war was won and that need for secrecy was no longer necessary.

On the afternoon of July 4th the President of the United States issued a proclamation to the people, telling them of the wonderful victory in Washington and assuring them that the country was safe, and set aside the following three days as holidays to celebrate and commemorate the victory of Independence Day. In his message he said that God had blessed the Stars and Stripes and given to America a lone man who had made inventions which had saved the country, and that a lone woman, Edna Kennelworth, with these inventions had protected Washington from destruction and captured over 50,000 of the enemy's airships without causing the loss of a single soul.

The President's Proclamation was given to the newspapers and every paper in the United States carried big headlines:

GREAT ATTACK ON NEW YORK AND WASHINGTON
    FAILS. MORE THAN ONE HUNDRED THOUSAND
    OF THE ENEMY'S AIRSHIPS HAVE BEEN CAP-
    TURED. HUNDREDS OF THOUSANDS HAVE BEEN
    TAKEN PRISONERS. EDNA KENNELWORTH, A
    LONE WOMAN, SAVED WASHINGTON WITH

SLEEPING GAS BAGGED OVER FIFTY THOUSAND AIRPLANES WHICH ARE NOW SAFELY HELD IN THE TUNNEL THRU THE AIR MADE BY SUPREME COMMANDER GORDON'S GREAT INVENTION. IT IS EXPECTED THAT THE ENEMY WILL MAKE A PLEA FOR PEACE ANY DAY.

When the President declared a holiday, Supreme Commander Gordon decided that this was the time to let the enemy know what our strength was as it was no longer necessary to keep the secret about our new wonderful inventions. He ordered the invisible noiseless planes to load up with hundreds of thousands of newspapers which told of the great victory, sail at great altitudes over the enemy's lines in the United States and bombard them with these newspapers. He ordered Colonel Morrison and Colonel Manson to take charge of the planes which were to distribute the papers over the enemy's lines. Ordered them to sail over the City of Mexico and distribute papers over the enemy's headquarters there. The Supreme Commander felt that this was the end, in fact he knew it, because after reading over Ezekiel again he saw that the prophecies were about all fulfilled and that in a short time the millennium would dawn and the world would be at peace. He read Chapter 10: 9 and 21:

And the cherubims lifted up their wings and mounted up from the earth in my sight; when they went out the wheels were also beside them and everyone stood at the door of the east gate of the Lord's house; and the glory of the God of Israel was over them. Everyone had four faces apiece and everyone four wings; and the likeness of the hands of a man was under their wings. And the glory of the Lord went up from the midst of the city and stood upon the mountain, which is on the east side of the city."

He knew that this was the glory referred to for the United States and that Ezekiel's prophecy, Chapter 14, 21st verse, had been fulfilled. It reads as follows:

For thus saith the Lord God: How much more when I send my four sore judgments upon Jerusalem, the sword and the famine and the noisome beast, and the pestilence, to cut off from it man and beast?

He knew that the noisome beasts were the airplanes, and that all of these things had happened.

He read again about the 7 days when they should prepare and purge the Altar and purify it and conse-crate themselves. He now knew that the time was com-ing when the Lord should rule on earth as he had prom-ised and war should be no more. The prophecies of the Bible had been fulfilled where it said that woman should be the equal or exalted above man. The Lord had said, "I will exalt the low and debase the high," and the Bible said, "The little ones shall become as a thousand." He was happy to know that everything was working out just as he had predicted it and happy because his in-ventions which he had worked on so unselfishly, had saved his devoted country and made the nations of the world realize that all power under heaven and earth was given unto the United States, the land of liberty. Knowing that the great power was now in his hands alone, he could proceed to destroy every living thing in every nation, but his heart was full of love and mercy and only thru mercy and without selfishness could the United States set an example to the world. He could retake the Pacific Coast, wipe out the Western lines of the enemy or put them all to sleep for 7 days and then make peace on any terms that he might dictate. He thought of all the rulers of the world, from the tyrant Nero down to the Kaiser, how each one had sought world dominion based on selfish greed, and each one had failed because God would not sanction such rulership. He thought of Marie and as he dreamed of her, forgot whether he was a man with Caesar or a God with Alexander. Not once was he tempted to use the great power within his hands, for he knew that love was kind and merciful. All the writings of St. Paul had put stress on love and charity. He decided that women and children must be protected and that not one of their lives should be taken in this final conflict. Now that the end was near, he must demonstrate in a way never to be forgotten the power that he held over the world and decided to use the sleeping gas.

CHAPTER XXXIX

ROBERT GORDON'S SEVEN DAYS

ON July 20th he had completed all preparations and had all his armies and all the airships and planes equipped with the sleeping gas machines. Instructions had been given that they should pass over the lines from the Gulf of Mexico to the Great Lakes, from Los Angeles to Seattle, and send forth the sleeping gas and put to sleep entire enemy armies so that they would be kept asleep for 7 days. He decided to notify all of the Commanding Generals of the Allied Enemy just what he was going to do so that they would realize and know what power he had, and instructed them to have all their commanding officers moved to places where they would not be molested or put to sleep, so that they might watch and know what was happening. The Allied Enemy were notified that they could make every attempt to protect themselves but that it would be useless, because they would be unable to see or hear the approach of the silent, invisible planes.

He called Colonel Walter Kennelworth and Colonel Edna Kennelworth to his headquarters. Thanked them for their services to the country; assured them of his appreciation of their loyalty and devotion and promoted them to the rank of General. He ordered General Walter Kennelworth to take charge of headquarters in

New York, operate the sleeping gas machine and to use the "Demon of Death" in case of emergency. However, he felt sure that there would be no more attacks. General Edna Kennelworth was ordered to Washington to resume charge in the Capitol Building and operate the machines for defense if necessary.

In bidding good-bye to his loyal comrades, he told them that he was going to take Marie the Angel of Mercy, and was going alone to London, Berlin, Moscow, Madrid, Tokio and destroy buildings in these cities and with the light ray put every city in darkness, put the people to sleep and leave them for 7 days. Then he would destroy or conquer every important city in the world in 6 days, just the same as God created the world in 6 days, and that on the 7th day he would return to New York City and await the action of the Allied Nations in regard to peace. He ordered all of the countries notified by radio that he would leave New York City on Marie the Angel of Mercy, which could make 1000 miles an hour, and when he arrived in London and other cities everyone should be out of the buildings which he would destroy with the "Demon of Death"; that this was to be a mission of mercy and that he would not destroy one life if possible but that he must demonstrate the power that he could destroy all life and buildings if necessary.

The world was astounded and amazed but of course did not believe that there was any such invention or any such power in the hands of any one man, or any one nation. At 7 A.M. on July 21st, Supreme Commander Gordon sailed away in the Marie the Angel of Mercy and in a little over three hours he was over London. He notified them to clear all the big buildings on Lombard and Downing Streets. They were unable to see his plane or hear it but they knew that he was somewhere over London in the air. The people were frightened and cleared out of the buildings. Women and children were taken away to safety and slowly the death ray started to do its work. The big buildings crumbled away, slowly melting down as tho they were butter. The people fell upon their knees in the streets and prayed to God to save them from this great invisible force. Many people believed that it was an unseen power from heaven that had come to destroy the world and that this was the end of the world. When he had completed the destruction of enough buildings to show them his power, he circled over London time and time again, sending forth the sleeping gas and the people all succumbed and went to sleep. With the power from his machine he extinguished all the electric lights in the city and left it in darkness. The news of this terrible disaster was sent from London to the Allied Enemy headquarters in the United States.

Supreme Commander Gordon then proceeded on the following day to Berlin. He intended to teach the Germans a lesson that they never would forget. He would show mercy that they had never shown because not one woman or child would be harmed, but protected. Not one human life would be taken, but he would make the destruction of buildings in Berlin so complete that they would never forget his visit. He would remind them that the Kaiser and all of the great German armies were powerless when Marie the Angel of Mercy sent forth its destructive rays and sleeping gas. He sailed over Berlin and notified everyone to clear out of the buildings. He destroyed all of the important buildings on the business streets, turned loose his sleeping gas and left Berlin in darkness, to sleep for 7 days.

When he had completed the bombardment of the buildings in Berlin, he sent a message to the President of France that he would be in Paris within the next hour to thank him personally for the great aid that France had given us in the war. The President notified him that France would declare a holiday and give him a reception greater than that tendered Captain Lindbergh when he landed there on May 21st, 1927. He informed the President that his time was limited, but in appreciation of the friendship of France he would anchor Marie the Angel of Mercy over Paris and arrange lights to play upon her to make her visible so the people could see this wonderful ship.

He left Berlin and was in Paris in a short time. France had sent thousands of her planes into the air signaling the "Marie." They could not see her and Supreme Commander Gordon communicated with them by radio and anchored near the same spot where Lindbergh had landed over five years before. He was taken aboard one of France's airplanes and carried to the President, who greeted him cordially, kneeled and kissed his cheeks and hands. Thanked him for the inventions which he had made which would end war for all time. Supreme Commander Gordon had brought a letter from the President of the United States thanking France for her support and assuring them of our loyalty and support forever in the future. He told the President of his plan for a United Kingdom of the World. How he was going to call all the nations to New York for a peace conference when the war was over, which he was assured would be when he returned to New York. The President assured him that France would be very happy to be the first nation to join with the United States in the brotherhood of man to make it a United Kingdom of the World.

He told the President of France that he had brought with him on board the "Marie" one of his Tunnel machines which he wanted to place in one of the tallest buildings, establish a Tunnel thru the Air between New York and Paris so that their airships could pass in safety thru the Tunnel to New York, or if any of the officers in Canada wanted to come home, they could proceed to New York and travel thru the Tunnel to Paris. He tested out this machine after it had been set up, sent one of the planes to New York thru the Tunnel and the round trip was made in one hour and thirty minutes. He explained to the President that by establishing a vacuum, it was possible to drive the machines in safety at a terrific speed. He instructed Louis Corday, one of the famous aces of the French Aviation Corps, how to handle the Tunnel machine.

Then Supreme Commander Gordon went to Lisbon and Madrid, Spain, destroyed their most important buildings and put the people to sleep for 7 days. Then proceeded to Rome where he destroyed all the fine cathedrals, business and government buildings. Before arriving there he had notified the Pope to get all the people out of the buildings and instructed him where to go for safety, telling him he did not wish to give him the sleeping gas but wanted him to be awake to pray during the 7 days while all the inhabitants were asleep. Told him that his people must be taught that God is more powerful than any ruler or potentate and that the time would come when there must be one religion, one United Kingdom of the World and one God.

From there he proceeded to the beautiful city of Vienna and having the people removed from the buildings, turned on the "Demon of Death" and melted the buildings down. Discharging sleeping gas from his machine, he said good-bye to Vienna and proceeded to Moscow.

The poor and uneducated people of Russia had been warned of his coming. The newspapers told them what had been happening in other cities, but the people refused to believe that they would not be destroyed. Many of them rushed to the waters and drowned themselves. Others went to the forests to hide. Moscow was more excited than ever before. People had been praying day and night before he arrived. Finally when he was over Moscow, he sent a radio message that they should clear all the important buildings which he was going to destroy. He descended very low and located the buildings and when he had been notified that the people had been moved to safety, turned on the "Demon of Death." As the buildings leapt into flames and the people could see them, they were sure that this was the end of the world and that God was destroying it by fire, because they were unable to see the source from which the destruction was coming, the destroying rays from the machine being invisible and Marie the Angel of Mercy being invisible. When he had finished the destruction of the buildings, he turned loose the sleeping gas, darkened the city and sailed for Constantinople.

He had notified the terrible Turks, who had sent such destructive airships to help conquer the United States, that he was going to open the Dardanelles from the air; and destroy the battleships in the Black Sea. When he arrived and all buildings were cleared, people were greatly frightened and some of them were praying to America's God to save them. Supreme Commander Gordon assured them that no lives would be taken. He then proceeded to destroy all their largest buildings, discharged the death rays into the water and blew up their ships; left the city in darkness to sleep in peace.

His next stop was at Alexandria and Cairo, Egypt. He visited the Pyramids, notified the people that they were placed there according to a divine plan and that he would not destroy them. He destroyed the main buildings and blew up the warships, leaving the people asleep as he had done in other cities.

He notified the people in Bombay, India, that they had taken sides with England against us and that they must be shown an example of the power of the Land of Freedom. He destroyed their temples and large buildings and put the people asleep. Then went to Pekin, China, where he destroyed buildings which had stood for thousands of years; discharged the sleeping gas and proceeded to Tokio.

The Japs had been the first to declare war upon the United States and make an attack and they must be taught a lesson which they would remember so long as the world stood. He ordered all the men removed from their battleships and proceeded to discharge the death rays into the water and destroy them. When he began to destroy the important buildings the people thought that it was another earthquake because they had not forgotten how their buildings had crumbled down years before. He assured them that no lives would be taken, that they would be allowed to sleep for 7 days in peace; leaving the city in darkness and the inhabitants asleep, he proceeded to Melbourne and Sydney, Australia.

Australia had remained neutral and was friendly to the United States. He carried a letter of thanks from the President of the United States to the people of Australia. Thanked them personally and told them that they were now invited to join the United States in forming the brotherhood of man in the United Kingdom.

The City of Mexico was next notified that they would have the final and greatest demonstration of the power of Marie the Angel of Mercy. The Mexicans and Spaniards knew that Supreme Commander Gordon was born in the State of Texas. They remembered the Battle of the Alamo and Goliad. The poor class of Mexicans refused to believe after Mexico had joined with Japan and Spain against the United States, that any Texan would spare their lives. They had prayed day and night since they learned that the Supreme Commander of the United States with Marie the Angel of Mercy was to visit them. He told them that this machine took its power from the air and that the rays were powerful enough to melt down the mountains and that he would destroy some of the mountains of Mexico and all the old pyramids. Before he reached the City of Mexico, he anchored over a mountain, turned on the death ray and the mountain crumbled to dust. The old pyramids were also destroyed. When he reached the City of Mexico, he informed them that he had destroyed the mountains to fulfill the prophecies in the Bible which said that every mountain should be laid low and every valley should be exalted. A large part of forces of the enemy and their officers were located in the City of Mexico and they were notified to flee to the mountains and hills where they could watch the destruction of the buildings. The Supreme Commander of the United States said that they would not be put to sleep because he wanted them to watch the silent, sleeping city while it remained in darkness for 7 days.

When he had completed his destruction of the City of Mexico, he sent a message by radio to New York and Washington that he was on his way home and would pass over the enemy's lines in California and in the central part of the United States, sending them messages all along giving his location and offering to let the officers take a shot at Marie the Angel of Mercy if they could see her. He knew that "Marie" could rise to a height of 60 miles or more if necessary and intended to fly at a height to which no enemy plane could ever ascend.

Supreme Commander Gordon sent a message to his old home town, Texarkana, Texas, that he would anchor there and give everybody a view of Marie the Angel of Mercy. When he arrived there he circled over his own old home out near Red River; then sailed the "Marie" down Stateline Avenue and anchored her in the air about 100 feet above the street. He turned on the lights and made his great ship visible, so the people could see what had accomplished the great victory. It was the greatest celebration that Texarkana ever had. The people went wild with joy. His dear old mother was the happiest woman in the world. She greeted him affectionately; told him that all her dreams about him had come true.

He could only make a short visit as he had to hurry on to New York. He notified Montreal, Canada, that he would arrive there early on the morning of the 7th day. Montreal prepared for a great celebration. He arrived there soon after sunrise, anchored the "Marie," and delivered a message to the people of Canada, thanking them for their loyalty and aid in our behalf. Invited them to be among the first to join in the peace conference in making the United States of the World. After bidding them good-bye, he sailed for New York, arriving just before noon on the 7th day after he had sailed away on his great trip around the world.

Marie the Angel of Mercy circled over New York and landed at the Mammouth Building. General Walter Kennelworth was on duty and reported what had happened during Supreme Commander Gordon's absence, altho he had kept in touch with him by radio all the time and informed him what was going on. Supreme Commander Gordon's orders had been carried out the day he left on his 7-day tour of the world and sleeping gas sprayed over all the enemy lines thruout the United States.

CHAPTER XXXV

THE Allied Enemy generals and officers knowing what could happen after the losses at New York and Washington obeyed the instructions of Supreme Commander Gordon and moved to a place of safety. After waiting three days and finding that their armies were still asleep they gathered near their various headquarters in New Orleans, St. Louis, Chicago, San Francisco and prayed for deliverance. They realized that the greatest power of the universe was now in the hands of the United States. Most of them credited this power to an act of God, and not to man. They had not yet heard what had happened in all the cities of the world where the Marie the Angel of Mercy had visited.

Late on the 7th day the Allied Armies of the enemy began to awake. Each day following for the next 6 days, the people in one city after another of the foreign countries where he had visited awoke. Supreme Commander Gordon released an electric light control and the cities were no longer in darkness. All wireless and radio stations refused to take any messages except what concerned news in regard to the Marie the Angel of Mercy and what had happened all over the world.

On the second day after Supreme Commander Gordon's arrival, the War Council of the United States and the President came to New York City to confer with the Supreme Commander. Reports had come from all parts of the world about his mission of mercy. Not one life had been reported lost. To say that he returned in triumph and great victory was to put it mildly. The President and the War Council decided that it was now time to permit all newspapers to publish the news all over the United States and let the people know just what had been happening during the past 7 days. Thousands of messages poured in to Supreme Commander Gordon. The world was at the Supreme Commander's feet. He was hailed as the greatest man since Jesus Christ.

On August 4th, 1932, all of the cities in the world where Supreme Commander Gordon had destroyed buildings, were heard from. Reports showed that everything was normal and that no lives were lost. Messages were pouring in from every part of the world to the Allied Enemy Commanders to make peace with the United States on any terms and never permit the return of Marie the Angel of Mercy. The Commanders of the Allied Enemy armies dispatched messages to the President at Washington, asking for an armistice and peace terms on any conditions. The President replied:

Peace terms are out of my hands. When this country was in dire peril and our cause seemed hopeless and lost,—when your demands were to take our country, our name, our honor, —at that time we placed our fate in the hands of a lone man Robert Gordon and made him Supreme Commander of all of the Armies of the United States. His will is law. You will have to deal with him, no one else has authority or will be given authority.

The communication was sent to Supreme Commander Gordon. He called a conference to discuss peace terms. The President, Cabinet officers and all the Army and Government officials attended. When the conference convened, General Pearson arose and said: "When we turned over the Supreme Command of the Armies of the United States to you we agreed to abide by your decision no matter what it might be. Your actions and the victories that you have won have justified our faith and confidence in you. You have proven yourself to be the greatest man in the history of the world. Your mercy and justice has been demonstrated. Our country and the world and its destiny are safe in the hands of a man like you. You have been guided by Almighty God and I make a motion that we say nothing, offer no advice, but leave everything in your hands. Whatever terms of peace you make, we will gladly abide by them."

When he had finished talking, Colonel Manson arose and said: "I second that motion. Let us make the vote unanimous by all rising." Every man rose immediately. The President grasped Supreme Commander Gordon's hand and thanked him for his great service to the United States and the world. Each Cabinet officer and army officer followed, and shook the Supreme Commander's hand, wishing him continued success. The President and Government officials were anxious for Supreme Commander Gordon to explain how he had accomplished the wonderful feat of going around the world in 7 days and destroying so many buildings. He told them that his new machine made a Tunnel thru the Air and that it had overcome resistance from gravitation and the machine was invisible. He explained how he had been guided in building this machine and all his other inventions by the Bible.

Supreme Commander Gordon decided to call a conference of all nations to take place in New York, on August 30th, 1932. They were notified and representatives were asked to be sent. Supreme Commander Gordon made a special request that the representatives from all the countries bring with them their wives or daughters as he had a special message for them and wanted them to take an important part in the Peace Conference. No one knew what the conditions of peace would be, but even the enemy felt that they were dealing with the most just man that the world had ever known, a man who refused to take the lives of women and children. When he had the power to put the entire Allied Armies of the Enemy to sleep and destroy them, he refused to do it. They were all willing and glad to leave their fate in his hands. All over the country Old Glory was waving from every building. Flags were printed with the picture of Supreme Commander Gordon on them and the picture of "Marie the Angel of Mercy." The flags bore the inscription "Tunnel thru the Air," "The Lone Aviator," "America's Savior."

Each day airplanes from all parts of the world began to bring the officials who were to be at the conference of all nations. Madison Square Garden had been engaged for the conference. Several millions of people had applied for admission but only Government officials and prominent men and women thruout the country were granted tickets. The Government officials of the United States led by the President and the Supreme War Council, decided that at the opening of the Peace Conference, General Walter Kennelworth should be designated to make the address of welcome to the delegates of all countries and also to make the speech of thanks for the United States to Supreme Commander Gordon, for the services he had rendered, knowing that he was his best friend and he knew him better than anyone else.

CHAPTER XXXVI

Peace Conference of the World

THE conference convened about 10 A.M. on August 30th. All of the officials were seated by 11 o'clock and shortly after, Supreme Commander Gordon escorted by the President of the United States, General Walter Kennelworth and his wife General Edna Kennelworth, arrived. The applause lasted for more than one hour. When it had died down, General Pearson stepped to the center of the platform, and grasped the Supreme Commander's hand and raised it before the vast throng and said, "Commanders, rulers, kings and officials of all nations, this is our lord and master, whose will is law. Whatever he says, we will abide by. I now introduce to you, General Walter Kennelworth, who will make the opening address. The applause again lasted for over a half hour, then General Walter Kennelworth began to speak:

"Brothers and Sisters of the world: This is the greatest council that the world has ever known, for never before in history has every nation gathered at a peace conference. We hope and verily believe this is to be the last war. We expect to be one united people and follow the law laid down in the Bible, 'Love thy neighbor as thyself.' Then there can be no more wars. It is my purpose at this time to introduce to you a man who needs no introduction, the prince of peace, a man of sorrow and acquainted with grief—the greatest and most just man since our saviour Jesus Christ was on earth. We placed our liberty in his hands and he saved our country and has been merciful to the enemy. Our gratitude to him can never be repaid. I now commend you to his care and keeping. Whatever terms he may make for peace, the United States Government will ratify and confirm. I now take pleasure in presenting to you our Supreme Commander Robert Gordon who will now address you."

Supreme Commander Gordon arose and tried to quiet the great crowd. Women were on their feet and men were shouting, "Hail the most just and merciful man in the world." There was a mad rush to try to get to the platform to shake his hand. When the noise had quieted down and order been restored Supreme Commander Gordon raised the Holy Bible and said:

"Brothers and Sisters of the United World:

"The terms laid down in this book are the terms of peace that I offer you. I am going to offer you peace on the same terms that Jesus would give you. The United States has always stood for liberty and as the land of liberty it must set an example of peace and brotherly love to the world as it has always done before. This country has never engaged in a war for personal gain. In the great World War, we refused to accept any indemnities. We made the fight for a principle, not for money or territory.

"Now the United States will make no demand upon any nation. There is no longer to be different nations of the world, but the United Kingdom of the World. The United States is to dictate peace to the world on the terms of brotherly love. We will take no territory nor demand any indemnity. We will retain the gold supply of the world but will follow the admonition of Jesus Christ when he said 'Feed my Lambs.' We will lend a helping hand to any nation that needs it. You are to return to your homes and loved ones and tell them that the spirit of God, which is all-powerful and able to destroy, is ever merciful and just and has spared your lives and liberty. We refuse to take your money or territory and in return only ask and demand that you do unto others as you would have them do unto you and as we have done unto you.

"Remember that Old Glory has never trailed the dust and she never will, because the God of the universe did not create this nation for any or all nations to destroy. He has placed the great power in the hands of those who would use it only in defense of right and not for selfish gain. When I am ready, I can touch a button and your great airships which are now held captive may proceed safely home and when you go, may you follow in the footsteps of Him who created the earth and who has saved you, and may you give reverence and praise to Him who is able to destroy not only property, but both soul and body. When the final articles are drawn and the territory of the United States is divided and allotted according to the plan laid down by Ezekiel and according to science, we will so direct that each of you can live in peace and harmony and according to the law.

"I demand that the terms of peace be signed by women as well as men. They are more just and merciful and will rule the country in the future. If women must continue to be the mothers of our men, they must have the right to decide whether their sons shall be sent to war or not. It will take time to arrange the plans for cities and countries as outlined by Ezekiel and I expect that the terms will be acceptable and signed by the good women of every nation.

"It is understood and agreed that the United States will retain all of the inventions we now have for the prevention of war and I warn you that if necessity ever demands it, for the protection of peace of the world, that a machine can be built which will destroy every living soul on the earth. It can be directed from New York City by a lone man without ever leaving here and do complete destructive work. This is only a warning and not a threat. You have seen the power demonstrated by Marie the Angel of Mercy, and mercy shown. You must respect this divine law and divine power. Remember that this victory is according to God's plan and God's will. I take no credit to myself and for myself and my country ask nothing, except that you live with us in brotherly love."

When Supreme Commander Gordon had finished speaking, the applause was the greatest ever known, lasting again for more than an hour. When it had died down, General Walter Kennelworth stepped to the platform and said, "It is next in order for me to make a speech of appreciation to Supreme Commander Gordon not only for our country, but I have in my hand a paper which has been signed by the rulers of every country in the world, asking that I make a speech of appreciation for them. Before proceeding with this address, I want to ask every man and woman in this audience who is willing to accept the terms of peace laid down by Supreme Commander Gordon to rise to their feet." In an instant, every man and woman in the building was on their feet, shouting, "Hail to the Chief, God bless him and long may he live."

When they were seated again, General Kennelworth proceeded, and turning to Supreme Commander Gordon he said:

"Supreme Commander Robert Gordon, Comrade and Friend: I now have the greatest honor that has ever been conferred upon any man,—that of presenting to you the highest medal that the United States can confer. This medal is emblematic of your great work and the duty and loyalty you have shown to your country. It is made of gold with a triple triangle in the three royal colors, purple, blue and gold. The words in the center of the triangle are 'I am God-Love.' Around the triangle are the words, Faith, Hope and Love. All of this and even more you have lived.

"Words are empty when I attempt to convey to you the appreciation and gratitude of this country and the world. I am instructed by the President of the United States to say to you that anything that the United States can give is yours without the asking. All the foreign countries now fall at your feet to worship you because you have proven worthy and have used the great power placed in your hands wisely. It has been well said that God never places a responsibility upon a man who will use it unwisely. God has made no mistake in selecting you, Robert Gordon, as the prince of peace. The United States is proud of you, the world honors you and we offer you our humble gratitude and all the praise that this world can give you. Name what you want as your reward and it shall be given to you."

Again the applause lasted for a long time. When it had died away Supreme Commander Gordon arose and said, "General Walter Kennelworth, Comrade and Friend, we have known each other since early youth and I am deeply touched to have you here to make a speech of gratitude for my humble efforts in behalf of my beloved country. You ask me what our country and the world can give me in return for my achievement.

"I am deeply grateful to you, my brothers and sisters of the world. I ask no credit for myself but owe it all to God who guided me thru love and inspired me to give my best to my country and to bring back with honor Old Glory's colors which have never trailed the dust, unstained by blood of innocent women and children.

"Above all the rest, I have kept a woman's trust untarnished and hope to some day see a new light of love in a woman's eyes. No reward is greater than this and I must still trust in God and wait. I have been loyal to her when all others have doubted her. Even when my country dishonored me, my faith never faltered, and when she disappeared, I hoped and prayed that she would live and still hope she is alive. I knew she had faith in me, love for me and the power of that love has given me the power to destroy the world, but her love has left charity in my heart and for that love I have dealt with the enemy with love and mercy. All the money, power and glory that you can give me are empty and cannot supply the aching void in my heart for her. The greatest gift that could be bestowed would be to return her to me with all the love and confidence that she had in me on June 5th, 1927.

"In speaking of the inspiration that has been brought about by my love for her, I want to say that I was always faithful to my mother and that I have honored and respected her. It was she who taught me loyalty to my country and it was for her that I remained loyal and faithful to the cause of my country.

"In closing, I request that one of the terms of peace shall be that New York City shall be the capital of the United Kingdom of the World; that the plan of the future shall be according to Ezekiel. The Bible is replete with references thruout of a rebirth. Jesus said 'Ye must be born again of water and of the spirit.' A change of name is referred to many times. Jesus said 'I will give him a new name.' The United Kingdom of the World shall be the new name. Jesus said 'I will be their God and there shall be no more War.' In Ezekiel 48: 35, his last prophecy was 'And the name of that city from that day shall be THE LORD IS THERE.' New York City, which is to be the capital of the United Kingdom of the World and which has been known as the most wicked city in the world, is now to be the capital of the land of love and liberty, because the victory which united the world was won from there. I christen it 'THE CITY OF THE LORD.' May you so live that the world may know by the acts and justice of this great city that THE LORD IS THERE. I thank you, one and all."

When Supreme Commander Gordon finished speaking, almost every man and woman in the audience were in tears. They had never known that such wonderful things were in the Bible and that all of these very events were foretold by the greatest prophet, Ezekiel.

The President of the United States stepped to the platform and suggested that they give a rising vote of thanks and three cheers for Supreme Commander Robert Gordon. When the cheering was over, the President said: "The conference is going to close for the evening and meet tomorrow when Supreme Commander Gordon will go over the plans for the future brotherhood of love. If you will have patience for a few moments, General Walter Kennelworth will make the closing address, but in the meantime I want to introduce to you America's greatest woman, one whom we hope that the good women of America will select to be the first woman to rule the United Kingdom of the World; one who made a supreme sacrifice and rendered her country the greatest aid in time of war. I present to you the wife of General Walter Kennelworth, and the aide of Supreme Commander Robert Gordon, the woman who saved the capitol at Washington—General Edna Kennelworth."

When the President had finished and the applause had

died down, General Edna Kennelworth arose. "Mr. President, Supreme Commander Gordon, Brothers and Sisters of the United Kingdom of the World: To me belongs no honor and I seek no glory. We owe it all to the genius of our Supreme Commander, Robert Gordon. I thank our worthy President and all the nations of the world who have shown their honor and appreciation to General Walter Kennelworth, my husband, and myself. I am happy to know that the cause of women has triumphed and that our Supreme Commander has set an example for the world and has shown what the love of a good woman can do. I thank you."

The women were all on their feet and gave Edna the greatest applause any woman ever received. It was now growing late in the evening and General Walter Kennelworth stepped to the platform and said: "Brothers and Sisters of the United World, I will not detain you long with this personal address to our Supreme Commander Robert Gordon."

Turning to the Supreme Commander he said: "I will no longer address you as the Supreme Commander Robert Gordon, but as my friend and comrade. This is the happiest moment of my life and I now realize that justice, mercy and truth always will be rewarded. You have been unselfish and since the day that you wrote the famous letter that won Marie and the Garden of Love, you have kept your promise and been unselfish. Your first thought has been of your country in time of need. You have been loyal to your mother, true and faithful to Marie and now I want to read Marie's letter to you written the day she disappeared. I know that you know it by heart because you have read it a thousand times, but I want this conference of men and women from all the nations of the world to know that you are a man among men—that you are one in millions and that you have set an example for the world· and that example will make better men. The letter reads:

" 'DEAREST ROBERT:

" 'According to your faith be I unto you. Love will always have faith, understand and wait. Time proves all things. You will get everything you want. I will come to you when I mean the most, and your need for love is the greatest.

MARIE.'

"Your faith has been supreme. Your love has given you faith and you have tried to understand. More than five long years have passed and no word has been received from Marie. In your speech today, the thought uppermost in your mind was for her happiness and safety. This shows that time does prove all things. It has proven your love for Marie and your faith and confidence in a woman's promise. Marie was a wise prophet. She knew better than we knew when she said: 'You will get eveything you want.' Robert Gordon, that prophecy has been fulfilled. You have accomplished your ambition and received everything that the world can give. All of your dreams but one have been realized. You have all the honors, all the gratitude that a world can give, yet I know that your heart is aching and after your duty is well done and the peace of the world is established, you will need Marie and her love more now than ever.

"What Marie Stanton had in her mind the night she wrote that letter and left the train on the way to St. Louis, I do not know, but I do know that she has rendered the greatest service of any woman to this country. Whether she dreamed or realized what she was doing, makes no difference. Had she proceeded on to St. Louis and married you, Robert Gordon, the great inspiration which has made you the greatest inventor of the world and the prince of peace, would have been lacking. The great desire for love and your longing for Marie has stimulated your ambitions, kept hope in your breast and endowed you with the power to subdue the enemies of the world and unite the world in the brotherhood of peace. This has all been brought about by the act of Marie Stanton. She deserves credit and above all, you deserve the greatest reward that can be given any man, and that is the love of a good woman.

"The last line of her letter read, 'I will come to you when I mean the most and your need for love is the greatest.' Robert Gordon, that last promise has sustained you thru all of these years. It has been the anchor that has kept your soul steadfast. You have trusted and never doubted. You have honored and respected the land that gave you birth. Your love and faithfulness to Marie Stanton has guided you to success and victory, because it was an unselfish love. The great God who gave His only begotten son to save the world that He loved has not been unmindful of you and your devotion to His wisdom. You have followed His example of love and mercy. You have kept the faith. You have preserved the life of your nation and the all-wise God in His wisdom and mercy, has preserved for you the life of Marie Stanton. Robert Gordon, my friend and comrade, I now take pleasure in presenting to you Marie Stanton."

Robert Gordon jumped from his seat as if in a daze. Marie Stanton shouted, "Robert! Robert!" and fell into his arms. General Walter Kennelworth turned to the audience and said:

"This is the proof of God's divine plan and the reward for those who obey His law. Love is indeed the fulfillment of the law. I may not be as great a prophet as Ezekiel or as our Supreme Commander Robert Gordon, but I predict that when we meet tomorrow we will have heard that the first marriage in the new city, The City of the Lord, capital of the United Kingdom of the World has taken place between Robert Gordon and Marie Stanton."

THE END